The Calling of Education

EDWARD SHILS

THE CALLING OF EDUCATION

The Academic Ethic and Other Essays on Higher Education

EDITED, AND WITH AN INTRODUCTION, BY
Steven Grosby

FOREWORD BY
Joseph Epstein

THE UNIVERSITY OF CHICAGO PRESS
Chicago and London

Edward Shils (1910–1995) was professor in the Committee on Social Thought at the University of Chicago and a fellow of Peterhouse, Cambridge University.

The University of Chicago Press gratefully acknowledges the assistance of the Exxon Foundation in the publication of this book.

The University of Chicago Press, Chicago 60637
The University of Chicago Press, Ltd., London

Printed in the United States of America

06 05 04 03 02 01 00 99 98 97 1 2 3 4 5

ISBN: 0-226-75338-7 (cloth)
ISBN: 0-226-75339-5 (paper)

Library of Congress Cataloging-in-Publication Data

Shils, Edward, 1910–1995.
The calling of education : the academic ethic and other essays on higher education / Edward Shils ; foreword by Joseph Epstein ; introduction by Steven Grosby.
p. cm.
Includes bibliographical references and index.
ISBN 0-226-75338-7 (cloth : alk. paper). — ISBN 0-226-75339-5 (paper : alk. paper)
1. Education, Higher—Philosophy. 2. Education, Higher—Aims and objectives. 3. College teachers—Professional ethics. 4. Universities and colleges—United States—Administration. 5. Education, Higher—Social aspects—United States. I. Title.
LB2325.S439 1997
378′.01—dc21 97-18654
CIP

♾ The paper used in this publication meets the minimum requirements of the American National Standard for Information Sciences—Permanence of Paper for Printed Library Materials, ANSI Z39.48-1984.

Contents

Foreword

The university was Edward Shils's field, milieu, turf, the scene of his best and strongest passions, and he was a very passionate man. He loved the university in general, and the Universities of Chicago and Cambridge in particular, and in the last decades of his life came to have grave worries about its future. Although he pondered a vast deal of things, higher education was never far from his mind. Nor, really, could it have been, for he lived the best part of his life in universities, and taught more than sixty years at Chicago.

Edward Shils thought the university a place of great privilege and the men and women who were able to spend their lives in it themselves greatly privileged persons. In a university one could devote oneself to books, science, paintings, documents, the study of languages, things of the mind—elevated things that put one outside the necessity of daily life with its mad crush and demanding insistence on earning a livelihood. He had great regard for anyone who had mastery over any serious craft; he also thought running a good shop a useful task; but if he had to point to one form of the good life above all others, my guess is that he would have designated the life of scholarship lived within a university.

Because Edward Shils loved the university so ardently, he greatly disliked inroads, not to say onslaughts, against it whose ultimate affect could only be to diminish it. People who were at the University of Chicago during the student disturbances in the late 1960s report that Edward Shils's role as the chief adviser to President Edward Levi was of key significance. No need to rehearse the history of those days here, but one can say, without much qualification, that the University of Chicago came away with its integrity less battered from those events than did Berkeley, Columbia, Harvard, Michigan, and nearly every other major American center of higher learning. Because Edward Shils knew what was at stake, because he knew from long study how delicately placed the university is in modern society, he was able to offer unequivocal advice, which came down, finally, to the advice to remember why the university is important, what makes it important, and why it was necessary not to equivocate with students who may have had all sorts of other goods in mind but not that of the university, the institution that he, Edward Shils, knew and revered above all others.

Edward Shils's understanding of the university can be likened to that of a great symphonic conductor to his orchestra. He knew the value of all its instruments and sections, he knew them separately and he knew their power when properly integrated. Early in "The Criteria of Academic Appointments," which he originally composed for the University of Chicago in 1970, Professor Shils made plain the balance that needed to be maintained between the parts and functions of the university if it is to perform as it is intended to do. "A university faculty is not merely an assemblage of individual scientists and scholars," he wrote, "it must possess a corporate life and an atmosphere created by the research, teaching, and conversation of individual scientists and scholars which stimulates and sustains the work of colleagues and students at the highest possible level."

Among Edward Shils's many gifts was that of superior perspective. His was a perspective formed by wide historical reading and relentless common sense. He never forgot how easily things in an institution as intricate as a university could go badly awry. Where standards are allowed to slip in one place, the slippage is certain to be felt in another. I can remember Edward Shils's anger at what he thought were poor appointments in departments at his own University of Chicago—appointments that, from the outside, one might not have thought central. But he didn't see it that way. Appointing a pretentious, or merely fashionable, or badly wrong-headed faculty member he saw as a form of letting down the side, no matter where it occurred. "Every appointment of a mediocre candidate," he wrote, "makes it more difficult to appoint a distinguished candidate later and it makes it more difficult to bring outstanding students to the university."

Professor Shils, who wrote a brilliant book on the subject of tradition, had the most lucid notion of the role of tradition in the university. I remember once asking him his opinion of the Institute for Advanced Study at Princeton. He didn't doubt the right, in intellectual distinction, of most of its members to be there, but what he regretted is that such a place took many distinguished scientists and scholars out of the stream of influence on students that they undoubtedly would have had in universities. He saw this as an unfortunate break in the necessary linkage of knowledge that passes from teacher to student.

But worse than unfortunate were those lapses in intellectual courage on the part of university administrators of the kind that he saw as more and more prevalent in an age when university presidents ceased to be educational leaders and more and more became chiefly fund-raisers and public-relations officials. Even worse than the want of intellectual courage on the part of university administrators and faculty was their true ignorance of their tasks. When in Randall Jarrell's novel, *Pictures from an Institution,* someone calls one of the characters, a college president, a hypocrite, the narrator retorts that this isn't an accurate description, for the man hadn't yet arrived at that stage of moral development in which it would be fair to call him that; to be a hypocrite, after all, one has to know right from wrong. So it is with so many people now running and teaching in universities who haven't the least notion of what constitutes academic freedom, the responsibility of teachers, the mission and place of the university in the larger society. Edward Shils knew all these things in his bones; he knew all the questions, and he never forgot the right answers.

I do not think it in the least an exaggeration to say that Edward Shils, owing to the most sedulous study and to personal experience filtered through meticulous understanding, knew these things better than anyone else in the world. The essays in this volume provide the core of Professor Shils's knowledge and wisdom about what might be called the first principles of higher education. As such, they provide a book of inestimable value for anyone who cares about the fate of higher education in our time.

Joseph Epstein

Introduction

The Academic Ethic by Edward Shils is the product of a study group of the International Council on the Future of the University.[1] It was first published in 1982 in volume 20 of *Minerva,* the journal of science, learning, and policy founded by Edward Shils in 1962 and edited by him with tireless scrupulosity until his death at the age of eighty-four on January 23, 1995. Since the first University of Chicago Press edition of *The Academic Ethic* (1984), there has been a steadily growing recognition of the essay's importance. It now reappears along with other of Edward Shils's significant writings on higher education.

This book underscores the importance of *The Academic Ethic* by supplementing it with an additional five essays, each of which takes up in greater detail its particular themes. Two criteria were employed in the selection: first, that these essays be representative of the best work of Edward Shils on higher education during approximately the last twenty years of his life, and second, that they had not already appeared in the three volumes of Shils's papers already published by the University of Chicago Press.[2] The essays chosen continue to speak very much to the issues, questions, and problems of higher education in our day.

The Academic Ethic is concerned with elucidating—and, by so doing, reaffirming—the ethical obligations of university teachers, researchers, and scholars. These are the obligations that arise from the methodical discovery and transmission of truth, and the integrity and freedom of inquiry integral to that discovery and transmission. In *The Academic Ethic,* Edward Shils promulgated a set of guiding principles to govern the academic profession's custodianship of knowledge in teaching and research, its role in the internal conduct of universities that sustain the academic life, and its participation in life outside the university.

According to Shils, the distinctive task of the academic profession is

1. For the history of the study group, see Edward Shils's introduction to "The Academic Ethic," *Minerva* XX/1–2 (Spring–Summer 1982): 105–6.

2. Edward Shils, *The Intellectuals and the Powers and Other Essays* (Chicago: University of Chicago Press, 1972); *Center and Periphery, Essays in Macrosociology* (Chicago: University of Chicago Press, 1975); and of particular relevance to many of the themes of *The Academic Ethic* are the essays contained in *The Calling of Sociology and Other Essays on the Pursuit of Learning* (Chicago: University of Chicago Press, 1980).

both research and teaching. In asserting the unity of research and teaching for the academic profession, Shils reaffirmed Wilhelm von Humboldt's ideal of the task of the university. He did so while being fully aware of the dramatically new conditions and demands on universities that have emerged over the past forty years, among them, the consolidation of the image of the mass "research university." Even though Shils grew more pessimistic about the academic profession's adherence to von Humboldt's ideal—to the point of fearing that Bonaparte's technocratic view of the university as an institution devoted to practical tasks in service to the state had become ascendant[3]—he never wavered in his own belief in the unity of the discovery of fundamental truths and their transmission as integral to the academic profession. This continued reaffirmation of the necessary unity of teaching and research is nowhere more evident than in "The Idea of the University: Obstacles and Opportunities in Contemporary Societies," included in this volume.

Along with clarifying the fundamental obligations to research and teaching, *The Academic Ethic* takes up, of necessity, the obligations of university teachers both to their own disciplines and institutions and to their surrounding societies. Among the most practical of such obligations is that of making academic appointments. It is through academic appointments that the commitment of the university teacher to his or her discipline, students, and university is concretely manifested, namely, in the adherence to both the criterion of achievement in teaching and research and the criterion of academic citizenship. Because the criteria employed in academic appointments directly affect the quality of a university, it was decided to include in this volume Shils's article "The Criteria of Academic Appointment." The article was actually the report of an official committee of senior members of the faculty of the University of Chicago constituted to clarify the criteria of academic appointment. The committee was chaired by Edward Shils and the report written by him. Shils consistently maintained the criterion of achievement in teaching and research in the face of demands that other criteria be employed. In particular, he took a strong position against the criteria of affirmative action and "pluralism of standpoints." The continuing controversy over these matters was another reason for including the article here.

The question whether permanent tenure is desirable in the light of its consequences for the adequate fulfillment of the obligations of the academic profession has increasingly been posed, especially of late in

3. See Edward Shils, "The Service of Society and the Advancement of Learning in the Twenty-First Century," *Minerva* XXX/2 (Summer 1992): 242–68.

the United Kingdom. One of the main arguments for tenure is that it is necessary for academic freedom. Given the continuing controversies over permanent tenure and academic freedom, it was thought worthwhile to include the essay "Do We Still Need Academic Freedom."[4]

Shils knew very well that relations between the academic profession and universities, on the one hand, and governments and their societies, on the other, have in the past forty years become increasingly complicated.[5] These relations are a major concern of *The Academic Ethic,* not least in the consideration of the different ways in which threats to the academic ethic arise out of the existence of mass, bureaucratized, and increasingly politicized universities.[6] The complicated relationship between government and universities in the United States was the topic chosen by Professor Shils when, in 1979, he was selected by the National Endowment of the Humanities to be its Eighth Jefferson Lecturer. Professor Shils delivered three lectures—the first in Washington, D.C., on April 9, 1979; the second in Chicago, Illinois, on April 10, 1979; and the third in Austin, Texas, on April 17, 1979. The themes of the lectures were, respectively, the claims of governments on universities, and the limits to those claims; the legitimate claims of universities; and a declaration of the rights and duties of universities. The decision was made to include all three lectures in this book despite a small degree of repetition because, taken as a whole, they are every bit as intellectually powerful and vital as *The Academic Ethic.*

Ten years after his Jefferson Lectures, in "The Modern University and Liberal Democracy" (the final essay in the present volume), Shils returned to many of the problems of both *The Academic Ethic* and his Jefferson Lectures. In this essay, however, he took a different approach to the problems by analyzing the modern university within the context of liberal democracy, its institutional arrangements, and the various, occasionally conflicting traditions that constitute liberalism.

Edward Shils was such a prolific writer that any collection of his papers could easily and properly be twice as long; and this is certainly true of his writings on the academic ethic, the pursuit of learning, and the problems of higher education—subjects on which he brooded throughout his long career. But it is the hope of the editor that the essays in this book

4. See also Edward Shils, "Academic Freedom and Permanent Tenure," *Minerva* XXXIII/1 (Spring 1995): 5–17.

5. See, for example, Edward Shils, "The Service of Society and the Advancement of Learning in the Twenty-First Century," *Minerva* XXX/2 (Summer 1992): 242–68.

6. See also, for example, Edward Shils, "The Academic Ethos under Strain," *Minerva* XIII/1 (Spring 1975): 1–37.

will encourage readers to turn to other of Professor Shils's writings—not only those on education. By so doing, they will discover that Edward Shils was a thinker who illuminated every subject on which he wrote.

Acknowledgments

I wish to thank four individuals whose efforts have greatly facilitated the appearance of this volume in a timely fashion: Mr. John Tryneski, editor at the University of Chicago Press; Edward Shils's fellow bibliophile, Professor Stuart Warner; Edward Shils's friend, Professor Naomi Farber; and, finally, Mr. Joseph Epstein, Edward Shils's good friend and the literary executor of his estate.

Steven Grosby

The Calling of Education

The Academic Ethic

An Inherent Commitment

The Task of the University

Universities have a distinctive task. It is the methodical discovery and the teaching of truths about serious and important things. Part of the task is to enhance the students' understanding and to train them in the attitudes and methods of critical assessment and testing of their beliefs so that they can make what they believe as free from error as possible. The discovery and transmission of truth is the distinctive task of the academic profession, just as the care of the health of the patient is the distinctive task of the medical profession, and the protection, within the law, of the client's rights and interests is the distinctive task of the legal profession. The teaching of specific truths postulates a more general affirmation of the value of truth about any specific object or about any general class of objects. That truth has a value in itself, apart from any use to which it is put, is a postulate of the activities of the university. It begins with the assumption that truth is better than error, just as the medical profession accepts that health is better than illness and the legal profession begins with the belief that the assurance of rights under the law is better than to be at the mercy of arbitrary power.

These concepts—truth, knowledge, rights, health—are none of them wholly unambiguous. The doctrine that there is such a thing as truth, that the quest for it is intrinsically valuable has become associated in many academic minds with "metaphysics," "theology," "idealism," "dogma," "religion"—in brief, with all those beliefs and modes of thinking against which many scientists and scholars have rebelled. There is abroad today a desire, more frequently expressed by academics in the humanities and the social sciences, to derogate or even to dissolve the idea that truths can be discovered and taught. Denial of the possibility of detachment, denial of the possibility of the disciplined and disinterested search for knowledge, denial of the possibility of objective knowledge,

Reprinted from *Minerva* XX/1–2 (Spring–Summer 1982): 107–208.

which is true independently of the passions or desires or "material interests" of the discoverer and transmitter have become more common in recent years in certain influential circles of academics. Some academics preach these denials day in and day out. Their actions, however, almost invariably belie their words. They still believe sufficiently in the possibility of rational argument issuing in truthful conclusions to think that what they say should, on the basis of the rationality of their argument and the evidence which they invoke, persuade their hearers and readers of the truthfulness of their denial of the possibility of truth.

The ascertainment of any truth is a difficult matter; the truth must be re-ascertained incessantly. These truths are changed continuously by new discoveries which may indeed be defined as the revision in the light of new observations and analyses of propositions previously held to be true. For these reasons, there must be elements of tentativeness and readiness to revise in the attitudes towards any truths accepted at present. This readiness to revise is not tantamount to relativism. It does not mean that any proposition is just as true as any other proposition or that the truth of a proposition is dependent on the social position or political orientation of the person asserting or accepting it. It means that the propositions held at any moment are the best that could be achieved by the methods of observation and analysis which are acceptable in scientific and scholarly communities. The acceptance of these propositions, with these qualifications, implies an admission that these particular propositions will not so much be proven to be wrong as that they will be shown to require revision and replacement by propositions sustained by better observations and better interpretations.

It is exactly their concern that their statements, made in their teaching or formulated in their research, should be as true as possible, based on the most methodically gathered and analyzed evidence, taking into account the state of knowledge in their own particular fields, that characterizes the academic profession. That is what justifies the academic life and the existence of the social institutions, especially the university, which sustain that life. The more specific obligations of the academic as such, as distinct from the obligations he shares with other human beings, all flow from his concern for truths about particular things and for the idea of truth in general. Just as if illness is a myth there is no point in having a medical profession, if rights are a myth there is no point in having lawyers, so if truth, objectivity, and rational argument are myths there is no point in teaching and research and no point in taking any particular care in such more specific tasks as making academic appointments, giving expert advice, and so on.

That all their work depends on this assumption is a fact which often disappears from sight when academics are immersed in their specialized research and teaching or are distracted by the demands of public engagement. Unless they are professional philosophers, academics do not spend their time thinking about the nature of truth or its relationship to their activities, any more than doctors daily ask themselves what constitutes health and how it differs from illness. They have specific tasks to perform, specific inquiries to make, specific things to teach; they take these tasks as given and they do not worry themselves about the fundamental principles which underlie their specialized activities.

That is why it is urgent to remind university teachers of what they committed themselves to when they entered upon the academic career. Their passionate desire to aid in the movement towards social equality or justice, and to meet requests and satisfy their own desires to contribute to the practical work of society, sometimes causes academics to forget that the cultivation of truth in all the fields which they study and teach and the respect for truth in their practical activities are essential to and distinctive of their calling. These other social objectives can well exist alongside the methodical search for reliable knowledge in research and its communication in teaching. However, without their primary activity of discovering and teaching the truth as scrupulously and as methodically as they can in the fields for which they are responsible, university teachers would be no more than agitators for social arrangements which they think desirable, or a special sort of leisure class, which is "kept" by society because some of its members, such as the teachers of medicine, law, chemistry, or engineering, perform useful services for society through their own research and their teaching and consultation.

There are, of course, two other views about the function of academics and academic institutions which we do not wish to ignore. We shall, indeed, often advert to them in what follows. The first is that the sole object of universities is to prepare students to fit into particular occupational roles; the second is that the function of universities is to be centers of revolutionary change. About the first view of the task of universities, it should be said that while it is certainly true that universities should, among other things, train students to perform effectively in certain occupations, not every form of training for an occupation is appropriate to universities. Only training for those occupations which rest upon a foundation of fundamental knowledge, as distinct from consisting almost entirely of practical skills, is appropriate for universities. The universities do and ought to educate for those occupations which demand of their practitioners a mastery of a coherent body of organized knowledge, a capacity to assess evidence and a readiness to look at situations afresh. A university education should not have as a task to prepare students for occupations which deal with routine tasks. It should offer education for those occupations which require a knowledge of fundamental processes, principles and methods of analysis. As to the argument that universities should be centers of revolutionary action, it should be emphasized that universities have often been the points or centers of origin of profound changes in the world at large. These have been changes based on an intellectual foundation; many changes in economic and social life have come about in consequence of the intellectual achievements of academic scientists and scholars, for example, in economics, sociology, physics, chemistry, and biology. But to think of universities as centers of political agitation is to assign to them a responsibility which properly belongs to political parties, not to universities. Indeed, the suggestion that students and their teachers should together stand for a particular political attitude which they can then impose on the world at large would be comically absurd were it not, in its effects, so tragic. They should stand together for two things: for intellectual integrity and freedom of inquiry. But that is not a political program, in and of itself, even if it has political implications.

Investigation, and teaching the manner and the results of investigation, are the things that universities know how to do and can do well. It is not more arbitrary to regard them as the function of universities than it is to regard healing as the function of physicians. Some doctors will put money-making or the elevation of their social status or the protection of medical monopolies before healing. But they are then poor physicians. So are those academics poor academics who fail to give primacy to discovery and teaching.

The academic profession is not singled out here for attention because it is worse than other learned professions. Nor are we discussing its ethical problems and obligations because the academic profession was once perfect and has since then fallen dangerously away. As the situation of professions changes, their ethical obligations need reformulation in the face of new tasks. It is not that the fundamental principles change but rather their application to new situations. There is no profession which is exempt from fundamental ethical obligations; there is none which does not constantly encounter conditions causing those ethical obligations cynically to be transgressed or innocently to be overlooked in the concentration of attention on the vigorous pursuit of subsidiary and quite legitimate objectives. There have always been such situations in academic life throughout the whole history of universities. The present situation of universities is one of these but it is also, in some respects, unique. Over the past third of a century, new conditions and new demands on universities have emerged. The world became busier, more things seemed to be happening. Politics became more interesting to more academics as the air filled with wars and rumors of wars, amplified by radio and television broadcasting. New opportunities for all sorts of extra-academic activities came into existence.

Students became much more numerous, universities became larger, and their teaching staffs expanded greatly. Many new universities were founded. More demands were placed on universities. The attention of university teachers was more drawn into the problems of the society which surrounded them. Universities became more dependent on and were more pressed by governments than was the case until the Second World War in liberal-democratic societies. More was demanded of universities and they also became more costly. Universities have become more exposed to public scrutiny than they used to be and many administrators and teachers have sought publicity for themselves and their universities. Universities now have many more administrative officers than they used to have. Universities have become more disaggregated than they used to be.

The past decade has been a period of straitened financial circumstances, of diminished opportunities for the younger generation of scientists and scholars to find appointments, of increasingly complicated relationships of the universities with governments and private business and political organizations. This decade of financial constriction has followed a quarter of a century of great expansion and almost euphoric optimism. The disorder both in the student body and in the teaching corps have all left marked traces in the diversion of attention from some of the central tasks of academic life. Many teachers have continued to do their duty, and, of course, great numbers of teachers have applied themselves unreservedly to research. Nevertheless, in recent decades, the sure moral touch has weakened and the self-confidence of the academic profession in its devotion to its calling has faltered. There is a need for the profession to clarify in its own mind and to reaffirm the fundamental obligations inherent in its undertaking.

The present report is intended to contribute to the reanimation of discussion regarding the proper end of academic persons and of academic institutions. Aside from a few fragmentary starts, which have been responses to particular abuses and grievances, the academic profession has done very little to promulgate a set of guiding principles which should govern its custodianship of knowledge in teaching and research, its role in the internal conduct of universities and its participation in the public sphere. Such a set of principles should be broad enough to cover the main fields of activities in which the academic profession engages in its concentration on the acquisition and transmission of knowledge at ever-higher levels of complexity. The principles should apply to all the activities in which academics participate, including not only their scientific, scholarly, and pedagogical activities and their conduct within academic institutions but also their publicistic and political activities and their performance of advisory and consultative services for government, private business, and political and civic associations.

The obligations of the university teacher are as many-sided as his[1] role. Important though the role of the teacher is, the university teacher is not solely a teacher. Teaching is only one part of the activity of one who is appointed to teach in a modern university. There is an expectation that university teachers should do some research; research is to be regarded, if with differing emphases and in differing proportions, as an obligation of the same order as teaching. Of course, not all teachers will distribute their intellectual energy and interest in the same pattern; some will do mainly teaching and relatively little research, others much more research than teaching. Nor will all universities have the same pattern; some will do much more research than teaching; some will do much more research than others. In those which do little research, it should be accepted as obligatory for those who concentrate mainly on teaching to keep abreast of the most important research for the purposes of their teaching. A university teacher is, furthermore, a member of an academic institution which is more than an administrative facility for his teaching and research; he is a member of a department and of the teaching staff of a university. He is also a member of a scientific and scholarly profession and of an intellectual community which runs beyond the boundaries of his department, his university, his profession, and his country. He is also a citizen of his own larger society to which he has, by virtue of his larger and more elaborate stock of rigorously founded knowledge, more than the obligations of the ordinary citizen.

The special obligations of a university teacher derive from his possession of a stock of knowledge such as other persons, who do not devote themselves to the systematic and concentrated acquisition of knowledge, do not possess. The belief that the knowledge an academic possesses is applicable to important practical concerns such as health, economy, military security, industrial production, etc., is a source of deference.

1. Wherever "he" or "his" is used to refer to the individual university teacher, both men and women are to be understood.

The granting of deference to a person in consequence of his possession of special knowledge on important topics is not the result of a deliberate search for deference on the part of the possessor of the knowledge. He does not owe gratitude to those who grant him that deference. What he does owe them is an obligation not to abuse their respect for him.

A body of substantive knowledge in itself has, simply as knowledge, no necessary implications for the conduct of its possessor; yet in certain ways, it does have such implications. It implies above all a concern for the truthfulness of what is asserted as knowledge. It is with this implication that we will be concerned. Knowledge of the various consequences of urbanization, for example, does not entail any particular course of action. It leaves open the question how these consequences are to be weighed against one another, which is something about which individuals can disagree. But when an academic makes an assertion of these consequences as constituting knowledge, he should do so only if he has done all he could do to ensure that they are indeed the actual consequences. In short, the possession and communication of knowledge implies respect for the rules or methods for the pursuit of knowledge; it entails affirmation of and strict adherence to the criteria of truthfulness as they operate in the particular field or discipline. This in its turn entails modesty in making proposals based, for example, on demographic and sociological studies of problematical validity. And this, in its further turn, has implications for the mode of transmission of knowledge, whether it be to young students, to the wider public, or to the powerful in society.

The academic ethic is the sum of these obligations which are involved in the pursuit and transmission of advanced knowledge and in roles and in conduct affected by the real or presumed possession of such knowledge. The academic ethic really exists. It is not something excogitated outside the academic realm and offered as an alternative to what goes on there. It is already adhered to by most academics, especially in their research. It is the aspiration of this report to articulate it more explicitly, elaborate some of its implications, and to help colleagues to think about what is entailed ethically in the life and activity of an academic. Conditions have arisen in recent decades in Western societies which have debilitated this ethical commitment. The debilitation must not be exaggerated but it must also be recognized that the present situation is not without its troubling aspects.

The Possession of Advanced, Complex, and Reliable Knowledge and Its Obligations

University teaching in the present century has been regarded as more than just an occupation through which a livelihood is obtained. When it is called a "profession," it is meant that, in some important way, it differs from other occupations, the fortunes of which are to be determined by the vicissitudes of the market or syndical power or governmental decision. It has been thought to be one of those occupations with special qualities which confer special privileges and obligations on those who practice them. Although in recent years, many occupations have sought to be designated as "professions," a profession still remains what it was thought to be for some centuries, namely an occupation the practice of which requires a more than ordinary amount of complex knowledge, acquired by persistent and systematic study and authoritatively certified. This is true primarily of law, medicine, engineering, and the academic profession. The first three are engaged in the practical application of knowledge about particular kinds of situations and objects. The first three of these professions deal with relatively restricted parts of the entire body of systematically studied and acquired knowledge while the academic profession, through its internal division of labor, covers the entire range of systematically studied, methodically gained knowledge, parts of which are applied in law, medicine, and engineering.

The primary task of the academic profession is the acquisition and transmission of knowledge, not its application. The academic profession receives, assimilates, and discovers knowledge by methodical study, and it interprets and transmits that knowledge; it transmits knowledge about the methods of discovery and especially of the validation of knowledge. Even when the teacher's concern is the application of knowledge to practical activities, he himself is not applying the knowledge which he teaches to practical activities. In the teaching of technology, for example, the teacher is transmitting knowledge about the application of knowledge. He teaches how knowledge of a particular substance is applied and can be applied to particular practical tasks. He is not applying that technological knowledge himself. The teacher of engineering in a university is not, in his teaching, performing the practical activities of the engineer. The teaching in a university of the principles and techniques of the application of knowledge in clinical medicine, legal procedure, architectural design, and engineering construction is the transmission of bodies of knowledge and of the rules or methods governing their application. A great deal of university teaching is not about practical application at all; it teaches what is known about particular phenomena and classes of phenomena and how to learn more about them. It tries to dispel error, confusion, and misunderstanding.

In modern universities, teaching is associated with research or at the very least, a sustained effort to keep in touch with what is happening in research. The teacher does research and he also bases his teaching on the research done by others and himself, where this bears on the subject of his teaching. Research itself is the methodical acquisition of knowledge, hitherto unknown. Knowledge languishes and fades if it is not cultivated by research. Teaching too languishes if it is not sustained by research. Even though a particular teacher himself does relatively little research, he has to be informed about the research which is being done on his subject. Knowledge is not self-sustaining; it does not grow of itself. It has to be actively sought and brought into teaching to remain alive. These are among the first responsibilities of the academic.

But if they differ in some respects, there is still a major similarity among all the learned professions. Each of them possesses large stocks of complex and advanced knowledge which have not been mastered by the laity of clients, patients, and students to whom the learned professions address themselves. This inequality in the possession of knowledge gives to the possessors of knowledge large opportunities to abuse that position of superiority.

The university teachers' possession of more and more intricate knowledge—greater in amount and in intensity, more fundamental and more strictly criticized and tested—than is available to the layman places special obligations on him. These differences in the amount and quality of the knowledge possessed by academics and by laymen are ultimately the ground for the invitation of academics to give "expert" advice to governments and private bodies. Academics are reputed to have not only specialized knowledge and achievement and the habit of objectively considering alternatives; they are reputed to have scholarly, detached, and dispassionate judgment. For a variety of reasons, the reputation of the academic profession is at present in danger of discredit.

In the academic profession, the privileges of university autonomy and academic freedom—the very considerable autonomy of decisions in appointment and promotion, in methods of teaching, in the definition of courses of study and of the setting and marking of examinations—as well as the far-reaching freedom of initiation and conduct of scientific and scholarly investigation and the freedom of publication are all, in principle, justified by the greater knowledge possessed by academics in their respective subjects, in comparison with the knowledge possessed by students and laymen. The corporate autonomy of universities rests also on certain legal traditions, which continue a principle of corporate self-government once shared by guilds and estates and which took form prior to the emergence of modern society. The main argument for the autonomy of universities, aside from more general arguments from tradition and for a pluralistic organization of society, is that the validity of the knowledge which academics teach and discover can be assessed only by those who have mastered it by long and intensive study.

The special privileges of university autonomy and academic freedom are accorded in consequence of the belief of the laity that academics possess knowledge which it appreciates and desires. These privileges in turn engender obligations. The obligations of the academic profession are inherent in the custodianship of the pursuit, acquisition, assessment, and transmission of knowledge through systematic study, in accordance with methodical procedures including observational techniques, rules of evidence, and principles of logical reasoning. The obligation to adhere to these norms is entailed in the acceptance of this custodianship. The commitment to rigorous methods of inquiry and of assessment of the results of inquiry is inherent in the decision to pursue an academic career.

A person who enters on an academic career might do so on the ground that it is an easy and quiet life, or that it is reasonably well remunerated, well regarded and likely to place the person who has chosen it in pleasant surroundings. Or he might, while at first being attracted to the academic life for academic reasons, come to have little interest in research and teaching, engaging in them in a humdrum way as one does a job which does not hold one's heart. There are undoubtedly many academics like this who have lost their zeal and who fall short of the standard which they know ought to prevail. Nevertheless, the ethical principle which is implicit in academic activity is not hidden from most of those who have chosen to enter the academic career; it is never far from their consciousness, however far they stray from it. Once their choice has been made, they cannot free themselves from their obligations as academics, even if they do not participate whole-heartedly in the life of teaching and research.

If one engages voluntarily in the activities of teaching and in research, of acquiring, assessing, transmitting, and discovering knowledge, one is committed to the acknowledgment of the differences between truth and falsity and to the greater value of the former over the latter. One commits oneself to adherence to the methods which help to distinguish between truth and falsity. One acknowledges that there are criteria outside one's own desires and convenience by which one may distinguish the true from the false; one acknowledges that there are techniques and modes of reasoning which help to distinguish truth from falsity. These include the adduction of evidence, critically assessed, by the use of the criteria of reliability and validity and of the rational comparison of alternative interpretations.

The acceptance of propositions is justifiable by more than a judgment of their convenience or of their practical value; it is justified by a judgment of the validity of the grounds for holding them. It is a judgment that they are more likely to be true and it implies an acceptance of criteria whereby that greater likelihood of truthfulness is arrived at and tested. The prospect that these criteria may become more precise with the passage of time does not absolve anyone from adhering to the criteria, which, at any given time, are as precise as it lies within human powers to make them.

Universities would never have achieved the status which they are accorded in civilized societies if they had not demonstrated that they sought, acquired, and presented reliable knowledge. Universities have passed through many vicissitudes and one of the main reasons why, from time to time, their status has declined and responsible parts of their societies have turned against them has been their negligence or indolence in the pursuit of truth by the best-known methods and by the best, currently possible, assessment of received and transmitted knowledge.

The New Situation of Universities and Its Challenge to the Academic Ethic

The academic ethos has grown out of a long tradition. It has its origins in the time when there were no universities, but only learned men seeking reliable and fundamental knowledge. It goes far back into the long period before the formation of modern science. It was practiced by devoted university teachers and by scientists long before it began to appear in very rudimentary formulations in connection with the reform of the German universities in the first decade of the nineteenth century. Even at the height of the glory of the German universities from the last third of that century, when German university professors thought themselves to be almost at the pinnacle of German society, the promulgation of an academic ethic was not taken in hand. Perhaps it was thought to be superfluous. Nor did it appear urgent to academics in the United States, Great Britain, and France as the universities in those countries entered into a new phase of creativity. The academic ethic must have seemed self-evident to the academics of the first quarter of the present century. In the United States, where academics came more frequently into conflict with the earthly powers of the state, the press, and the economy, much attention was given to the assertion of the rights of academics. Obligations were accepted as self-evident.

Meanwhile, societies were changing and with them the universities were changing too. The obligations which were given in the calling of science and learning have not changed but the conditions in which they are to be brought into action have changed. The universities have become very much larger; more services are demanded of them; their members have become more demanding financially. The universities have been more closely observed by the larger public and they themselves are more aware of this public attention and more desirous of it. All of these changes have affected the morale of the academic profession.

The "Mass University"

The "mass university"—the university with more than twenty thousand students—is not universal. In Great Britain it does not exist; in the United States many of the leading private universities are smaller. Yet, even short of this arbitrary figure, the universities nearly everywhere have acquired some of the features of mass universities. Mass universities and approximations to them present challenges to the academic ethic which have not been resolved.

The sheer increase in size in both student body and teaching staff has rendered it difficult to maintain the kinds of relations among students and teachers and among colleagues which are necessary for a university to maintain a high morale in its devotion to the advancement of learning through teaching and research. In its more extreme manifestations it has alienated students from the teaching staff and it has isolated many teachers from many of their students. Many individuals in each category are proud of the eminence in science and scholarship which has been attained in the particular mass university with which they are affiliated and of the excellent education and training which they received there. Many of the teachers in mass universities in the United States, where the state universities have been large for a long time, are proudly attached to their universities through their pride in the achievements of their most eminent colleagues; they are also sustained in that attachment by their simultaneous membership in the larger academic and scientific communities which transcend the boundaries of any single university and which have their branches or sections in parts of many universities.

This experience of intense intellectual activity and high achievement in some teachers and students at some of these mass universities casts a light, which is both awakening and deceptive, over the mass universities.

It has been an awakening light to some of those who have come into contact with it and who have been quickened by it into an intellectual curiosity and exertion which they did not know before and which they might not have reached had it not been for their contact with those persons in the teaching staffs and student bodies who have been the bearers in those mass universities of the scientific and academic ethic.

It is also a deceptive light because it has covered and transfigured to the larger society the rest of the university on which it shines. It has obscured the laxity in standards of teaching, the listlessness of many of the students and the perfunctoriness of their performance in the university.

Even in universities in which the academic and scientific ethos were at the highest level and which were relatively small, there were many time-servers and shirkers or persons whose talents and exertions did not measure up to a high standard. The most famous German universities in their greatest days had a sizeable proportion of members who did little that was significant in teaching and research. It is true that there have always been blank and dreary spots in teaching—if there had not been, there would not be such pleasure in recalling "famous teachers." It is also true that in the Continental universities, which did not share in the tradition of the principle of *in loco parentis,* the professors took little interest in their students except for the very outstanding ones. The seminars, however, did permit a closer intellectual contact with students who showed promise of becoming scholars or scientists. This has now become more difficult with the increased size of seminars.

One of the things repugnant to the academic ethic which has happened in the mass universities, especially in the United States and the Federal German Republic is that many of the students in the humanities and the social sciences have been abandoned by their teachers to the domain of the unreclaimable. This has not been an explicit decision; it has become part of the culture of mass universities in a number of countries; it has become a part of what is taken for granted. It is based on a conviction that the capacities of the students are weak and that they cannot master an exacting syllabus. They are assigned intellectually shabby text books and thin reading lists. In the mass universities of the United States, they are consigned in many places and subjects to junior teachers who, because they teach the lower years, feel that they have been cast into a lowly status, teaching according to a syllabus which they did not design themselves. The junior teachers themselves tend to be neglected by those above them.

The mass university increased the proportion of the area covered by the blank and dreary patches. The mass universities have grown too greatly and too rapidly in the size of their teaching staffs for the supply in sufficient numbers of teachers of outstanding talents, discipline and devotion to their calling. Furthermore, teaching large classes of uninterested students has a discouraging effect on teachers. Uninterested teachers bore their students. The very large numbers of undergraduates and graduate students have made it difficult for the intellectually most aspiring and most talented students to find their way to teachers who should guide them and who should respond to their intellectual gifts and potentialities; there are of course some teachers in mass universities who seek out such exceptional students; in some cases, special provision is made for exceptional students, as in undergraduate honors programs.

In the period of great expansion, a euphoric attitude about the prospects of universities led paradoxically to negligence about the criteria of appointment, especially about the criteria of teaching ability and interest. This negligence contributed to the appointment of indifferent teachers. The size of the newly appointed teaching staffs of universities and, even more important, the large proportion of such newly appointed teachers in many departments have made it difficult for younger teachers to become adequately assimilated into the academic and scientific ethos which some of the older teachers practiced.

The mass universities are not only much larger than all but the very largest universities used to be but they have also larger numbers of students who, although they have met all the formal qualifications for admission, are not well qualified for studies at the level of a university. Changes in the syllabuses of secondary schools have resulted in many of their graduates not having the knowledge which earlier in the century was regarded as prerequisite for work at a university. This creates difficulties for teachers as well as for the students. Teachers must teach at a lower intellectual level than they like or they teach "above the heads" of their students. The students are bored or made miserable and as a result "drop out" or prolong their studies over too many years.

Some of the problems of the mass universities had also been problems of the "elite universities" of fifty or seventy-five years ago but they are now vastly exacerbated. There were undoubtedly persons holding permanent appointments in such universities who were not pleased with the academic career and who fell short of its standards; there were some who flouted the standards of the academic profession, who neglected their teaching and their students, who did little research and who did it with little interest or conviction and who did not care about their institutions.

These problems have become more severe as a result of the relatively rapid growth of the mass university.

The mass universities are here to stay for the foreseeable future and the academic ethic must be practiced by the teachers of the mass universities as well as by those in universities with smaller student bodies and smaller teaching staffs. Indeed, emphasis on the academic ethic is even more necessary for the present-day mass universities than it was in the smaller outstanding universities of the past century and a half. In the latter, it was more readily assimilated and did not need to be explicitly stated. There was really little need to discuss the academic ethic in the German university of the 1890s or in Oxford and Cambridge in the first half of the present century or in the leading American universities in their best years between the two world wars. Even at that time, there were universities which were little or no better in their respect for the academic ethic than are today's mass universities but since the numbers of students they educated were smaller than they are now, their influence in their respective national higher educational systems was less pronounced.

Some departments in some of the larger universities have become so large that senior teachers do not know their juniors, even by name and face. Something like this has happened in the smaller universities too; in these, senior members might know their younger departmental colleagues but they are ignorant of the younger members of adjacent departments. This is injurious to the assimilation of the younger generation of teachers and to the internal solidarity of the teaching staff as a whole and to their attachment to the university. The teaching staffs of departments with closely connected subject-matters have become more separate from each other. The increase in the size of universities and their constituent faculties and departments has also increased the spatial separation of departments and disciplines from each other; they have increasingly been housed in separate buildings so that their members seldom meet each other. This spatial separation of faculties was always more common in Continental universities, less so in American and British universities. The separation has now been aggravated in both the Continental and the Anglo-American universities.

It might be said these are merely ecological matters and that they have nothing to do with what the universities have as their concern, namely, intellectual things. It should also be said that spatial separation is not new; universities which do not have a single campus have experienced it for a long time. Nevertheless, the increased size of the universities both in numbers of students and in numbers of teachers has accentuated this condition. Furthermore, spatial and social separations do affect intellectual matters. Universities became what they were in their great days because they helped to bring intellectual traditions into focus and concentrated them on individuals by bringing persons of intellectual talent and disposition into contact with each other. The universities enabled them to find each other and to benefit from each other's stimulating and disciplining presence. Their mutual presence—of teachers with teachers, teachers with students and students with students—had the effect of making them more inclined to exert themselves and to stretch their capacities. One deficiency of the mass university is the isolation of the intellectually serious, highly talented student who has the capacity to become a productive scientist or scholar. This kind of student, under present circumstances, is frequently left to himself until fairly late in his career as a student, when he has a better chance of finding a mentor who can help him. This isolation obtains not only among students, between students and teachers, but also between teachers and teachers. The academic ethic and the scientific ethic are both inculcated through face-to-face contact and they are maintained at a high level of intensity by such face-to-face contact. Mutual isolation reduces the pressure generated by the presence of other lively, curious and actually and potentially productive minds. The present-day mass university makes this process of the mutual discovery of talented and interested intellectuals more difficult and it thereby hampers—although it certainly does not prevent—the intensification of intellectual exertion.

The constraints of the mass university are exacerbated in the "reformed" mass university of the Continent where malformations consequent on rapid growth to very large size and the ill-considered responses to those malformations have been petrified into law. The *Gruppenuniversität* in Germany and the "democratized" universities of France, the Netherlands and the Scandinavian countries have made the rehabilitation of the academic ethos more difficult because they have aggravated conflict, withdrawal, and bureaucratization. The reforms have denied the postulate of the academic ethic; they have denied that there can be consensus and solidarity about common aims in the university and that the university can be a community devoted to intellectual things, despite the divisions of age, function, status, and specialization. As a result of these spuriously "democratic" reforms, many teachers who would have liked it to be otherwise have withdrawn into their own scientific and scholarly research with a few of their more intellectually advanced students and left the rest to the political factions which have been given constitutional status and official resources. Others work under discouraging conditions, separated from their students by the impersonality of large classes and by the distrust, which is intermittently given a dramatic and disruptive expression by a minority of radical students. Efforts to provide for the future of higher education in science and scholarship by discovering at an earlier stage the more talented students who wish to make academic careers and by trying to help them by drawing them out of their isolation are resisted by the "anti-elitist" pretensions of the present period.

The mass university has been criticized for bringing into itself many young persons who have little intellectual interest. This may be true but it does after all teach many of these young persons the specialized technical knowledge which will be necessary for the practice of their occupations and which is sufficiently desired by society to support that kind of education and to pay for the service of those persons after they graduate.

It is, however, not only the small number of highly talented students who are often overlooked in the mass universities; the much more numerous, less distinguished ones also suffer from neglect. They are given an education which is often little more than a simulacrum of a university education. They, like the better students, are usually taught in large classes and receive little attention from senior teachers. Syllabuses have been allowed to run down in the belief that the ordinary students cannot measure up to a higher standard of performance or that they will balk if too much work is required of them. The university teacher's idea of his obligation to these students tends to become pale and blurred. Many teachers working under these conditions, especially those who are zealous in research, come to regard their teaching of undergraduates as of secondary importance. This is not so true of their attitude towards their own group of research students or of the handful of brilliant undergraduates whom they discover by deliberately searching for them or who deliberately seek them out. They have tended to think of these students as prospective scientists and scholars and their association with them is regarded as closely connected with their own research. The teaching of the other students is often regarded as a chore. This does not always happen; famous scholars and scientists sometimes teach the introductory course in their respective fields but the pleasure in the delivery of polished lectures to large numbers of students does not extend to a sense of obligation to deal with the mass of these ordinary students in smaller groups.

It has always been an issue as to whether academics of outstanding scholarly ability should devote as much time as is done by teachers in

Oxford and Cambridge colleges to students of mediocre talent. This question need not be decided here. What is clear, however, is that for a variety of reasons in the mass university many teachers look with some revulsion on teaching large numbers of students of whom they know nothing, whose faces they forget or do not notice and whose names they never know.

One could go on multiplying this list of obstacles which the "reformed" and "democratized" Western European mass university and the mass universities of North America have thrown up in the way of the academic ethic but enough has been said to make clear the magnitude of the task and the urgency of rescuing what can be rescued.

The Service-University

Universities have always been integrated into the practical life of their societies. They have always included among their functions the training of lawyers and physicians; later, they introduced courses for civil servants and advanced secondary school teachers as well, and later still, courses for engineers and scientists who worked in government, agriculture, and industry. In the present century, they have continued to do all these things as well as to educate their own succession in science and scholarship and the practitioners of many occupations, such as journalism, librarianship, and social work, which did not exist in their present form until quite recently; nursing education has also become in some places a responsibility accepted by universities. For quite a long time in American and British universities, they have also provided training for the management of private business firms.

Despite these perfectly obvious facts, the charge that universities are ivory towers has been a common one throughout the present century. The charge has been made by narrow-minded political zealots who resented the studious detachment of universities in the pursuit of truth in numerous fields of intellectual work and the training of their students to face the facts of life, without dogmatism or rigid prejudice and to apply the best established knowledge in their professional careers. It has also been made by social reformers and radicals who thought that their causes—sometimes good causes, sometimes pernicious ones—could not wait any longer for their realization, and who required that everyone throw himself into the battle without regard for balanced judgment based on carefully assessed knowledge. Similar criticism of universities used to be made from the quite different standpoint of the "practical man," usually the businessman, who could not see the point of intellectual activities which did not show a profit or which did not contribute directly to industrial and agricultural production. The criticism of the university as an "ivory tower" has greatly diminished in recent years. Both businessmen and humanitarian reformers, both civil servants and politicians have accepted that the university is not in fact an "ivory tower."

Similarly the universities have practically ceased to be criticized for being too "utilitarian." This was a common view especially in the United States in the early part of this century but such criticism has nearly disappeared. The universities are now regarded by academics, both in principle and by their own individual engagement in practical activities as rightly serving the intellectual–practical demands of their societies. There is a general consensus inside and outside the universities that they should be and are involved in the practical concerns of their societies in so far as these activities have a substantial intellectual—above all scientific—content.

Universities are now regarded as indispensable to more practical activities than were ever conceived before as requiring systematic knowledge, and hence, higher education for the acquisition of that knowledge. There is general agreement about this between most academics on the one hand and the leaders in practical affairs on the other. Local and state governments and national governments in almost all Western countries, private business firms, and civic organizations now think that the knowledge which universities produce is necessary to them. They do not think that it is sufficient for them just to appoint the graduates of universities who have had these necessary kinds of fundamental knowledge imparted to them as students before taking up their appointments and who have learned at universities how to acquire the fresh knowledge which their tasks will require.

The prospective "users" of the knowledge and of the techniques of gaining new knowledge which their employees have acquired in universities have, however, begun to demand something more immediately practical. The first steps were taken about a century and a half ago when enterprisers in chemical industries began to solicit individual academic chemists to do research on problems which were of practical importance to the chemical industry. They began to invite academics to do research designed for immediate practical use, alongside or instead of concentrating on the advancement of fundamental knowledge. More recently they have wanted universities to offer special training courses for already employed persons in order to provide them with very particular kinds of knowledge which have been created since those persons had been trained as regular students. Academics, for their part, began to offer advisory services to help governments or business enterprises to deal with highly specific current problems. These expectations and the positive responses of academics became very common after the Second World War.

Also after the Second World War governments became persuaded that the well-being of their societies, or of particular parts of their societies, would in the future depend on having sufficient numbers of persons with the necessary higher educational qualifications; the "planning of high-level manpower" in one form or another was widely recommended and taken seriously. The universities came to be regarded more specifically than ever before as the places where immediately usable scientific research was and could be performed and where the scientists and other persons could acquire the scientific and technological knowledge which was to be immediately applied in the technology and management of the affairs of industrial and commercial firms and governments. This belief was one of the major reasons for the greatly increased financial support for universities. Although this was not a sharp disjunction from what had been developing over the preceding century, the specificity and insistence of the demands for these practical services in research and education have become much more prominent elements in the conception of the tasks of the university.

This pressure on the universities for the provision of specific "services" in research and training has not been exerted solely by the immediate "users" of these services; nor have the "services" been devised and "pushed" by the universities although the universities have responded very energetically to the new possibilities. Some of the pressure has come from agencies of propaganda like the Organization for Economic Cooperation and Development (OECD) and organs of the United Nations as well as from many foundations, associations, publications, and individual publicists arguing for making the universities more "relevant." A large volume of popular writing in books and periodicals about universities was produced after the end of the Second World War. Much of this literature contended that universities must "serve the interests of society" much more directly and deliberately than they had done before. This literature, when combined with the demands made and opportunities offered by governmental and civic bodies, philanthropic foundations and private firms, generated a wave of belief which carried many university teachers and administrators with it.

When in more recent years in the United States, the federal government became more active than it had ever been before in attempting to overcome the disabilities of certain sections of American society, it used its financial power over the universities to make them become its instrument for that egalitarian objective. Teaching hospitals in the poorer sections of large cities which were parts of the institutional system of medical education found themselves becoming "community hospitals" as well. The resources of universities located in large cities were pressed into the provision for groups in their vicinity of certain social services although the beneficiaries of these calls on the revenue of the universities were in no sense members of the universities. This has gone far beyond activities of the "settlement movement" which flourished in British and American universities from the 1880s onward.

The universities perform nonacademic services not only for bodies outside the university but for groups inside the university as well. Anglo-American universities traditionally took quasi-parental responsibilities for their students; much of this was informal. Latterly, universities have assumed many additional functions for the welfare of their students and teaching staffs alongside the traditional functions of record-keeping, examining, financial procurement, etc. As they have become larger, and as the number of students having no direct contact with their teachers has increased, specialized offices of advisers and counselors who are not teachers have also become more numerous. Medical, dental, and mental health services for students and staffs became fuller. Day-care centers for the offspring of students and academic and auxiliary staff have in varying degrees been taken on by universities in a number of countries. Similarly, the provision of entertainment and cultural performances for members of the university and the larger public have appeared among the new services of universities, going beyond the provision of athletic spectacles, which was practically unique to American universities, and of dramatic and musical performances by students. In all these and other ways, universities have acquired a number of functions which they never had previously. Whatever their moral, social, and economic desirability, these activities all increase the size of the administrative staffs of the universities; they bring into the universities a larger number of persons who have no primary interest in intellectual matters and who in the course of time possess vested interests in their own activities and offices. When the financial resources available to the universities are reduced or cease to grow, these non-academic activities, including those which bring no revenue to the universities but which entail only costs as well as those which are associated with the acquisition of revenue, such as "offices of research contracts," are very strong claimants for their share of the budget of the university.

It is not that all these services are useless or despicable. Some of them are outgrowths of the success of the universities in scientific research and in professional training; they are results of the prestige won by the universities through these successes. Many of these services are valuable to society and to the members of the university. Some of them bring revenue to the university which provides them. Nevertheless, they extend the nonintellectual preoccupations of the university and they are distractions from its central responsibilities for teaching and discovery.

The Political University

In the past, churches and governments demanded the faith and loyalty of university teachers. Over the past century and a half and especially in the past half-century, the churches have largely abandoned their demand for the faith of the teachers in the diminishing part of the university world which they controlled. In some countries, governments took the loyalty of the teachers for granted; in others loyalty was required of university teachers as persons with the legal status of civil servants. In countries as different as the German Empire and the United States, this loyalty was assured by the dismissal of teachers who were charged with sympathy with or participation in subversive activities or who were affiliated with organizations with allegedly subversive goals; it was also assured by the refusal to appoint persons suspected of such activities or opinions. In wartime, university teachers usually served their governments in various ways as members of the armed forces, as scientific research workers, as administrators and as intelligence officers. Apart from rare instances—more frequent in some countries than in others—university teachers were assumed to be loyal to the existing social order even when some of them were in sharply expressed opposition to it. Revolutionaries also believed that university teachers were loyal to the existing order and they expected no help from the universities in their conflict with it.

The university as an institution was generally accepted as part of the "establishment," i.e., the constellation of the major churches, the leading newspapers, the government itself, and the economic leadership of the country. Except for occasional ceremonial affirmation of loyalty and in wartime, the highest officials of the universities, such as presidents, rectors, and vice-chancellors, acting on behalf of the universities as institutions, asserted no corporate position on political issues. As institutions, universities espoused no partisan attitudes, whatever the attitudes of their individual members. By and large, this situation still obtains and universities have generally been able to avoid being drawn into political controversies in which they would have to declare a position as a party to the controversy. They have on occasion, but not frequently, issued corporate and joint declarations regarding academic freedom or regarding governmental policies in the financial support for universities; associations of vice-chancellors or presidents have sometimes issued statements to inform the public regarding the financial problems of the universities in their respective countries.

In more recent years, this has begun to change. For example, a few years ago, certain leading American universities, acting in their corporate capacity, have declared themselves as *amicae curiae* in controversies regarding affirmative action in universities other than their own. This was an unusual step but it was in tune with the spirit of the times. Much more often there have been demands made by students and by members of academic staffs of American universities that their universities, in their corporate capacity, should make public declarations expressing the attitude of the university as a whole denouncing the war in Southeast Asia in the 1960s and 1970s or about the policies of racial segregation of the South African government. Both radical students and some university professors and presidents have declared that the university should become a "critical university." By this, they have meant, among other things, that a university, as a corporate body, should, through its officially appointed representatives, make public declarations on all kinds of public issues about which some of its members have strong feelings and convictions, regardless of whether these issues touch directly on the university as an institution of teaching and research. Another related demand has been that the university should train their students to develop and express critical attitudes towards the existing social and political order. A small number of radical teachers have in a moment of enthusiastic fantasy tried to turn the precincts or buildings of their universities into asylums for evaders of conscription, terrorists sought by the police, etc.

These demands have on the whole been unsuccessful, although university presidents have since the late 1960s become increasingly disposed individually or collectively to make public declarations on political issues. Another related phenomenon has been the increased frequency over the past several decades with which university teachers have been signatories of partisan "open letters" about political issues to which not only their own names but the names of their universities have been attached. (There has been an increasingly critical attitude towards the attachment of the names of the universities but the practice has continued unchecked.)

Underlying these particular developments has been a heightening of political interest within the academic profession as a whole and particularly in the social science and humanistic faculties. University teachers have long been interested in political issues and a small number of them, in France in the nineteenth century, entered upon political careers. This animation of political interest within the academic profession has been rather pronounced since the agitation about the case of Captain Dreyfus in the last decade of the nineteenth century. In Italy, the United States, and Germany, and to a lesser extent in Great Britain, academic social scientists played a significant part in public discussions on political questions and they seem to have had some influence on public opinion. The period since the Second World War has seen a considerable expansion of this kind of activity and an intensification as well. It is against this background that the high degree of sensitivity and the increased force of expression about political matters on such matters as the war in Southeast Asia, the control of armaments, and the developments in formerly colonial territories are to be seen.

University students in liberal-democratic countries have intermittently been drawn into political activities. They have been more inclined towards extreme positions than have their politically interested teachers and their politics have been more demonstrative. The political activities of students in the 1960s and 1970s were probably more fervent and more extensive than ever before and the politically active students made more political demands on their teachers. They also concerned themselves more with the substance of their course of study and with the internal administration and academic appointments in their universities than they had in the past.

One manifestation of the vigor of political partisanship in the universities has been the movement in the social sciences and in the humanities to make appointments with fairly explicit references to political criteria. The view that a department should have representation of "the Marxist view" or "the radical view" is put forward not infrequently by senior members of university departments or of appointive committees who themselves are not Marxists, or it is put forward by members of the department or of the appointments committee who are sympathetic with the radical political standpoint which they wish represented. It is explicitly argued that the Marxist or the radical viewpoint is scientifically distinctive, that it represents an intellectually legitimate approach and that the "pluralism of standpoints"—meaning, in fact, certain particular political standpoints although not usually so explicitly stated—requires the appointment of a Marxist. This argument is apparently seldom adduced when the appointment of non-Marxists is being discussed.

The foregoing observations do not imply that university teachers should be indifferent to the political problems of their societies or of the world at large and they do not imply either that they do not have the same political rights as other citizens. They do point, however, to a phenomenon which can distract academics from their responsibilities for teaching and research in accordance with the best methods available for ascertaining what is true regarding any of the particular subjects and problems they deal with. Among the consequences of politicization is the appearance of a current of academic opinion which asserts that such truths are not ascertainable by these methods, that all intellectual activity is political by its nature, and that the aspiration for detachment and objectivity is vain and illusory. This opinion hits at the very heart of the academic ethic.

The Governmentally Dominated University

In many liberal-democratic countries, universities were founded on governmental initiative, have depended on the financial support of governments, have had their charters authorized by governments, and even had their constitutions and statutes promulgated and enacted by governments. In the Anglo-Saxon countries, governments nearly always issued the charters of universities which permitted them to exist legally as corporate bodies, to own property, etc. In the United States, first in the southern and middle western and then in the western states, the state governments founded universities and supplied the funds for their support. Alongside these there were many private universities which had no financial support from governments. Being supported by government did not mean that the universities were simply instruments of governmental desires and decisions. Governmental financial support was quite compatible with far-reaching autonomy of the universities in Germany as well as in Great Britain and the United States.

Apart from those countries and states in which a secondary school diploma or certificate automatically entitled its holder to have a place as a student in a state university, universities were generally free to set the conditions of admission; except for state examinations, the setting and marking of examinations were entirely in the hands of the teaching staff of universities. Universities generally appointed members of their teaching staffs and promoted or discontinued them, if they had not been appointed on permanent tenure. They decided what was to be the content of the various courses of study, although they had to bear in mind the requirements for admission to and practice of the various professions for which the university offered training. Professors decided what research should be done in their university institutes or departments.

Governments generally did not attempt to influence the choice of subjects which students might make, nor did they attempt to influence the proportion which "major" subjects made up in all the subjects studied by the students. When governmental approval of proposals for appointment had to be obtained, it was mainly granted as a matter of course within the list of candidates submitted by the faculty, or the universities were asked to submit an alternative list of proposed candidates. Direct governmental appointments were relatively rare. Universities were entirely free to decide who should be granted degrees and what classes of degrees were to be awarded to students on the basis of their performance on examinations, in research or in their performance in the classroom or in seminars.

Universities have had to move on an intricate pathway in their relations with churches and governments to establish and maintain university autonomy and academic freedom. The paths have varied from country to country. Still, by and large, both the autonomy of the university and academic freedom did become established. In at least one country—Germany—academic freedom in teaching and research came to be guaranteed by the constitution. In other countries, it was achieved through conventions which were generally observed even though they did not have the force of law.

With the coming of totalitarianism, this pattern, which was mainly a creation of the second half of the nineteenth century, underwent drastic modification. In the totalitarian countries teachers were appointed on political grounds; other teachers were dismissed on political, ethnic, and religious grounds. Admissions of students and the contents of courses of study were regulated according to political criteria. Academic freedom in the sense of freedom to do academic things, e.g., to choose what to teach and how it was to be taught, was far-reachingly curtailed; the civil freedom of academics was of course abolished with that of all other citizens. Universities became infiltrated with academics who, whatever their past performance, became agents of the ruling party. Certain subjects in the natural sciences and humanistic subjects, which were relatively remote from the doctrines espoused by the monopolistic party, continued to exist in a shrunken and obscure condition. Disciplines on which the party's doctrines touched or on which the leaders of the party had views were utterly distorted.

Nothing at all close to this has occurred in the universities of liberal-democratic countries. Nevertheless, governments in such countries, too, have greatly enlarged their interest in and influence over universities. The interest and influence of governments were expressed and intensified by their unprecedentedly large expenditures on universities. The immense expenditures were in fact an expression of their confidence that the universities could, if appropriately provided for and conducted, meet the "needs of society" on behalf of which governments spoke.

Governments have never been completely indifferent to universities, even in Great Britain, where no universities had been governmental institutions except in the sense that they received charters from governments and in the sense that in the provinces and Scotland representatives of local governments sat on the highest governing bodies of the universities. The central government of Great Britain on a number of occasions appointed royal commissions to inquire into the conduct of universities. In the United States, private universities had no connections with governments except for the receipt of a charter from a state government; others were supported by but not closely supervised or regulated by state and municipal governments and they had practically no connections with the central government. In France, Spain, and Italy, universities were dependent on the central government for their budget, appointments, the setting of syllabuses, etc. In Germany, universities were legally institutions of the state which provided practically all of their funds, authorized the appointment of their teachers, and drew up their constitutions or statutes. Nevertheless, these varying arrangements did not entail very close and continuous surveillance of teaching and research. Most of the universities of liberal-democratic and more or less liberal monarchical countries enjoyed a considerable degree of autonomy, some by law and some de facto. Nevertheless, this autonomy has not made the universities immune from the consequences of variations in governmental policies regarding education and scientific research.

Without requiring any change in standards of admission, governments have greatly influenced the size of the university student bodies. They have done so by promoting the completion of courses of study in secondary schools, which has, in turn, resulted in more young persons acquiring the qualifications for admission to universities; to this, governments have added the provision of grants or loans to pay for fees and maintenance and of grants for the construction of new buildings at universities and for the payment of the salaries of larger teaching staffs. This movement towards the "mass university" has not been a result of direct command by governments to the universities nor has it been entirely a product of governmental policies—there has, in fact, been a tremendous surge of belief throughout Western societies in the desirability and necessity of becoming "educated." The universities themselves welcomed the governmental policies which expanded the size of the student bodies, increased the numbers of universities, etc. The many-sided expansion of the universities owes a great deal to governmental policies.

Likewise, the policies have produced the present embarrassments of universities which enlarged their plant and equipment and their teaching staffs on the assumption that governments would continue to provide, because, in recent years, governmentally supplied financial resources have been contracting more than student bodies and teaching staffs and the costs of operation. The contraction or stabilization of the appropriations made to universities both for the support of students and the support of research have caused many difficulties for universities which had enlarged their staffs and their facilities during the period of expanding financial resources. (Quite recently, the British government has imposed a reduction in the number of students.)

Furthermore, once central governments began to spend huge sums of money on universities and particularly for research in universities, they also became insistent that their money be properly spent. "Accountability" has become a governmental concern which affects universities as recipients of governmental funds. This has been thought to require much closer surveillance over universities. Their expenditures have been more closely watched; the ratio between teachers and students has likewise been more closely watched in a number of countries and the teachers' use of their time has also been questioned as never before. Although there have been efforts by governments to influence the distribution of students among different fields of study, the substance of what is taught has been left untouched. By and large, however, the specifically academic freedom and the civil freedom of university teachers have scarcely ever been greater in the history of universities, as far as intervention and restriction by governments are concerned. Nevertheless, governments have moved nearer to the heart of the university. For one thing, the new system, now nearly half a century old, of the support of research in universities by central governments has made universities more dependent not just for funds—in Continental universities, they were already very dependent on central governments for the financial support of research at a time when universities in English-speaking countries were still largely independent of such support—but on the decisions of governmental officials as to which fields of research would be supported. Governments, spending so much money on research and attributing so much importance to it, have sought to instate "science policies;" they have succeeded in doing so with very varying degrees of efficacy and coherence. These science policies are much influenced by the advice given by academic scientists. Nevertheless, general decisions regarding the allocation of funds among the different fields and groups of problems in which academic scientists work are now being influenced by governments in a greater measure than was the case before the First World War or between the two world wars.

This dependence has by no means been a totally external imposition against the will of academics. In this recent development, the advice of academic scientists has been sought regarding which particular proposals for research should be supported and it has normally been heeded; still, the decision has remained the decision of government officials who at the moment of decision are neither scientists nor university teachers. In decisions about the allocation of funds among the main fields of scientific research, e.g., between astronomy and nuclear physics, the decisions have been made by politicians in cabinets and legislatures and by high civil servants; here too, however, the decisions have usually been made after hearing the views of scientists in various capacities as scientific advisers, university administrators, and officials of academies and learned societies.

This shift towards government of the center of gravity in the making of decisions about the choice of problems for research is much more pronounced in the kinds of governmental research designated as "mission-oriented." While much of this research is done in governmental laboratories, in research institutes which are more or less governmentally supported, and in the laboratories of private business firms which work on contractual terms for governments, a considerable proportion of it is also done in universities on grants and contracts. The decisions as to which of the problems of mission-oriented research should be investigated are made by governmental officials. It is true that academic scientists, in the countries in which the universities do mission-oriented work, are not compelled to work on these problems and there are indeed many who do not work in mission-oriented research and who are able to obtain funds from other sources which permit them to work on problems of greater interest to themselves. There are, however, many who are content to work on interesting problems set by "outsiders" and for whom the contracts are important because they are enabled thereby to support graduate students or postdoctoral fellows whose scientific careers are dependent on the income which these contracts bring. A great deal of very important work is undoubtedly done in mission-oriented research and it could not have been done without the large sums made available by governments. The fact remains, however, that the increased prominence of mission-oriented research in universities is tantamount to the displacement of the power of decision from within the universities to governments.

American universities have been more directly affected by governmental actions in matters of appointment in ways which have gone far beyond the traditional Continental practice of the requirement of ministerial approval for the creation of new professorial chairs and for the appointments of particular candidates.

In the United States, the federal government for some years has threatened—it still does so—universities with suspension of the financial support of research or funds for the payment of tuition fees if they do not appoint Negroes, women, Mexican-Americans and Puerto Ricans in sufficient numbers. Nothing like this has happened in other liberal-democratic countries. The Continental universities have been subjected in a different way to a far more comprehensive intrusion of governmental authority into their internal affairs. This has occurred through the legislation of the past two decades which has transformed the system of internal government of universities and severely affected their intellectual level and the policies of universities regarding the appointment of university teachers. By transferring much of the power to make decisions regarding the substantive content of syllabuses and courses of study and in some cases, the appointive power as well, to teachers in lower ranks, students and administrative and custodial employees, many European governments have intervened into the internal affairs of universities more penetratingly than has ever happened in liberal-democratic countries. They have done all this while nominally maintaining the academic freedom and the autonomy of universities which in the past were justified by the argument that they guaranteed the predominance of intellectual criteria in the making of decisions about the most important elements of academic life. It is true that the governments of Continental countries have, over the past century and three-quarters at least, had the legal right to frame the constitutions and statutes of universities. Nevertheless, except for the period of National Socialism in Germany, these powers have never been used before to subvert so crucially and systematically the predominance of intellectual academic criteria in the making of decisions on academic matters.

The arrangements vary from one Continental country to another with respect to the composition and powers of governing bodies but whatever their composition, the governmentally guaranteed autonomy of the university from government means that "interest groups" within the university are encouraged to contend for their "interests." These are often political and economic interests.

The Bureaucratized University

The growth in size of the university in numbers of students and teachers, the greatly increased sums of money involved in the operation of a university, the increased intensity and complexity of relations with government, the increased provision of services by the university, and the reluctance of university teachers to take responsibilities for activities beyond their own research and teaching has brought about a situation of increased bureaucratization in the administration of universities. Max Weber made the bureaucratization of the university one of the main themes of his analysis of science and scholarship as a vocation. He compared the new conditions with the situation which had obtained in the early part of the nineteenth century when professors still worked in their own private libraries and used their own premises and equipment. He remarked on the bureaucratization of the university as one aspect of the bureaucratization which had been going on in many spheres of society during his own lifetime. "Self-administration" was one of the characteristic features of the German universities. Except for the *Kurator,* who was the representative of the state government in the university, all higher administrative posts in Continental universities were filled by academics for short periods after which they returned to their regular academic duties. The ancient universities of England were not far removed from this pattern. The American universities, the modern British universities and, since the 1930s, the Australian universities, have had a stratum of full-time administrators. Some of them had been university teachers but they ceased to be so on becoming full-time administrators, appointed for long terms, and others were never university teachers.

The amount of paperwork has grown as universities have become more dependent on and accountable in greater detail to governments for the support which they receive, and as every new research project requires a new application of many pages and in many copies. More administrators are needed to deal with these papers and to certify them before passing them on to the next higher level of authority. Governments demand more information about what is being done to observe their regulations, and not only regarding the expenditure of funds which they have awarded to universities. The more exacting the laws regulating the conditions of employment of industrial and commercial employees, the more records the universities have to keep and the greater the number of nonacademic staff they require for the purpose because the universities are employers of manual, custodial, and clerical workers, just as are private, industrial, and commercial enterprises. The care of animals used for biomedical research has increasingly aroused the concern of governments and hence more records must be kept; the universities must employ persons who will watch over and enforce conformity with laws and decrees of government concerning the care of experimental animals.

It is in the nature of bureaucracies to extend themselves. More tasks, quite reasonable tasks, are discovered; it then becomes necessary to increase the administrative staff for that purpose. So, at least, it seems to administrators. As a result, the administrative staffs proliferate and academics find themselves surrounded on all sides by administrators, who want forms filled out, who wish to have their permission sought to do things for which older academics do not recall having had to seek permission. Rules, forms, and "channels" become more prominent; informal understandings and conventions become less prominent in the administration of universities.

In some universities, the activities of teachers are subjected to minute scrutiny in order to assure maximal "productivity." The amount of time spent in classrooms and in consultation with students is expressed in "contact-hours," and a certain number of contact-hours is stipulated as obligatory. There have even been indications on the part of governmental officials that teachers should be present in the university during "working hours," contrary to the traditional view that teachers should be free, apart from scheduled classes and office hours, to spend their time wherever they found it most convenient to do their academic work.

With all this proliferation of administration and of administrators around research and teaching, these two central activities are, at their hearts, untouched. In liberal-democratic countries with academic freedom and university autonomy, once a scientist or scholar is in his classroom or seminar room or laboratory or library study, he is, as he has been for a long time, the master of his own intellectual actions. Nevertheless, he does not always feel that way; instead he feels himself hemmed in, pushed and pulled hither and thither, by administrators who are alien in spirit to his vital intellectual concerns. This fosters a sense of alienation from "the university," which he sees as dominated by the bureaucracy and in essential antagonism to what he thinks are his main obligations.

The Financially Straitened University

The growth of the "mass university" in the period after the Second World War would not have been possible without munificent financial support by governments. Scientific research has, for the most part, been supported by governmental bodies separate from those which supply the funds for capital and current costs of conducting the instructional activities of universities. Many new universities were founded and were equipped at great expense; large teaching staffs were appointed. In a number of countries, and most of all in the United States, funds provided by public bodies were supplemented by funds provided by private bodies and individuals. It became possible through these greatly increased funds to appoint more teachers, to construct new buildings, to purchase more and more powerful and refined scientific equipment, to purchase more books for libraries, to appoint more administrators and to increase the services and amenities for students, as well as to pay the fees for many of them and even to pay for their maintenance. Grants for tuition fees and maintenance were supplemented in the United States by loans from the federal government.

The easy and unprecedented availability of funds from governments and philanthropic foundations caused a euphoric attitude to grow among university teachers and administrators. Young persons shared this euphoria to some extent. All were confident of the future. Unceasing public favor and largesse were taken as assured. The universities went on increasing the size of their academic and administrative staffs and adding to their physical plant with relatively little anxiety that the resources to pay the salaries, support the research, and maintain the buildings and equipment might cease to grow or even diminish. Nevertheless that is what has happened. The universities in most countries have had in the past decade to reckon with the cessation of the growth in their income, and many higher educational institutions in the United States and an increasing number in Europe have seen their budgets decrease. Demographic changes have contributed to this but more important has been the governmental decision to reduce the allocation of funds for education at all levels.

We need not concern ourselves with why nearly all governments in liberal-democratic societies have tapered off their enthusiasm for universities. They have certainly not ceased to expect the universities to meet all the demands for training, service, and research which had been directed at them previously.

Governmental allocation of funds for scientific research, although ceasing to grow at the same rate as in the several decades which followed the Second World War, have continued to grow slightly or to remain approximately constant. The funds for instruction, the "regular" budget from which salaries of teachers are paid, have stopped increasing and in some cases declined. This has meant a marked reduction in the numbers of new appointments and this in turn has meant that young scientists and scholars who have recently completed their studies have found it very difficult to obtain appointments.

As part of the rapid expansion of the 1950s and 1960s, many persons were appointed to permanent tenure at early ages or were granted such tenure fairly shortly. In consequence of this, universities for the coming years are amply and expensively provided with teachers in most subjects at the higher levels of salary and with a large number of retirements scheduled to fall due only towards the end of the present decade or later. Until then, there will be serious obstacles to the careers of young aspirants to academic careers. This has also aggravated the situation since mistakes in appointment committed in the period of great expansion cannot be corrected by new appointments of more able young persons. The damage done by earlier misjudgments cannot under these conditions be undone. Any postponement of the age of retirement such as has recently been enacted into law in the United States will reinforce these obstacles.

This has very discouraging effects, not only on those who have acquired the qualifications for an academic career and have in some cases already begun those careers, but also on those who would otherwise be inclined to seek those qualifications. There is, in short, the danger of a loss of an academic generation. This is a personal tragedy for the individuals so affected and an obstacle to the growth of knowledge which is dependent on the creative powers of younger workers in each field. It is injurious to the universities in many other ways. It widens the always threatening cleavage between senior and junior teachers. The threat of redundancy generates anxiety about personal fates and about whole courses of study, especially in fields in which there are few students and which are relatively costly to maintain. All this distracts young academics from the tasks of teaching and research and it worries older academics who are solicitous about their subjects, their institutions, and their professions.

In the countries under discussion here, governments played a decisive role in the promotion of the expansion of the numbers of students and academic staffs and in the establishment of new universities. The academics welcomed the expansion with much enthusiasm. They were very exhilarated by the increase in the size of the teaching staffs of their departments and they gave little thought to the duration of expansion and the possibility and consequences of its cessation. Incumbent professors, particularly the older generation, should have thought of the morrow. It should have been readily apparent to them that the expansion could not continue indefinitely.

The University in the Eye of Publicity

For much of their history, universities were not widely noticed in their societies. The mass of the population ignored them, except for the small groups of employees who served them in various menial capacities, local shopkeepers, innkeepers, and lodging-house keepers who gained a livelihood from the students, and the townspeople who were occasionally made aware of them by rampaging undergraduates in altercations between town and gown. Some students engaged in revolutionary and nationalistic political activities in France and Germany but they were more attended to by the police than by the wider public. The major activities of universities were not of much interest to the working or the middle classes. The fame of universities existed mainly for academics and for learned persons outside the universities and for the rulers of society: the universities were very remote from and shadowy to the workaday larger world.

This state of affairs had persisted over many centuries. Even after the development of the popular press in the second half of the nineteenth century, the universities received no treatment in its columns. The superior press published brief articles and letters by professors, announced jubilees, and deaths. Some professors entered on political careers but this did not attract attention to the universities. It is really only in the twentieth century that universities became "news." The ceremonial dedication of major academic buildings and scientific installations and spectacular achievements touching local pride also received some attention. In English-speaking countries, athletic competitions and games began to attract popular attention. In the present century, scientific discoveries, archaeological excavations, great steps in surgery and medical therapy began to be reported outside the scientific press. But even though such subjects began to be treated in the press, there seems to have been no "science writers" in popular newspapers before the First World War.

The universities did not seek publicity. It did not occur to academics and university administrators to seek it. Individual academics did not yearn to be "in the news." American universities in the 1920s did employ "press officers" but their task was to prevent the universities from being placed before the public eye when some possibly embarrassing event occurred; it is unlikely that any continental European university had a press officer. There was no call for such a person. The press, apart from the handful of superior newspapers, did not concern itself with universities and was not interested in receiving "press releases" from "public relations officers" of universities. The wider public, even in the middle classes, had no interest in reading about universities in the daily press; the working classes scarcely knew that universities existed and had little interest in learning what they were. Occasionally universities drew the attention of the press; the undergraduate debate on the "defence of king and country" in the Oxford Union, the conflict over the cancellation of Bertrand Russell's appointment at the City College of New York, the troubles of Professor John Anderson at Sydney or of Scott Nearing at Pennsylvania and of McKeen Cattell at Columbia were *causes célèbres* and very much out of the ordinary run of events.

A very dramatic change took place after the Second World War. Universities entered much more extensively into the consciousness of their contemporaries. The increased numbers of students, the increased appearance of university teachers as advisers, the successes of academic scientists during the war, the brushing of universities by Soviet espionage, the implication of a small number of university teachers in espionage, and the rumors and accusations of the connections of larger numbers in such activities as well as the general conviction that universities held the keys to a happier, more prosperous future made newspapers begin to attend more seriously to the activities of universities. Universities became, in a sense, part of the "beat" of newspapermen. The achievements and the claims of scientists became "news." The fortunes of the universities became "newsworthy;" the activities of their students, the opinions of their presidents and the views of their teachers about all sorts of public events became material for journalists. The social sciences joined the natural sciences as "news;" the natural scientists reported their discoveries, sometimes through press conferences which they or their universities convoked. Social scientists were frequent sources of assessments of contemporary economic, social, and political questions. Legislative investigations repeatedly summoned academics as expert witnesses.

University administrators were in step with this mood. Since the universities were being conducted in a more and more costly fashion, funds from governments, private foundations, and individuals had to be raised—in different proportions in different countries. To attract and hold the favor of legislators and political leaders, university administrators, singly and collectively, had to try to reach them; the printed press, radio, and television seemed to be the appropriate instruments for this. Thus, both sides seemed to approach each other, the universities approaching journalists in order to gain attention and appreciation for their achievements and an understanding of their problems, journalists approaching the university as a source of interesting news.

The student disturbances of the 1960s and 1970s made universities into even more eagerly observed sources of dramatic "news;" in fact, the publicity which was so readily available helped to extend the student disturbances nationally and internationally. The student disruptors' desire for publicity was in fact one manifestation of the quest for publicity which has become very widespread in Western societies.

Many academics seek publicity for themselves and their work. In some universities, teachers who are in dispute with their colleagues break the confidentiality of the proceedings of governing and appointive bodies by "leaking" to the press. The press is drawn into academic disagreements and aggravates them. Aggrieved members of the universities turn to the press as well as to the courts to vindicate their cause and to remedy the wrongs which they think they have suffered.

Confidentiality, which had long been regarded as right in university proceedings, is no longer thought to be so, especially in the United States. Courts in two separate American jurisdictions have ordered members of appointive bodies to disclose how they voted for a particular candidate. The federal government has legislated a prohibition of confidentiality in the assessment of students and the federal bureaucracy demands that confidential assessments of candidates for appointments be taken into their custody. (Once in the possession of the federal government, these assessments are open to anyone who wishes to obtain copies of them under the Freedom of Information Act.)

Some of the publicity given to significant scientific and scholarly discoveries is desirable as a form of public education and it might also be beneficial to the universities by enabling ordinary citizens to learn about and to appreciate their achievements. But much of it is a distraction to many of the academics who seek it, some of whom come to regard a broad publicity as a good in itself; others do so because it enables them to raise their prestige in the academic world. Some of them regard it, rather than the judgment of their qualified colleagues, as evidence of the merit of their achievements.

The "Research University"

The idea of the modern university was shaped by Wilhelm von Humboldt who thought that the university should be a place of scientific and scholarly research where young persons were inducted into and educated through research. The "unity of teaching and research" formulated this idea, which reached into the life of universities throughout the world. It guided the reform of existing universities and it set the pattern of newly established ones. Although some universities placed greater emphasis on research and others placed more emphasis on teaching, it was not generally believed that these two activities were in a mutually exclusive relationship with each other.

The situation changed after the Second World War. Research in the

United States became in some of the leading universities more prized than teaching, particularly the teaching of undergraduates. Research came to be regarded as the primary obligation; the desire to do research spread to higher educational institutions which had previously placed primary emphasis on teaching. It was not difficult to understand why this change took place after the great triumphs of scientific research during the Second World War. The availability of large sums for the support of research, the high public prestige of research and the tendency to base decisions on academic appointments and promotions on achievements and promise in research all placed research at the top of the agenda of the university teacher. Many persons who would have preferred teaching to research felt they had to do research. Many were swept into research by the strong currents of academic opinion.

Under conditions such as these, which were very favorable for research, universities which were already distinguished in research shot further ahead of the others in their accomplishments. They were the most esteemed and the most talked about. Other universities seeking to hold their own in the increasingly acute competition for eminence also placed the criteria of achievement in research in the forefront. Those who did not succeed in research were regarded by others and themselves as inferior. Many individuals who did not have a very strong propensity to do research felt themselves compelled to do it. Whatever the scientific or scholarly significance of their results, the activity of research itself became a condition of minimal academic self-respect.

The disturbances in the universities caused by the agitation of the 1960s and early 1970s aroused some uncertainties about this elevation of research in the hierarchy of academic values. They led some academics to turn against the academic ethos and to denounce the obligation to do research, to deny the possibility of objectivity in research and to deride the devotion to science and scholarship as no more than an "ideology." Others reacting in the opposite direction were led to feel aversion from universities, to reduce their teaching and to concentrate on research and to working with graduate students.

Although European universities did not fall prey to the classification which separated "research universities" from "other universities," the conditions of the "mass university," the student agitation, and the subsequent university reforms alienated many teachers from the existing pattern which coupled research and teaching. In Germany, the "Humboldt-pattern" was declared to be no longer practicable; research, it has been said, can no longer be done by teachers in the ordinary universities.

According to this idea ordinary universities should concentrate on teaching; special universities should be provided for the conduct of research.

From the high value accorded to research, it follows that the university teacher tends to be assessed in accordance with his achievements in research. Achievements in research are easier to assess than are achievements in teaching; the results of research are visible in published works, the results of teaching cannot be seen adequately either in marks on examinations or in the approval of students for the pedagogical merit of a particular teacher. For these reasons all teachers and especially younger teachers, wishing to assure their reappointment and promotion to permanence of tenure, often engage in research with an intensity which goes much beyond their intellectual interest in the problems they study. Even where the university teacher is deeply interested in the problem of his research, he often feels himself additionally compelled in his research by the belief that his success in its completion, publication, and acceptance will affect his academic career, either in the university in which he holds an appointment or in one to which he wishes to be invited. This state has two consequences which are worth noting; one is that it calls forth additional effort in the talented inducing them to devote themselves to research with a degree of concentration which they might not otherwise demand of themselves. In such cases, the demanding atmosphere and considerations of advancement in the academic career add a beneficial impetus to the production of work of high quality. The other consequence is not so beneficial. This occurs when the individual who might be an excellent teacher and who might take seriously the necessity of "keeping up" with publications in his subject but who has little desire to do research is constrained in order to secure his reappointment or advancement to do research in which he has less interest and aptitude than he has in teaching. Inasmuch as most universities nowadays wish to be "research universities" and hence regard achievements in research as paramount criteria in appointments and promotion, many persons, the results of whose research add little that is valuable to the stock of knowledge, are forced, willy-nilly, to be "published" scholars and scientists.

The widespread desire of administrators and senior academics that their universities be research universities is reinforced by the prevailing methods of granting financial support for research by bodies external to the universities. In the United States, at least, the universities have become dependent on grants for particular research projects in order to obtain the funds needed to pay the salaries of many of the members of their academic staffs. Teachers are pressed therefore to seek grants for research in order to help to pay their salaries. This increases the pressure on individuals to engage more intensively in research than they otherwise might do.

The elevation of the criterion of the publication of the results of research to a dominant position creates special difficulties for younger academics. Although the publication of short papers in scientific and scholarly journals is relatively easy because of the large number of journals in every field, the publication of books and monographs is less so. The increased costs of printing, paper, and binding have greatly raised the costs of publication of academic books and thereby reduced their sale. Publishers are therefore reluctant to invest their resources in the production of books which will have an excessively small market. Thus, while universities concerned to enhance their reputation as "research universities" attribute more and more importance to the publication of books and monographs as well as shorter papers, the obstacles to the publication of such larger works by younger scholars have grown in recent years. To be sure, many books and monographs still continue to be published both by commercial publishing firms and by university presses.

Another of the consequences of the increased emphasis on research is that teachers have become more interested in and more attentive to what goes on in the "profession," constituted by those who are doing research in their discipline regardless of where they are, than they are in their colleagues within their own university or in the problems of their own university. It is inherent in the present-day organization of learning that teachers inform themselves about what is being accomplished in their own field of study, wherever that work is being done. A teacher who does not keep up with current work in his field is giving his students less than they should have from him. But, granting this inevitable and desirable external direction of intellectual interest, the great weight laid on achievement in research as evidence of success in the academic career has been associated with an increased indifference to the affairs of one's own university. It is obviously possible to maintain a dual loyalty and many university teachers are able to do so. Nevertheless, the balance of concern has shifted outward to the detriment of academic citizenship.

The Disaggregated University

A university has to have some minimal institutional arrangements for decisions regarding the allocation of resources among its parts, for the performance of certain services common to the whole university such as the maintenance of buildings, grounds and libraries, for the purchase of equipment and supplies, for the keeping of records, and for the acquisition, administration, and expenditure of financial resources. All these activities are services to the individual members of teaching staffs, to the departments, and the student body. These arrangements do not, as such, require a sense of membership in a corporate entity on the part of the beneficiaries of these various services; they do not inevitably require or give rise to a sense of solidarity on the part of the teachers with each other, and of their students with each other and with their teachers. They do not necessarily entail a sense of responsibility on the part of each member towards the other members of the university nor do they necessarily generate stimulating intellectual interaction among the individual members of the teaching staff, or the intellectual influence of some individuals on other individuals within the teaching staff. The administrative functions of a university do not involve the dependence of each individual on the silent but significant proximity of so many other persons engaged in the same undertaking of discovering and teaching reliable knowledge. All of these intellectual functions depend on but do not necessarily arise from the bare existence of the university as a legal entity and as an administrative machine performing indispensable services for its members. Nevertheless, a well-functioning university is more than a legally recognized corporation and an administrative machine; it is an intellectual corporation.

Probably no university has ever been completely without conflict or egotism; no university has ever been the object of the solicitude of all its members, each recognizing the intellectual benefits which he receives from his membership in it. Universities have always been divided into faculties, departments, colleges, and other segments. Universities have always been cut across by the lines of generation and ranks. There have always been rivalries among teachers and cleavages between teachers and students. All this notwithstanding, universities which have a single campus and where teachers live near their universities and have studies in them are likely to have more corporate spirit than universities in which faculties are scattered spatially and where teachers live far from the university, appearing there only to teach and absenting themselves at all other times. The universities of Latin Europe have been the most dispersed in this respect. But even where there was wide spatial dispersion, it was not decisive, and the formation of an intellectual corporate spirit did occur to some extent. Outstanding universities have always approximated wholes which have been greater than the sums of their parts.

In the past few decades, the internal unity of universities has been under strain. When the student bodies of universities expanded in size and more funds were available for the appointment of teachers and for research, not only were new recruits to the academic profession brought in, but academics who had already entered upon their careers moved about from university to university in search of more stimulating, more pleasing, more remunerative and more honorific appointments. The expansion of the number of universities increased the intensity of the game of "musical chairs." Teachers shifted from university to university to a far greater degree than they had when universities were increasing very little in either number or size. It is no criticism of the right of individuals to seek appointments which are more suitable to their talents, tastes, and interests and which are more remunerative and honorific, to observe that the movements sometimes have an unsettling effect on the universities those individuals leave or join. In general, a restless seeking for opportunities to go elsewhere has a weakening effect on the morale of a university; it is also a consequence of a weakness of morale or attachment to and care for the institution where the individual in question holds an appointment.

Specialization has similar effects. The unceasing advancement of specialization in scientific and scholarly research, coupled with the greater attention given to research, has caused individual scientists and scholars to be more interested in what colleagues in their own fields of specialization outside their own universities are doing than they are in what is being done by their colleagues in their own universities who are working in neighboring or remoter fields of scientific or scholarly enquiry. Furthermore, the greatly increased size of departments has reduced the likelihood of talking to persons outside one's own department within the same university. The newer modes of providing support for research projects by extra-university patrons has also a tendency to cause academics to have their minds focused more intently on the world outside their own universities.

The centrifugal inclinations of individual academics in universities in the provinces are nourished especially in countries in which life in the capital city is very much more attractive than life in the provinces. In such countries as France and Italy, there are many professors who hold appointments in the provinces but who live in the capital, appearing at their universities only at the hours when they are scheduled to teach.

The tradition which provides that only deans and heads of institutes have rooms at the university in which to work and to receive students and colleagues also serves to disconnect the teachers from each other, from their students, and from the university as an intellectual corporation. These factors have certainly not been insuperable, as many Continental universities have shown, but they have hampered the unity of the university.

The existence of a large proportion of students who have no interest either in their academic studies or in the collective life of their university has also the effect of diminishing the inward direction of affections and attachments. The mass university has brought into the university many young persons whose foremost and perhaps exclusive aim is to obtain a degree and to enter a remunerative occupation. These students have little intellectual interest and they are often not open to sentiments of attachment to their particular university.

The new university laws in Continental Europe have also added to the centrifugal tendencies within universities. These laws have declared—more explicitly in some countries than in others—that the different sections of the university have "interests" which are in principle incompatible with each other. The students are said to have interests which are antithetical to the interests of teachers, the interests of young teachers in the lower ranks are treated as antithetical to the interests of older teachers in the higher ranks. Administrative and custodial employees are also said to have their own distinctive interests, which are said to be different from the interests of teachers of different ranks and of students. That is why, according to this legislation, each of these interests must have its own spokesmen. According to this conception of the university, justice is to be done to these various divergent interests by giving them representation in governing bodies, the primary task of which is to arrive at compromises among these fundamentally conflicting interests. This enactment in legislation of the idea that the university is a constellation of conflicting interests has deepened and made more rigid the conflicts which upset the university during the time of the student disturbances; it has not reconciled them. The legislation based on this idea has added one more seriously disaggregative impulsion to the already existing tendencies towards disaggregation arising from large numbers, specialization, external financial support for particular research projects, and the intensification of attention to government and politics which is characteristic of all modern societies.

As the central governments in all modern societies have acquired more and more tasks and powers, their constituent institutions have all become much less self-contained. One of the many consequences is that these institutions dwell within themselves much less than they used to and are more turned outwards into the arena of political controversy and governmental action than was the case prior to the Second World

War. University teachers and students have become politicized, which means being more inclined to give precedence in attention to things external to the university and to bring those external matters into the university. Since politics is by its nature contentious and partisan, the strengthening of such attitudes in universities has disaggregative results.

The University with Shaken Morale

Whole universities, particular departments, and individuals have from time to time suffered crises of confidence. The loss of a number of eminent members, severe internal conflicts, distracting misfortunes, and sometimes the stagnant state of a discipline have all at one time or another injuriously affected the pride and self-confidence of the individual or the institution. There are disciplines in which the practitioners think that the discipline has not fulfilled its promise, or cannot go forward to new tasks and new problems and techniques. Withdrawal, resentful criticism of their disciplines, and an arbitrary thrashing about are characteristic of such an intellectual condition. Disciplines of which their practitioners were once proud and confident can fall within a few years into this state.

In recent years this has been somewhat more common in the social sciences and the humanities than in the natural and technological sciences. The change has occurred mostly in the younger and middle generations. Some of them have felt that they made a mistake in entering the academic career. Some of them have thought that there is nothing of significance in their subjects. They have been led in some instances into political activity as a way of doing something significant. Some, in recent years, have come to think that their subjects as generally practiced over the past several generations are just "ideologies" supporting the "ruling classes" and serving as instruments of "imperialism" and "colonialism." Others have attempted to prove that as hitherto practiced, their entire discipline is a fraud. There has been much denunciation of their professional colleagues and particularly of some of the acclaimed leaders in their disciplines. They sometimes have sought the admiration of their more antinomian students by denouncing their subjects and disciplines in class.

This situation was sorely aggravated by the student disorders of the late 1960s and the early 1970s. This disaffection of the students shook the moorings of some teachers who did not have sufficient confidence to withstand the muddle-headed attacks on their subjects which some of the more vociferous students were making. They had never previously been asked to construct such a defense and it is not surprising that they did not have one at their fingertips. The traditions of their discipline had existed and interested them and that had been enough. But once they looked critically at the research which they had done, they decided that it had not been satisfactory. Some of them concluded that they had chosen the wrong career. Others concluded that universities were a "racket." This kind of demoralization is to some extent a reaction against the overbearing pride and optimism which some university teachers felt about their subjects during the period of demographic and financial expansion.

The Persistence of the University as a Center of Learning

The phenomena which we have called the "mass university," the "service university," the "political university," the "governmentally controlled university," the "bureaucratic university," the "research university," the university seeking the "eye of publicity," and the "disaggregated university" are undeniable features of academic life of the past third of a century. In some cases, they have been present for a longer time, in others for a considerably shorter time; they are by no means equally present in all universities within any single country; there are also differences in the extent to which they affect the university systems of the various countries with which we deal. Still, despite variations, these features in various combinations have affected the situations of university teachers quite tangibly. Each of them has placed a strain, in various ways, on the performance by university teachers of their fundamental and central tasks of teaching and research. They have in extreme cases rendered the performance of these tasks very difficult. They have all contributed to changing the situation of the university teacher from what it was in Western countries in the period of somewhat more than a century prior to the outbreak of the Second World War.

The situation of universities within the larger world of learning has also changed. A great deal of research is now being done outside the universities. Research in the laboratories of industrial firms and governmental departments has grown greatly. Independent research institutes, privately and governmentally supported and doing a certain amount of the basic and theoretical research which had been in most countries practically a monopoly of universities have become much more common. Institutes of advanced study which were extremely rare before the Second World War have become fairly numerous and have become havens into which scientists and scholars escape from the distractions of the mass university and the other aspects of university life in recent years. (At one time universities themselves provided exactly such havens for undistracted study and reflection.) The training of a small number of graduate students has been provided by a few independent, industrial, and governmental research institutions; in this respect, however, the universities still enjoy an approximate monopoly.

Despite these erosions and arrogations, universities still remain the major centers of learning in their respective societies. The pursuit of fundamental knowledge still goes on within them with great intensity. Much else goes on there, too. Not all of it is by any means practically useful or intellectually valuable; some of it is pedantic and "academic" in the pejorative sense of the term. Very important research is still done in universities and the induction of students into the works of the mind, to the mastery of principles of understanding and habits of thought likewise goes on there. These vital functions, without which no society can be a good society, are nevertheless exposed to distraction and constrictions. They can still be performed and effectively performed as long as university teachers are aware of their obligations and are eager to carry them out, out of the conviction of the value of their tasks and out of love for the knowledge which they possess and pursue.

The carrying out of these obligations will be well served if university teachers are reminded from time to time of the commitments which they took upon themselves when they entered upon the academic profession. The following observations attempt to clarify these commitments and to draw out some of their implications.

The Academic Obligations of University Teachers

All the particular obligations of university teachers to students, to colleagues, to their universities and to their respective societies derive their binding force fundamentally from their obligations to ascertain what is true in their research, study, and teaching, to assess scrupulously what has been handed down as true, and to cultivate and propagate an active quest for truth as an ideal.

The Obligation of Knowledge

To be in a university postulates a common commitment on the part of all of its members to a belief that some grounds for the acceptance and espousal of a proposition or conception are better than other grounds.

Teaching and research are about the pursuit and transmission of truths, the methods of distinguishing between truth and error, so far as that is humanly possible, and the distinction between fallacious and valid evidence and argument. To speak of knowledge is to accept the validity of methods of acquiring and assessing evidence; it is to speak of reason and of rigor in its exercise. A teacher who knowingly presents to his students erroneous and baseless beliefs while purporting to present them as demonstrated knowledge is clearly departing from his primary obligation, regardless of whether he intends to curry the favor of established authorities or to overturn them, and regardless of whether he wishes to please his audience or is simply careless.

A university teacher who knowingly or carelessly presents a false account of his observations in a report of his research is no less culpable than one who deliberately teaches false accounts of the subject for which he is responsible.

Hence we may say that the first obligation of the university teacher is to the truth about the subject matters which he teaches or investigates. Of course, to determine what is true about an important matter can be extremely difficult. What is thought to be the truth about a particular topic or subject matter is inevitably subject to change but the changes are not arbitrary. The changes are subject to disciplined methods; they are subject to the substantive tradition of the subject, even though that, too, undergoes changes with every increment to and revision of the stock of knowledge about any particular topic. There are also huge grey areas where reliable knowledge is patently not available. These are the areas where it is very tempting to a teacher to heed his predilections more than his intellectual scruples. But these situations impose the obligations of hard work, good judgment, scrupulousness, and self-discipline. The apparently definitive areas of knowledge—the black, well-established areas—must be faced with a readiness to change one's belief about them because even though they look final, they are bound not to turn out to be so as knowledge grows. The grey areas, if they are important, are the areas where new research is called for and the judgment of his equally qualified peers in his own university and elsewhere throughout the world of learning is needed to keep the university teacher on his mettle. Much teaching has to be done in these grey areas, indeed many disciplines fall almost entirely within the grey areas; in teaching them to students less experienced in the subject than himself, making them aware of such uncertainties is obligatory for the teacher.

To present as an established truth what is nothing more than an unsubstantiated opinion or a tentative hypothesis is nearly as great a defection from the obligation of a university teacher as it is knowingly to put forward a false proposition as true or to disregard the existence of available new evidence which throws doubt on what has previously been accepted. The teacher, of course, will inevitably have to exercise a degree of responsible personal judgment in such matters; he is not a calculating machine. He is entitled to express his doubts about the supposed new evidence, to express his own conviction that a still-tentative hypothesis will turn out to be true. Inevitably, he will sometimes be wrong on both these points. All that is demanded from him is honesty and modesty about what is and what is not, at a given time, seriously controversial, and about what is simply not known. This does not entail that he ought to become a Pyrrhonian sceptic. There are better grounds for holding some views than there are for holding others, even when they are subject to revision. He should help his students to learn to make such comparative judgments about competing interpretations and to learn to be ready to revise their judgments when better evidence and reasons are available.

The situation is little different when the university teacher is engaged in a role involving his knowledge outside the university. Perhaps the situation is more testing morally when the teacher is acting outside the university because the standards of truthfulness generally insisted on in political controversy or in the public discussions of alternatives of policy are less exigent. In the heat of controversy, the temptations of triumph are very powerful but the obligations to discriminate between what one has good grounds for taking to be true and what is doubtful are not less great than they are in academic settings.

The obligation of a university teacher to discover and enunciate the truth about the particular objects of his investigation entails a corresponding obligation to investigate whatever he regards as important intellectually and practically. This means that he has an obligation, while respecting the methods or rules of inquiry, to refuse to accept the domination of current popular, political, and academic prejudices regarding what it is permissible to investigate. The fact that a subject is "unpopular" must not be allowed to deter a scrupulous scientist or scholar from studying it, as long as he adheres to the methods of scientific or scholarly investigation. It does not mean that an academic may disregard the obligations which govern, for example, experimentation on human beings or which forbid damage to the persons studied or to those who are working with him, nor is he exempt from the obligations regarding publication such as submission to review of his results by his professional peers. It does mean that he must insist on his right to the freedom to investigate whatever he deems to be important.

The obligation to promote the growth of knowledge implies an obligation to share with colleagues the knowledge produced through research. A scientist or scholar is not under obligation to disclose his results to his colleagues before he has satisfied himself that they are as sound as he can make them but, once he has satisfied himself in that regard, he is under obligation to publish them in such a way that colleagues can study and assess them. The obligation to knowledge is met through investigation and "open" publication; secrecy is alien to the obligation of university teachers. There might be exceptional situations in which certain particular results obtained by a scientist working on a project supported by government might be kept secret after consultation between the scientist who has made the discovery in question and a qualified government official, but it must be treated as an exception. The general obligation is to undertake research which is publishable. The scientist who does research which he knows in advance must be kept secret should do such research in a governmental laboratory and not in a university.

His obligation to knowledge does not require that the university teacher become an author of large numbers of scientific or scholarly papers and enough books to fill a small shelf. Universities are institutions of research and teaching, but this does not imply that every teacher must be so active in research that practically all his time when he is not in a classroom should be spent doing "original" research in a laboratory or a library, or "in the field" if that is the kind of research done in his discipline. Nor should a teacher regard it as an obligation to exceed his colleagues in the number of his published works.

To do research does inevitably entail the multiplication of works which repeat one another in some respects. New research, even very original research, must inevitably have its point of departure in previously done research. Works by the same author repeat each other and so do works by different authors. Originality is scarcer than the number of publications. Yet the situation is hard to overcome. Research should be published if it meets the standards of responsible referees. Under present arrangements of financial support, every project which is supported has to culminate in publication. If it does not, then the research worker in question will be unable to obtain financial support for his research in the future and he will be discredited. The urge to publish in order to contribute to the growth of knowledge, to gain respect for one's achievements, and to advance in one's career is reinforced by the expectations of the patrons of research. Research, the results of which are not communicated to others, cannot in the nature of the case be a contribution to knowledge.

The urge to publish has grown with the increased prestige of research in the academic world and with the attention given to lists of publications as a criterion in appointments, including reappointments and promotions. The quantity of published works is easier to estimate than the quality of those works and teachers who compose with some fluency sometimes become indiscriminate in what they publish. Nevertheless, research workers must attempt to publish the results of their investigations if they are up to standard. Publications of scientific and scholarly works must be accompanied by truthful attribution of their authorship. Since careers in the academic profession are oriented towards the recognition and reward of individual achievement, plagiary of the work of others and claiming credit for the work of others infringe on the derivative obligation to acknowledge the achievements of colleagues. The presentation of reports of observations made by others regardless of whether they have been published, as if they were observations made by oneself, is a defection of this derivative obligation. Claiming the exclusive authorship of a work done in collaboration or claiming primary authorship of a work to which one's contribution was marginal is a grave impropriety.

The service of knowledge entails not only the discovery of new knowledge but also the transmission of the best of established knowledge to students. No teacher should allow himself to go on teaching as if the body of knowledge in his field has remained constant. Even in humanistic fields where there is an approximate canon of works to be taught and studied, new commentaries and interpretations require both the recurrent re-study of the canonical works and a well-informed awareness of the best interpretations of the works. Of course, to be abreast of "the literature" should not be confused with fashionableness. The growth of the body of knowledge in any particular field is not furthered by the espousal of fashionable topics and interpretations. Neither the body of knowledge in the field nor the students who study it are benefited by the multiplication of trivial or fashionable publications. The serious teacher will, of course, attempt to inform himself adequately about recent publications in his field of scholarship but as much to give his students the best that is known as well as to protect them intellectually from nonsense which they might otherwise accept.

Research is obligatory for those who can do it; it should not be regarded as equally obligatory for those who show little talent for it. For such persons the obligation regarding research is to attend to its results and to incorporate them into teaching to help their students to understand what research in their field is and to assimilate them into the outlook which pervades research. Those academics who do little or no research are under obligation to pay close attention in their teaching to the results of research in their field.

Obligations to Students

The Humboldtian ideal of the unity of teaching and research remains a valid one. The university is not a research institute. It is an institution of teaching and research. Teaching is as important as research in a university. In principle, all persons holding regular academic appointments in a university should do both teaching and research but not necessarily always in the same proportions. Teachers in liberal arts colleges may legitimately distribute their time between teaching and research differently than teachers in universities, where there is a greater emphasis on research. Some teachers might concentrate on the teaching of the most advanced students, the supervision of graduate students, and the conduct of research seminars. There may even be a small number of "research professorships" but their multiplication is contrary to the requirements of the academic ethic. A university in which teachers shirk their pedagogical obligation in order to advance "their own work," as if their sole obligation is to do research, infringes on the academic ethic. Properly understood, "their own work" includes teaching.

The ideal of the formation of the mind—and character—by research must also apply to teaching. Teaching is not merely the transmission of a body of substantive, factual, or theoretical knowledge. It must aim at conveying understanding of the fundamental truths in the subject and the methods of inquiry and testing characteristic of their subject.

It should go without saying that negligence in the performance of pedagogical tasks ought to be abhorrent to a university teacher. It is not only a puritanical praise of assiduity or the ordinary principle of commercial honesty which asserts that the acceptance of payment entails the delivery of the goods paid for that requires industrious preparation of teaching. A teacher cannot hope to arouse the spirit of inquiry in his students or to get them to see the need for care and imagination if his teaching is desultory. This implies, among other things, that the teacher must inform himself of the best scientific and scholarly achievement of the best workers in the subject which he is teaching. To do less is to present to the students as unchallenged truths what might have been subjected to severe criticism. Given the present volume of production of scientific and scholarly works, this ideal can probably not be completely achieved. This does not make the striving for it less obligatory.

The postulate that the university is an institution, the primary obligation of which is the discovery and teaching of important and serious scientific and scholarly truths, does not require that teachers should eschew the assertion of their political and ethical beliefs before their pupils. It does however mean that university teachers must avoid allowing it to appear that their political or ethical statements are scientific or scholarly statements; it also means that they must not allow what they put forward as truthful knowledge to be determined by their political or ethical ideals and sympathies. University teachers must also avoid discriminating among their students on the basis of the students' own political or ethical ideals and sympathies. (It goes without saying that for teachers to discriminate in the assessment of their students on the basis of the students' sex, religion, pigmentation, ethnic or social-class origin is absolutely antithetical to the academic ethic.)

The only immediate guarantee of the university teacher's observance of his obligation to teach what is true and important to his students is the seriousness with which he takes his calling, his belief in the value of the knowledge that he teaches and his conviction that the truth about his subject matter is eminently worth knowing and propagating. Conformity with this obligation can come only from strictness of conscience and conviction of the worthwhileness of the intellectual activity in which he is engaged. The teacher's conviction is manifested in his patent seriousness and pleasure in the intellectual value of his own subject; his commitment to knowledge is evident in his tone. It is this perception of these dispositions as much as the substantive knowledge which the teaching imparts that arouses and compels students.

The teacher has to be careful not to fall into dogmatism in the exposition of his subject or to attempt improperly to exercise influence on his students by demanding that they become adherents of his own particular substantive and methodological point of view. He must enable his students to know that his own point of view is not the only reasonable one and that other scientists or scholars have different interpretations and approaches, of which the students should be aware. To yield to the temptation of dogmatism is to be unfaithful to the obligation to communicate the truth.

With rare exceptions, the teacher knows more about the subject he is teaching than do his students. In this respect, he has the upper hand over his students. Their only defenses against intellectual exploitation are indifference and challenging questions. In most situations, especially in the earlier years of study at universities, they do not have enough knowledge to correct him and he has therefore the opportunity to take advantage of them intellectually and hence to be unfaithful to his obligations with impunity. The students might indeed render judgments on the teacher informally or in response to questionnaires but they are in fact not often in a position to assess the truthfulness or intellectual importance of what he tells them. This is especially the case if the body of readings he recommends is so chosen as to suggest that his views are universally accepted. The acceptance of the obligations which a teacher incurs from his greater possession of knowledge extends to an obligation to take seriously his students' intellectual queries and quandaries. A teacher has an obligation to be open to the students' questions about the validity of the propositions he puts forth.

The intellectual probity of a university teacher in his classroom can be reinforced by the interest of his pupils. The egg and the chicken who lays it and who is born from it are equally important to each other; so are teacher and students as far as adherence to demanding intellectual standards is concerned. The intellectual exigency of the student strengthens the seriousness of the teacher. This is the only worthwhile sense in which teachers and pupils form a mutually sustaining intellectual community. It is not an obligation of a teacher to please his students; the attempt to please the students often gives rise to supine and degrading flattery without intellectual substance. Meeting the demands of intellectually exacting students is a different and far better thing than pleasing them. The high expectations of the best prepared and most exigent students are a spur to a teacher to exert himself to meet them. Teaching which is addressed to the capacities of the lowest quartile of the student body will render the other students apathetic; apathetic students, in their turn, engender apathetic teaching. Indifferent students do not call out the best qualities of their teachers. Yet, teaching "over the heads" of the majority of the students in a class and addressing only the very best can also have a dispiriting effect. Nevertheless, teachers should try to make their students extend themselves intellectually.

In some of the very large mass universities there has developed a widespread belief among some teachers that most of their pupils have little capacity to master the more difficult aspects of the subject taught and cannot be aroused to try to do so. The students are not taken seriously enough by these teachers; they are too often treated as children or as dullards. One of the obligations of the teacher to the students is to treat them respectfully and seriously, as if they are capable and desirous of learning difficult things. The students must be pressed to attain the highest level of knowledge which their immaturity, their capacities, and their previous acquisitions permit. This is one of the obligations of the academic profession which is neglected by some teachers in many mass universities. With the emergence of higher education for much larger proportions of the generation between eighteen and twenty-two years of age, many teachers in American and European universities, whatever their political views, have slipped into the belief that little is to be expected of their students. The results is an intellectual poverty of the syllabuses and, resulting therefrom, the intellectual poverty of the students educated according to these syllabuses.

The devotion of a university teacher to his teaching obligations is buttressed by the seriousness with which his colleagues approach their own teaching. This is why the maxim about Mark Hopkins and a student on a log is too simple. One teacher, on his own, is seldom enough. The teacher's seriousness is supported by the proximity of other serious teachers, just as the seriousness of the student is nourished by the presence of other serious students. The seriousness of his colleagues about their teaching supports him in his acceptance of an exigent standard regarding the teaching of undergraduates. The maintenance of intellectual integrity is not only a matter of strength of character but it is also a function of the immediate environment of a teacher within his department and his university. Consciences reinforce each other in intellectual matters as well as in others. The academic community thus supports the academic ethic in teaching, but it does not do so through the watchfulness expressed in the assessment of particular published works, such as occurs in the scientific community, or by polls conducted among students or by occasional visits of colleagues to classes.

It is admittedly very difficult for a teacher or his colleagues to know how well he is teaching. Some teachers have a short-term effectiveness; others exert a more permanent influence over the minds of their students. Some fill their students with well-ordered information; others arouse their curiosity. Some teachers help their students to acquire methods of observing and thinking. Formal tests of effective teaching, such as conceived by educationists, are bound to be unsatisfactory because the modes of effectiveness are numerous and some of them cannot be assessed except over a long time. An assessment of poor teaching is difficult to demonstrate except in cases of very patent defections from duty such as frequent absences from class. Obvious failure to prepare and indifferent answers to the questions raised by students are not easy for assessors who have not observed the teacher's activity in class in a systematic manner.

One indirect way of assuring a high sense of obligation of teachers to their students is through watchfulness over the process of appointment, so as to exclude candidates who seem to be likely to be negligent about their teaching. Here, too, similar difficulties in the assessment of teaching reappear.

How then can the teacher's attitude of seriousness towards his subject matter and towards teaching and his freedom from dogmatism be guaranteed? There is no directly operating institutional mechanisms for the observation of teaching through which the diligence, alertness, conscience, and conviction of the teacher can be perceived and assessed in the way in which published scientific and scholarly works can be assessed by the judgment of peers. Persons who are outside the classroom cannot see or pass judgment on the teacher's fulfillment of his obligations to his students. Only continuous presence and adequate knowledge permit that and the students, who are the only ones continuously present, do not have adequate knowledge.

The matter comes down, therefore, to each teacher's own sense of obligation and his voluntary submission to it. The bearing of a conscientious teacher affects the attitude of his colleagues towards their own teaching. The sense of obligation of a teacher is strengthened by the awareness of the strength of that sense of obligation in his colleagues. This is not a tautology; it is a self-closing circle of reciprocal influences.

Students must not only be taught. They must also be assessed and they must be assessed fairly by their examiners. The assessment is important because it affects the students' chances in their subsequent studies and in admission to their professional careers. Assessment also affects the students' attitude towards their studies and towards themselves. Just assessment is as necessary for society as it is for the individual student.

Unfairness or arbitrariness in assessment of a student's performance may be a result of carelessness on the part of the examiner. It might also be a product of the examiner's personal attitude towards particular students—in those situations in which the examiner can identify the students being examined. Unfairness or arbitrariness in the assessment of the work of students might not be a result of carelessness or of the personal relationships between particular students and their teachers. Political sympathies can also have a similarly distorting effect on assessment, resulting in giving some students higher marks than their achievement merits and others lower marks.

No less important is carelessness on the part of the examiner in the maintenance of a stable standard of assessment. This is a difficult matter to control. "Double assessment" is one way of avoiding unfairness to students; this is more feasible when there is a common examination taken by the students of different teachers. The American system of either "continuous assessment" or "course examination" involves, in practically all cases, a single teacher and a single examiner who are the same person. The maintenance of a single standard under these conditions is not so easily controllable by institutional arrangements.

In the assessment of the achievement of students in mass universities which, at least in the United States, also have continuous assessment and course examinations, the assessment is frequently done by "teaching assistants." Many of these assistants teach small sections of a common course. Under the latter conditions double assessment is possible. But where assessment deals with performance in class as well as in terminal examinations, double assessment is impossible.

There is no institutional arrangement for reliability guaranteeing adequacy in examining. The collective review of questions to assure that they correspond to the syllabus cannot apply where there is continuous assessment and where the syllabus of each course is determined by the person who teaches it. Numerous devices for assuring the fairness of questions can be imagined but they tend to be so cumbersome that their application would place an intolerable burden on teachers. Hence, as in the performance of obligations in teaching, the adherence to a standard which reduces to a minimum arbitrariness, dogmatism, favoritism, and excessive severity or indulgence in setting and marking examinations depends on the self-discipline and scrupulousness of the teacher-examiner.

In some universities, ecology and tradition both favor the meeting of teachers and their students outside classrooms or laboratories. This is common in universities in which students reside on or close to the campus and where the teachers spend much of their time at the university. Even in universities in which these conditions do not obtain, opportunities for teachers to become better acquainted with their students occur at more advanced levels when classes are smaller and the intellectual interests of students and teachers are closer to each other. These relationships are often very valuable pedagogically. They afford opportunities for informal discussions about subjects beyond the limits of the syllabus. The friendly atmosphere of meetings between teachers and students is appreciated by some students; it often makes them more responsive to teaching in the classroom. The student feels more at ease in the university when he is in friendly relations with some of his teachers; the subject matter becomes more inviting.

Informal relations of teachers with students are therefore to be welcomed. They do, however, bring with them certain dangers. One of these dangers is that in such relationships, the teacher might be inclined to favor some students over others, to give them more opportunities to enter into discussions in classes or seminars, to devote more attention to their term papers or their research and also to be unfair in the assessment of the achievements of students in the sense of favoring those with whom he is friendly outside of classes over those with whom he has no such relationship. Even if the teacher does not discriminate in favor of those students whom he knows and especially those with whom he is friendly, some students will assert this; disaffection is stirred by such rumors and the students who think themselves disfavored avoid teachers from whom they could learn. It is therefore very important that teachers attempt to avoid not only the reality but also the appearance of discrimination in favor of some students and against other students.

This is a very complicated matter and a very subtle one. It is desirable that teachers should be friendly with students and it is also inevitable that they will be more friendly with some than with others. There is nothing wrong with this in itself. It is only its intrusion into the assessment of the achievements of students in the acquisition of knowledge or its intrusion into the teaching itself that must be guarded against.

It is important too that teachers should not take advantage of their status and their power over their students. The occurrences of sexual relationships between teachers and students is certainly to be avoided. The fact that the development of sexual relations between teachers and students can result in discriminatory assessment of the student's academic achievement is only one important ground for the strictness with which the obligation to avoid sexual relations with students must be observed. Academics must be scrupulous in their avoidance of any actions with respect to their students which will bring the academic profession into disrepute and which will damage the good name of their university among present and future students as well as before the larger public.

Teachers are often forgetful of the role which they play in affecting the future of their students. The desire to have more graduate students and assistants should not be allowed to influence the advice which teachers give to students who seek guidance about whether they should go on to work for advanced degrees. At the same time, teachers should not refuse admission to graduate students who really wish to study particular subjects and are adequately qualified even though the prospect of obtaining a satisfactory appointment in the subject is poor. A student who has reached the point of having taken a first degree should be regarded as capable of making responsible decisions on his own.

While a teacher must respect the choices which students make on their own responsibility and with some awareness of the risks involved, the teacher must also avoid giving his blessing or encouragement to the less responsible decisions made by students. The teacher must not support students who engage in rash actions which are sometimes injurious to themselves and damaging to the university as a place of education and research. This element of the academic ethic is especially in need of emphasis in view of the conduct of many university teachers during the agitations of the 1960s and early 1970s. University teachers owe it to their students not to encourage the students' hampering of their own education, hindering the education of other students and also disrupting the conduct of research and administration. Even where the teacher is not unsympathetic with the proclaimed political objectives of the students, he must abstain from fostering the disorders of which passionate and volatile students are capable.

University teachers, particularly in the social sciences, often find it difficult to abstain from the expression of their political beliefs. Many do not attempt to do so and even say that it is impossible. Max Weber desired the exclusion of the expression of political and ethical preferences from university teaching because the relationship between teacher and students in the lecture hall rendered their criticism of his assertion unfeasible. Weber did not say that a social scientist should avoid expressing his value judgment in seminars or in classes in which there were small numbers of students and in which they could presumably question him about his value judgments and express their own. Weber also thought that the student should be taught "to face the facts" and this also obliged the teacher to avoid the exposition of his own political and ethical views. Teaching "the facts" as truthfully as they can be ascertained in the subject being taught would leave the student free to make his own political decisions.

It is certainly desirable that the teacher avoid exploiting the authority which is attributed to him by virtue of the fact that he has more knowledge of his subject than have his students, by expounding to them views of nature or society which are not as true as the best available techniques and the existing body of scientific and scholarly literature can sustain. It is not that a teacher in a university must suppress his own political or moral beliefs in his classes in, for example, economics, sociology, political science, or any of the fields in which the subject matter is pertinent to public controversies. But he must not claim for his assertions which touch on those subjects which are enmeshed in public controversies greater veracity than the best scientific and scholarly evidence can justify. His obligations to truthfulness should prohibit the exploitation of an audience which knows less about the subject than he does.

It must be recognized that the teacher who "sticks to the facts" might be duller than the teacher who expresses his own preferences on political and social questions. At the same time, the teacher who wishes to assert his political and social value judgments should not spare the effort needed to make clear that he is doing so and to make as clear as he can the difference between what is supported by the most carefully assessed scientific or scholarly evidence and what is the political or moral standpoint from which he evaluates the situation. (One thing, however, is clear: the university teacher is under obligation not to use the classroom to win adherents to his own political standpoint or for his own political party.)

It is very difficult to find a plain and simple way to escape the dangers of indifference, selfishness, arbitrariness, favoritism, or the imposition of extraneous beliefs. All the more urgent therefore is it to lay stress over and over again on the scruples, circumspectness, and self-discipline of the individual teacher and to remind him over and over again of his obligations in teaching, examining, and in other relations with his students.

The Obligations of Generations of Teachers

No academic department, unless it wishes either to terminate its existence or to suffer complete discontinuity, can allow itself to have most of its members of approximately the same age. In so far as individual academics participate in the making of decisions regarding academic appointments, they must bear in mind the necessity that the academic staff of the university as a whole and of each department should be spread over a wide range of ages.

The most important reason for this is that the courses offered by a department should be diversified both in subject matter and in methods of research. Otherwise the department cannot fulfill its teaching function in relation to its field. New subject matters and new methods in a discipline are frequently, although not always, cultivated primarily by its younger generation. A department, to say nothing of a university as a whole, which has little place in its teaching for new interests and fields and new techniques of research, will do harm to the intellectual development of its students. It will also diminish its attractiveness to students and also place its graduates at a disadvantage in the competition for appointments with graduates of other universities. More important, it will handicap them in their own research because it will leave them uninstructed about the newer problems and newer techniques which emerge at the frontiers of knowledge in their respective fields.

There is another reason why heterogeneity of age is necessary. Teachers over forty-five years of age often seem very old to students; they seem remote and sometimes too awe-inspiring. Under these conditions an undesirable gap can emerge between students and teachers.

Appointments committees must be very sensitive to the considerations of age in their deliberations about the merits of candidates. Often the dilemma is avoided because the post which is to be filled stipulates the rank of the appointee and this usually determines, within wide limits, the age-cohort from which the appointed candidate comes.

All this, however, is incidental to the obligations imposed by the academic ethic on teachers of different ages in their relations with each other. The relations between senior and junior members of the teaching staff now run across the entire range of academic activities—the design of a course of study, what subjects should be taught, the allocation of courses and subjects among the teachers of a department, the appointment of new staff members, the fixing of the syllabuses for the teaching of particular courses, the setting and marking of examinations, the reviews of students' achievements and problems, the allocation of prizes and studentships, the admission of new students, and many others.

In every one of these categories of activities, now that they are usually no longer settled by the decision of the head of the department, the relationship between senior and junior teachers raises problems. When the departments were autocratically ruled, there were apparently no such problems since no one but the head of the department had a voice in the matter. Now, however, that there has been a dispersion of authority within departments and within the university as a whole, problems in the relations between senior members and junior members have come to the surface and must be faced.

It is not possible to deal with all of these problems or with any of them in any degree of detail. The most general consideration is the necessity for some intradepartmental consensus about the standard to be maintained in dealing with intellectual tasks. Mutual respect and trust among colleagues, regardless of their age, is one of the preconditions for the effectiveness of a department as an educational institution. The solidarity required is not merely a matter of personal friendliness among colleagues; it is also a matter of intellectual solidarity about the substance of the subjects taught and investigated and of belief in the value of the subject or discipline, but this does not entail complete unanimity about approaches and methods.

Departments usually have traditions of substantive emphasis and interests within the field which has been in their jurisdiction and they also have appropriate standards of achievement. It is important that the younger generation of teachers be assimilated into these traditions; no less important is the provision of opportunities for the new recruits to a department to follow new approaches and to pursue the intellectual problems which they regard as most pressing.

The intellectually flexible solidarity of a department is important for the senior members and for the students but it is especially important for the younger generation of teachers who otherwise are placed in the dangerous position of being caught in a crossfire of polemics among their colleagues. Where there is conflict within and between generations, the students too often are victims of these conflicts. They become alienated from some teachers and submissive towards others and they thereby lose the benefits which are to be gained from studying with a wide range of teachers.

The traditions of departments are microcosms of the traditions of a scientific or scholarly discipline in the large. The traditions must be constantly revised and improved. Although the younger teachers and other newcomers to a department should share in them, these traditions must not be allowed to stifle the potential originality of the younger generation. The worst thing is for these younger members to feign conformity with one or another of the department's traditions while not genuinely believing in the validity of any of them.

If the intellectual traditions of a department are not kept alive and assimilated by new members the new generation of teachers will lose the intellectual benefits in what these traditions have to offer. If the existing traditions of the department are completely disregarded, the department will more easily break up into several groups, each concerned with its own subspeciality. This is true, not only with regard to the intellectual substance of the discipline for which the department is responsible. This alienation will extend across departmental lines joining the unassimilated younger members of many departments with the result that they form a bloc within the university as a whole. If a young academic feels himself to be an outsider in his own department, he might also feel himself to be an outsider in the university as a whole. If young teachers fall into this state of mind, they will gravitate towards the discontented students and they will infuse a cynical and resentful attitude into the student body, as well as embitter themselves, and reduce their intellectual effectiveness.

The opposite alternative is also possible; the older generation of teachers in a department might conceive of themselves as being left behind intellectually, if the younger members, sometimes in association with one of the older members, push the older representatives of the traditions of the department to the wall. This is a condition which is injurious to the students who are usually swept in the wake of the victorious faction in the department and who are thereby deprived of what is vital in the stock of understanding possessed by the older tradition. Still another alternative is for the older members of a department to press for the appointment to junior posts only those of the same substantive views and to refuse to allow the appointment of junior colleagues of other views. This might assure departmental solidarity but it does so at the cost of the advancement of their field of study and at the cost of their students who are prevented thereby from confronting alternative approaches in their subject.

The conditions referred to here are not only the result of personal antagonism between the older and the younger generations of teachers within any given department. They are also consequences of the development of disciplines and subdisciplines. The introduction of new ideas is often the work of a pioneer in the older generation whose ideas are taken up and developed mainly in the younger generation. The very enthusiasm which is associated with new discoveries in a field can lead to the exaggeration of the disjunction between the new and the old and perhaps to an attitude of condescension of the exponents of the new towards those who do not follow them on their new paths.

A common responsibility of all the generations and ranks in a department and in a university is to maintain the academic ethic and the institution which it serves. It is not just a matter of "keeping the peace" within the department and within the university. Nor is it primarily a matter of treating the newly appointed younger teachers with hospitality and affection. The reason for doing these things is that they are conducive to the assimilation of the new academic generation into the academic ethic. The obligation of the longer established members must be to move them on to the path which in the course of years will make them into the co-responsible custodians of the well-being of the university as an intellectual institution.

Being loyal to one's department and being faithful to the ideals of one's discipline do not require uncritical subservience to the ideas of the reigning middle and older generations. That might maintain internal peace but it would do so at the cost of the advancement of knowledge.

Members of the older generation owe it to the ideal of the advancement of knowledge in their discipline not to be rigid in their adherence to its traditions. They owe it to their departments, to their students, and to the younger generation of teachers. The responsibility lies on all sides—on the older generation not to dig their heels in to resist innovations in the field to which they have devoted their careers, on the younger generation not to act as if the ideas which their elders espoused were simply mistaken. It lies particularly on the middle generation of scientists or scholars in their forties who still have enough connections intellectually and socially with both their elders and their juniors.

For all of these reasons it is important that the younger members of a department be assimilated socially and morally into the department. This is a special responsibility of the senior and the middle-aged members of the department. The execution of this responsibility is not easy. Social incorporation and personal amiability are necessary but they are not always sufficient to eliminate dissatisfaction over the degree of equality in the conduct of departmental affairs. Some might think that there is not enough equality; others that there is too much. Yet there is bound to be a certain amount of inequality in the relations between junior and senior members of the teaching staff. These inequalities are present in many situations in which it would be wrong to attempt to eliminate them, regardless of consequences for the quality of teaching and research and for the maintenance of the university as an effective intellectual institution.

The issue of the inequality of senior and junior members of a department in the making of appointments does not arise when appointments are made by committees consisting largely of persons from outside the university or department in which the appointments are to be made. Still, even if the appointment of professors rests with mainly external appointment committees, junior appointments in these same universities are usually made by committees constituted by members of the department, elected by the department as a whole, or appointed by the head of the department or by some higher authority within the university. In universities in the United States, there are seldom external appointments committees except in an advisory capacity. The appointments there are internally made or proposed.

How then are the powers of decision to be allocated among the generations or ranks in such cases? Should the lower ranks have a vote? Should they be consulted? Should young teachers in large departments have a "caucus" separate from a "senior caucus"? Should young teachers who themselves are in the department on short-term appointments and who are not yet the masters of their subject which senior members are expected to be, have an influence of equal weight with their seniors? Should those, who are committed to their university and department by long service and by the likelihood of spending the remainder of their careers there, have no more weight than those who are likely to be less committed to the university and department in consequence of the uncertainty of their future there? It is probably not advisable for junior members in short-term appointments to have a voice—or a vote—equal to that of persons who are committed to the department and the university by long service and permanent tenure.

What then should be the rights of junior members? In the case of senior appointments it is desirable that the junior members should have access to the dossiers of candidates—and that their assessments should be formally or informally solicited with a clear understanding that the confidentiality of the contents of the dossiers will be strictly observed and that their assessments will be considered seriously as advisory opinions by those who make the decision. Where the decision does not agree with the assessment of one or more of the junior members, the ground for disagreement should be explained. Perhaps the entire department should hold a preliminary, plenary discussion about the leading candidates but this discussion should not culminate in a vote by all those who participate in that discussion.

Senior members of departments should not agree to having junior members pass judgment on whether junior members who are their own colleagues and at the same time, competitors with them, should be promoted or given permanent appointments; junior members of departments should not claim this as a right. It is difficult in the egalitarian atmosphere of contemporary Western intellectual circles to exclude junior members, who are appointed on short tenure, from decisions about present and future colleagues without causing affront to them. Nevertheless their own interests are so involved that one could not be sure that the interests in their own future do not affect their assessment of the intellectual merits of their colleagues. It would also be anomalous to have persons whose stay in the university is still of uncertain duration to be given the opportunity to fix its future in a binding way.

It is felt by many nowadays to be embarrassing to argue in favor of inequality in general or in particular situations. Yet this embarrassment ought to be set aside and the junior teaching members of a department should be informed from the beginning about their responsibilities in matters of appointments. That follows from the need to make paramount the academic obligations of the department.

In decisions regarding the content of courses to be taught and the setting of examinations and marking them, there should be complete equality among teachers of different ranks. In teaching, junior members should not be disproportionately burdened by routine or disesteemed tasks; they must be encouraged and enabled to do research. Concentrating routine tasks on them stands in the way of their doing research.

In the decisions as to what courses should be taught in any given year and who should teach them, the junior members should be given as much opportunity as possible to choose at least some of the courses which they will teach, in so far as this was not settled when they were appointed. At the same time, care must be taken that this arrangement does not result in the students being presented with a number of highly specialized courses which do not adequately introduce them to the subject as a whole. This imposes responsibilities on senior members as well as on junior ones. Senior members have an obligation to prevent the segregation of junior members in the teaching of elementary and unspecialized courses; senior members should regard themselves as under a shared responsibility for this type of teaching. There should also be joint courses taught by junior and senior members.

The segregation of teaching responsibilities in a way which results in junior teachers being given the responsibility for teaching introductory courses for the youngest students while senior teachers teach advanced courses for advanced students is not desirable for a number of reasons. For one thing, it prevents the junior teachers from developing their own interests in research; it also generates a belief that they are being treated as helots or as "hired hands" and hence fosters the formation of a kind of stratification within the department which is injurious to departmental solidarity. Perhaps even more important, it deprives the first-year students of the benefits of having the more comprehensive and more mature views of the subject such as are likely to be available from more experienced members of the profession, when they teach the introductory courses. If older, more senior teachers, especially those who are fairly eminent figures in their respective fields, teach younger students, it heightens the students' sense of their dignity within the university as a whole. The teaching of younger students also has benefits for the more senior members of a department because it forces them to take a wider view of their subjects; if they teach only advanced students on the specialized topics on which they are doing research, they increase the always present danger that they will become so specialized that they will lose the perspective needed to appreciate fundamental issues.

Junior members should be helped by senior members to progress in their research. This flows from the dual obligation of all academics to advance knowledge as well as to transmit it. If the junior members do work together on research projects with senior members, great care must be taken that they should not be treated in the role of research assistants. Otherwise they will not learn how to stand on their own feet as investigators and they will not be stimulated to make the maximal efforts in research of which they are capable. They should be encouraged to undertake their own research and be helped in obtaining funds where funds are required. They should be very generously provided with free time, such as a term or a whole session for their research. Staff seminars and "workshops" should provide opportunities for junior members to present their research and to defend it and senior members should act in the same way. It is not desirable to allow the junior members to become isolated in their own research seminars. They need the help and the criticism of their seniors.

In all these categories of academic activity and beyond them, the senior members must avoid the peremptory exercise of their authority, which is partly official and partly an informal function of achievement. They must exercise authority; it cannot be renounced without danger to learning but it must also be done tactfully and with consideration for the dignity of those over whom it is exercised. Otherwise it is bound to arouse harsh feelings and to lead to fruitless dissension. It is very important for the work of the department and for the development of its individual members as investigators and teachers that each member of it, however junior, should have an opportunity to mature in independence, within the context of the tradition of inquiry.

To summarize: the obligation of each senior member in a department is to act in a way which will assimilate each junior member into the department and the university, to make him appreciative of its traditions and to leave him room for the development of his own intellectual individuality. The practice of a proper conviviality is among the obligations of senior members of departments, not only out of friendliness or affection but above all as an aid in the assimilation of the junior member to the academic ethic in general as well as into the particular department and the particular university.

It is pertinent at this point to say something about the obligations of junior teachers. It is important that they not give such primacy to their research that it leads them to neglect their teaching. It is also important that they regard themselves as members of their departments and of their university, even though their tenure is of uncertain duration, and take seriously any administrative duties which fall to their lot. It is not easy, in a period when many senior academics have allowed, or even aided, the disaggregation of their universities, for the new generation of teachers to develop a sense of the university as a corporate body collectively engaged in intellectual work. Nevertheless junior teachers are under obligation, if they envisage an academic career for themselves, to become aware that they must share in the collective responsibility for their respective universities as well as for their own departments. They must see that their departments and their universities are more than administrative conveniences and sources of funds and services. They should be willing to allow themselves to be drawn into the life and spirit of their universities.

Obligations of Colleagues

(i) The relationship among colleagues in a university is first of all a relationship within a department. It is also a relationship with colleagues in substantively neighboring departments; it is also a relationship with colleagues scattered throughout the university, and the universities elsewhere in the country and abroad.

Since it is desirable that a department offer to its students and the learned world a variety of established and new lines of interpretation and techniques, it must be accepted that an entire department should not be of a single intellectual stamp. Just as it is not good for the students to learn only one part of a field, only one approach to it, only one set of techniques for studying it, and only one theory for interpreting it, so it is not good for colleagues to be surrounded by a homogeneous intellectual environment. But even where there is general agreement about approaches, techniques, and theories within a department, there are still bound to be disagreements. Some of these disagreements will be intellectual, some of them will be an outcome of uncongenial temperaments, or of disagreements about academic and public policy. There are also bound to be disagreements between colleagues in a department about the merits of candidates for appointment and promotion, about the content of courses and the like. All these academic disagreements are quite legitimate and even desirable but they should be conducted in a restrained manner by those who are parties to them.

Senior academics have an obligation to contain both those disagreements in which they participate and those disagreements among their departmental colleagues to which they are witnesses. They should try as hard as they can to "purify" their own and their colleagues' disagreements so that they are disagreements about purely academic matters, and to exclude or suppress such disagreements as derive purely and simply from their own personal, temperamental, political, and other extraneous considerations. This calls for restraint by each person on his own expression of such tendencies and his resistance to allowing himself to be drawn by the expression of such tendencies in others. These are obligations of civility, respect, and courtesy within one's own university and beyond. It is contrary to the obligations to colleagues to disparage them before students or in public. It is perfectly within the boundaries of academic citizenship to criticize the work of colleagues in writing or orally before peers or students; personal vilification is not within those boundaries.

The head or convenor of the department or faculty must play a major role in trying to keep an amiable peace among its disagreeing members. He can do this by evenhandedness and patience in meetings and by trying to reconcile individuals in conflict with each other by talking with them individually. Without solidarity, mutual trust, and mutual respect among the senior members of the department, the junior members, worried about their own future in the department, will become partisans. The chairman must avoid giving the impression that he is in the hands of a clique or of one powerful personality in the department. Confidentiality will be broken in the search for allies and rumors of conflict will spread among junior teachers and from them to students, with resulting fears on the part of the young members—teachers and graduate students—about being on the wrong side. Cynicism about the department and the discipline among the students will result.

Relations with colleagues in other departments or faculties should be fostered for the intellectual benefit that might accrue since important new problems are often to be found at the boundaries of disciplines, and also so that the university should form a coherent corporate body and not be simply a convenient administrative context for the pursuit by each individual of his own specialized intellectual interests. The cultivation of friendly relations with colleagues in adjacent departments is an obligation on all members, senior and junior. Wherever possible and appropriate, courses should be given jointly by members of different departments and joint appointments in several departments should be sympathetically considered.

Opportunities should be taken and arrangements made for members of different departments to meet informally, to become aware of each other, to become aware of the intellectual problems they face in teaching and research and which are of significance beyond the boundaries of individual departments. The quality of a university can be benefited by the concern of its teaching staff about the standing of the university as a whole, as well as about the quality or intellectual achievement of particular departments other than their own. A university needs an "invisible senate," a stiffening spine which, outside the formal and official committees and boards, spreads its concern for the university beyond the boundaries of departments and up to the boundaries of the university. This "invisible senate" cannot be planned; it must emerge from the relationship of colleagues throughout the university. It arises from a sense of obligation to the university as an intellectual institution. This is not the same as being an "academic politician"; it means acting in a patently disinterested manner in a way which gains the general acknowledgment of colleagues.

Good relations with colleagues in other universities should be maintained. This is necessary for the benefit of each particular discipline. It is also desirable for the purpose of promoting the solidarity of the academic community as a whole within particular countries and across national boundaries. The republic of learning runs beyond national boundaries and its maintenance and prosperity should be one of the concerns of those who are committed to the academic ethic. Jealousy and disparagement of other institutions, regardless of whether they are of approximately the same rank of eminence or higher or lower, should be avoided.

Some differences in the status of individual universities is inevitable. It is important, however, that this differentiation not be allowed to enter into the relations of colleagues. In countries in which universities are dispersed over a wide range of eminence in terms of scientific and scholarly achievements, age, location, wealth, quality of students attracted, etc., the problem of the relations between universities higher in the hierarchy of deference and those which are lower emerges.

It is important that persons who teach in the less eminent universities not become discouraged because their universities are not so highly regarded by the outside world. The tasks of teaching and research are just as incumbent on members of less famous universities as they are on members of more famous ones. The tasks of academic citizenship are urgent in all universities, both the famous ones and the obscure ones.

(ii) One of the obligations of every teacher and of everyone who does scientific or scholarly research is to scrutinize the tradition of his subject, to winnow out the valid and important from the invalid and unimportant. This must be done both in teaching and research. The critical scrutiny of the tradition and particularly of the most recent increments to it is an obligation of a university teacher to his colleagues in his own university and at others, present and future, even where it requires that he render negative judgments on their work.

This obligation is also performed through reviewing recently published treatises and monographs in scientific and scholarly journals partly in the form of book reviews, for which ordinarily no monetary remuneration is received, and partly in the form of "reviews of the literature." The relative importance of these two forms of the assessment of recent literature in any field varies from one field to the other. In the natural sciences, the review of the literature is more important than book reviews; the reverse is probably the case in the humanistic and social science disciplines.

Book reviews and reviews of the literature are indispensable parts of the institutional machinery of learning. They not only inform colleagues of the existence of books, monographs, and papers which they might otherwise not learn about—at least not for a long time—but they sort the wheat from the chaff. More than that, they even improve the wheat by critical comments, supplementations and corrections. Book reviewing and the writing of reviews of the literature are onerous tasks; to do them properly requires hard work. Yet, it is in many fields very painstakingly done. Indeed it is a testimonial to the strength of the academic and scientific ethos that scientists and scholars who have so much else to do go to such trouble and spend so much time to serve their colleagues with minimal financial remuneration, if any, and not very much glory. There are also fields in which the standard of reviewing is not so high. In such fields it behooves editors of journals to try to raise the standard by instructions to invited reviewers and by greater care in the selection of reviewers.

At an earlier stage in the process of serving professional colleagues through improving the intellectual tradition of a subject is the reviewing of manuscripts which have been submitted for publication, either as papers in journals or as books and monographs. Whatever the "average level of quality" of published papers and books in any given field, it is undoubtedly higher than the "average level" of what has been submitted for publication. This first winnowing relies upon the readiness of university teachers to devote some of their time and energy to the burdensome task of "refereeing" papers, writing specific criticisms of them, and often, numerous and lengthy suggestions for revision and improvement. Much that sees the light of publication has been rendered fit for entry into that state by the careful and self-sacrificing—also financially unremunerated—work of referees and editors.

It is the same with respect to the publication of books and monographs by commercial and academic publishing firms. Here university teachers do not possess such exclusive responsibility for the quality of what is published as they do in the publication of scientific and scholarly journals. They have to share their influence with publishers' editors, who are often inexpert in the subjects dealt with and directors of firms who have to consider commercial profitability, the prestige of the firm, and other factors which are not always closely correlated with scientific or scholarly merit. Nevertheless the academics' obligation should be unaffected by these nonacademic considerations.

Another service to colleagues is the critical reading of manuscripts of other academics prior to submission for publication. Although each scientist and scholar bears the full responsibility for whatever he publishes, he often requests a colleague in his own field to read his manuscript and to recommend improvements. To do this well is a time-consuming work but whoever is asked to do so and who agrees to do it owes it to his subject as well as to his colleagues to do so as stringently as he can. It is an equal obligation of the person who makes the request to take seriously the criticism and suggestions made by the colleague who has read the manuscript.

(iii) One of the assumptions of the academic ethic is mutuality in the exchange of knowledge among colleagues. The open publication of the results of research is not only an obligation on university teachers; it is also a right which university teachers are entitled to expect from their colleagues. The asymmetry of secretiveness on one side and openness on the other is an infringement of the academic ethic. This raises the question of how those who are knowingly committed to and observant of the academic ethic should conduct themselves towards university teachers who do not adhere to that ethic.

Some special problems arise regarding the secrecy of research which is done with the financial support of governments or private business firms. The general obligation of openness is contradicted by the obligation of secrecy. Should a scientist who has done research for a governmental institution which desires that a particular paper not be published agree to meet that request? Should an academic scientist agree to disclose the results of his research before they are published, to a foreign colleague who will convey that knowledge to a governmental body or private firm in his own country which will in turn use it to place his country in a position of military or commercial advantage over the country of the scientist who has done the research? Should an academic scientist serve as a consultant to a government or to a private firm on scientific matters which are to be kept secret?

As to whether an academic scientist who has, with governmental financial support, produced a particular paper which the governmental body supporting the research wishes to have withheld from publication, should agree to the withholding, is a matter which the individual and the governmental body in question should decide between themselves in each case. If all of the results of the scientist's research emerging from the particular project are to be kept secret, then he should not seek to do that kind of research in his capacity as a member of a university. If the problem arises only occasionally, no major difficulty arises.

With regard to the question of whether an academic scientist should refuse to allow a foreign colleague of good credentials to know the results of his research before they are published, there is little harm in such disclosure prior to publication if the results are going in any case to be published. The loss of technological advantage to a competing country occurs less through the publication of scientific research than through the commercial sale of equipment embodying the technological innovation. Control over this kind of loss should be done, if it is to be done at all, by governments or private firms or both in collaboration; it is not something for individual academics to attempt on their own.

On the question whether an academic scientist should provide consultative services to a government or a private firm regarding scientific matters which must be kept secret, there is no problem at all if the consultation does not require that the research of the consultant-scientist be kept secret and if the consultative services do not intrude into the performance of the scientist's primary obligation of teaching, research, and academic citizenship. It would be contrary to the academic ethic if the scientist in question spent most of his time in the provision of such consultative services at the cost of his research and teaching, just as it would be if all of his research was classified as secret. But if he spends only about one day weekly on such services, no problem would seem to be raised.

The principle is clear: research done by academic scientists and scholars should be made available to their academic colleagues within their own country and in other countries. Free communications of the results of research is one of the conditions of the advancement of knowledge. Exceptions to this principle should be decided from case to case, with the burden of proof lying on those who desire the exception.

The Obligations of University Teachers in Academic Appointments

The extent of adherence to the criterion of achievement in teaching and research in matters of academic appointment affects the quality of a university. It is true that the intellectual intensity of the internal life of a university does indeed affect the quality of the performance of its teachers but even universities of the highest quality cannot make silk purses out of sows' ears. A poor university can ruin a good or promising scientist or scholar; a good one can induce a good scientist or scholar to exert himself up to the level of his potentiality; it can induce him to extend himself. But the talent and the intellectual passion must be there already, although sometimes hidden from a casual eye. The task of every appointive committee is to seek out these qualities in the candidates whom it has invited or who have been called to its attention by application or recommendation. Its task then is to choose the intellectually best person who can be appointed, given the salary available and the prestige of the university.

It is the high quality of achievement and no less the sense of the imperative of high quality of achievement which gives to a good university the tone which brings out the best in its teaching and research and which communicates itself to its students. Mutual trust, mutual respect, solicitousness for younger members, and the like are all indispensable but they cannot compensate for the absence of rigor in the choice of new members for the academic staff of a university; the decisions to discontinue, reappoint or promote persons already appointed must apply the same standards as are appropriate to the appointment of new members.

How are appointments to be made? The net must be widely cast. In countries where academic appointments are advertised, appointments committees should not regard themselves as confined to the consideration only of persons who propose themselves. They must look over the whole field, as well as they can survey it, on the basis of their knowledge of the published literature and recommendations by qualified persons. They must study the writings, published and unpublished, of those who are willing to be candidates and they must interview those whom they consider seriously. They should never think of merely filling a post on permanent appointment because one is vacant; if there is no candidate of the caliber which they think the salary, status, privileges and resources which their university offers should attract, they should leave the post unfilled. Short-term appointments which may be extended to permanent appointments should be made by the same standards as permanent appointments. Incumbency should not be one of the criteria of reappointment or promotion. Necessary and routine teaching for which no already appointed member is available can be done by rigorously delimited temporary appointments, which should be kept temporary, until a person worthy of a regular appointment can be found.

Every promotion from a post on short tenure to one on permanent or long tenure should be treated as a new appointment; the whole field should be scanned to see, whether, for the salary, opportunities, and resources to be provided for the post, the candidate for promotion is the best possible person available in the country, or internationally, at the time. If he is not, his promotion should be refused and a better person appointed in his stead. Friendship and personal familiarity must be relentlessly and absolutely resisted as criteria of appointment.

It is difficult to assess teaching which one has not observed over an extended period, or experienced as a pupil and reflected on in later years, but an assessment of teaching ability must nonetheless be made. Distinction in research is somewhat easier to assess since its results are public but that is not easy either. External referees should be consulted but their testimonials should be taken with a grain of salt because external referees are often generous at the expense of a university which is not their own. National origin, race, color, friendship, sex, religion, politics and personal charm must be completely excluded from consideration as irrelevant to the teacher's task. The chosen candidate must also be a person who will do his duty to the university and the academic world as a loyal and responsible academic citizen, but a disposition to "rock the boat" must be disregarded if it is compensated by high quality of teaching and research. A person of outstanding intellectual qualities in teaching and research who is inclined to "rock the boat" from vanity or selfishness or the sheer pleasure of being a bull in a china shop, should be told, if he is invited to take up an appointment that he will be expected to behave himself in a gentlemanly way with due consideration for his colleagues. This might be difficult to do but it might sometimes be necessary. Academic citizenship should be considered together with proficiency in teaching and research.

Fifty years ago, it would not have been necessary to stipulate the adduction of the criterion of academic citizenship. After the experience of the 1960s and the 1970s, it is now necessary to consider it explicitly. Does the candidate believe in the possibility of the disinterested pursuit of truth, however tentatively that truth is to be held and asserted? Does he believe that academic freedom is the freedom of an academic to place political ends above intellectual ends in the university? Does he believe that the proper end of teaching is to win the student for a particular political party or movement? Obviously, questions like these cannot be asked directly or in as simple a form as they have just been put but the implicit or explicit answer to such questions are things that members of an appointment committee must take into account in assessing the fitness of a candidate for an appointment to a university.

This emphasis on academic citizenship is not intended to supersede or subordinate devotion to teaching and to discovery. But since under modern conditions nearly all advanced teaching and a great deal of basic research take place predominantly in universities, the disordering of universities damages both teaching and research. The politicization of universities by those who believe in the primacy of politics everywhere, including universities, is a menace to the intellectual efficacy of universities. It is inimical to disciplined learning, to teaching, study and research.

A Note on Pluralism

It is appropriate at this point to insert some observations about "pluralism" or, as it has come to be called in recent years, "pluralism of standpoints." In universities fifty years ago, when there was one professor in a department, it was the professor's conception of the scope of the subject, the basic ideas, and the most appropriate techniques that prevailed. Nowadays, in many universities, there are numerous professors in many departments and departments tend to have numerous members, with a fairly large proportion in the higher ranks. The uniformity of definition and outlook characteristic of the older type of department is no longer necessary or acceptable. For one thing, many disciplines include many subspecialities. There are also different views about the relative importance of particular problems, about interpretations of certain phenomena, and about the best methods of investigation. It is obvious that any department which wishes to educate its students adequately must do justice to these legitimate differences in approach towards scientific and scholarly matters. It must also maintain a certain catholicity with respect to the constituent specialities, although it is not incumbent in every department to cover all the fields of specialization.

In the past fifteen years, there has emerged a demand for pluralism of standpoints. This demand for pluralism is usually not for the substantive and technical heterogeneity of the various disciplines, although it sometimes speaks in that idiom. It is rather a demand for the academic establishment of a particular political standpoint, usually Marxism, in one or more of its recent variant forms. Under the guise of "methodological pluralism" or the "pluralism of paradigms," the argument for the "pluralism of standpoints" is frequently an argument for the appointment of Marxists.

Marxism is, of course, a prominent political program and it has in the course of time also developed a fairly large body of literature, some of which is substantive, and much of which is doctrinal polemic. Since it is important to avoid political criteria in appointments and to avoid political propaganda in teaching, this kind of pluralism must be viewed very skeptically. It would be a serious disservice to higher learning to allow political criteria to be used in the appointment and promotion of staff members. At the same time, substantive and technical diversity within a department must be carefully nurtured.

What is wanted is intellectual diversity, the diversity of legitimate standpoints of objects, methods, and interpretation, within the various scientific and scholarly fields. It is difficult sometimes to see clearly a boundary line between legitimate and illegitimate diversity. It is not possible to promulgate a criterion in formal terms—but this is like much else in life. Nevertheless, good will, conscientious reflection on experience, and knowledge of the subject matter allow reasonable judgment.

In any case, arguments for the representation of political standpoints must not be given countenance, regardless of whether the political standpoint is liberal, radical, or conservative, revolutionary, moderate or reactionary. No person should be excluded from consideration because of his political standpoint; no person should be preferred because of his political standpoint.

Academics have an obligation to respect the confidentiality of deliberations regarding appointments. The disclosure to the press, or to the persons whose appointments have been discussed or to other persons, of the details of the deliberations of appointive bodies or of the testimonials submitted to them, and particularly to disclose how the individual members of the committee voted is an infringement on the obligation of confidentiality.

In matters of appointment academics play an important part as referees regarding candidates for appointment in other universities. It is part of the obligation of a teacher to write to prospective employers about his former and present students or colleagues when they seek to obtain appointments in universities, private business, research institutions, and governments or when they are applying for research grants, graduate studentships, assistantships, or research fellowships. This is a demanding and unceasing obligation of university teachers. University teachers are also often requested to assess the work of a person who has been neither their immediate colleague nor their student and who is being considered for appointment at another university.

Of course the letters of referees are not decisive but they are certainly often taken into account. One of the reasons why they are not taken into account as much as they might be is that the members of the appointment committee to whom they are addressed often distrust them. Although they have usually been solicited, those who have solicited them may suspect that they exaggerate the merits of the particular candidate about whom they have been written. The referees themselves are often in a false position. They write on behalf of a former student whom they wish to help to make his way academically; they also wish to tell the truth but they fear that the candidate on behalf of whom they are writing will be at a disadvantage if his faults are described as well as his virtues because they believe that the other referees will mention only the merits of their candidates and will even exaggerate them. For this reason, a very useful mode of advisory assessment is rendered unreliable and even useless. This is especially the case where the candidate is just at the beginning of his career and his referee wants to help him to get started. (In the United States, the dilemma is especially acute since the confidentiality of the referees' letters cannot be guaranteed.)

There is no simple solution to this vicious circle of inflation of testimonials. As in other situations, a more widespread probity is necessary.

Note on the Right to Participate in Decisions regarding Appointments

Any discussion about the obligation of members of appointment committees must face the problems raised by earlier negligence, lightheartedness, sheer mistakes, or the failure of a well-chosen candidate to realize his promise. It is obvious in every university that some departments are weaker than their past standing, the resources available, and the standing of the university as a whole justify. Vigilance over new appointments cannot undo past errors in appointment, except over a long period. But even this curative vigilance is unlikely, if the departments which are the victims of those errors and faults have the power of appointment, with only perfunctory scrutiny of its recommendations by the higher authorities of the university. In that case, the result will be self-perpetuation, at the same level of mediocrity, through the appointment of their own former pupils and friends and other persons of indifferent qualities. The question may be put as follows: are members of weak departments entitled to the privilege of selecting or recommending for appointment their new members?

Academics who have been careless in the application of stringent criteria of achievement in making or recommending appointments are not entitled to participate in decisions regarding appointments. For this reason academics should recognize the appropriateness of a governing body or officer of the university to suspend a weak department's right to propose appointments. This procedure is applicable mainly in universities in which appointive decisions or recommendations rest substantially with departments or committees made up of members of the department to which the appointment is to be made. Such arrangements obtain chiefly in the United States, but even in countries where the final decision is made by government officials in ministries of education, the power of recommendation is usually in the hands of the department or faculty to which the appointment is to be made. The situation is somewhat different when the power of appointment or of recommendation lies with committees for professorial appointments made up largely of external members, and the proposals made here do not apply.

It would take much courage on the part of the university teachers and administrators to restrict a department's or a faculty's power of appointment in a university where the tradition of departmental or faculty autonomy is well established. It could only be done where the governing bodies and the influential members of the teaching staffs are alert to the damage which poor appointments do to the intellectual quality of the university and if academic citizenship is stronger than the desire to let sleeping dogs lie.

Note on Permanent Tenure

Permanent or indefinite tenure is one of the major objects of the decisions of appointments committees. It has been generally accepted that senior academics should be appointed on permanent—or indefinite—tenure and the attainment of that state is a crucial feature of the academic career. An academic who has attained permanent tenure is genuinely regarded as having "arrived." It is worthwhile to inquire into the question of whether permanent tenure is desirable in the light of its consequences for the adequate fulfillment of the obligations of the academic profession.

There is no clear reason why academics alone in the world should claim permanence of tenure without the possibility of removal. Even the Roman Catholic Church can defrock a priest. Why should the universities, which have taken the pattern of permanence of tenure from the church and more immediately in some countries from the civil service, retain a teacher permanently when he has clearly been unfaithful to the unspoken commitment which he has undertaken on entry into the academic career? Furthermore, why should an academic who has become indolent and negligent about his obligations in teaching, and who does no research or who does poor research be guaranteed security? A teacher who is frivolous in matters of academic citizenship may, if he has permanent tenure, be so with the confidence that nothing can be done to terminate his appointment. Permanent tenure can turn an academic post into a sinecure with rights and without obligations.

Why in the first place, should university teachers be appointed with the assurance that they are guaranteed incumbency until the age of retirement? One of the main arguments for permanence of tenure is that it protects the academic from the menace of dismissal as a sanction for the independent expression of politically and intellectually heterodox views. Permanence of tenure allows an individual scientist or scholar to embark on potentially important investigations which might run over many years and which might not yield results until a long time has passed. The need for short-term investigations of less importance in order to demonstrate that the person is worthy of reappointment is reduced by permanent appointment. These are strong arguments for permanent tenure.

There are other good arguments for the maintenance of the institution of appointment on permanent tenure. One of the consequences of permanent tenure is that it holds in check the noxious effects of the extent of mobility. A teacher appointed on permanent tenure in a particular university is more likely to regard the university as the institution in which he will probably spend the rest of his career. He is more likely therefore to be concerned about its well-being and its good name for achievement in teaching and research. That this does not always happen is quite evident but it is equally evident that it does happen in many cases. The elimination of permanent tenure would increase the amount of movement between universities, partly because the appointments of many more persons would be discontinued and partly because many more individuals would seek appointments elsewhere if they were not assured that they could remain indefinitely where they are. A university depends for its intellectual well-being, in some measure, on its "invisible senate" which is made up of teachers who are concerned with more than their own scientific and scholarly achievements, their own teaching and their own departments. Such individuals who are at best a small minority within any university would probably become fewer and the smaller number might be less influential if permanent tenure were to be eliminated.

It is also possible that, since the elimination of permanent tenure would entail periodic review and deliberation about the merits and deficiencies of every member of the academic staff, it would entail either an immense addition to the work of all colleagues who were called upon to assess the achievements of the colleague under review, or it would be done in a perfunctory and slipshod way. It might result in "logrolling" and in the formation of cliques and factions made of persons who support each other in the periodic assessments. As a result of the elimination of permanent tenure, conflicts and divisions might become even more common than they are at present.

If permanent tenure were eliminated it is certainly possible that indolence would be reduced. So its critics assert. Academics might, under the threat of the discontinuance of their appointments, be more conscientious in their teaching; it is also likely that more of them who do little research and who publish little under conditions of permanent tenure would do more research and publish more papers. The latter outcome would be a very doubtful blessing. Research conceived and conducted under the threat of the loss of an appointment is not likely to be inspired by intellectual curiosity; it would probably be rather humdrum work of which there is too much already.

Thus although the present arrangements for permanent tenure do give rise to abuses, it is not certain that the alternative scheme of periodic reassessment and reappointment or dismissal would not have equally injurious consequences for the realization of the idea of the university as an institution of research and teaching at a high level. This does not mean that the present system might not be modified with advantages to the academic ethic.

The Obligations and Interests of University Teachers

"Interests" are prospective advantages or benefits which would accrue to individuals and groups under certain conditions. These benefits are usually understood as pecuniary benefits and physical conveniences. Members of the academic profession like all other members of society have interests. They are interested in having the highest possible salaries, the most congenial working conditions, the shortest working week, etc. How are these interests to be dealt with in the light of the obligations of the academic profession? "Interests" are often in conflict with obligations. Should interests override obligations? Should obligations override interests? Is there always a conflict between obligations and interests, and if there is, how can a way be found which assuages this conflict?

There is no necessary incompatibility with the academic ethic if university teachers, through an organization, negotiate about their salaries, conditions of work, insurance benefits, etc., with a national body which determines academic salaries. It may be argued that there is no infringement on the academic ethic if university teachers, through their representatives, bargain as a trade union with the administration of their university regarding their salaries, conditions of work, pensions and insurance benefits, etc. If it is done in a matter-of-fact way, and if the bargaining is about classes or ranks of persons, there need be nothing injurious in this. Nevertheless, the formation of a trade union of university teachers and its proceeding in the style of ordinary unions raises grave questions for the ethos of the academic profession.

If decisions about reappointment, promotions, and the granting of permanent tenure of individuals are made into objects of negotiations by trade unions with academic administrators, and if incumbency and seniority are to be made into criteria of appointment—and more especially of reappointment and promotion—damage will be done to the particular university in which it occurs and in the course of time to universities in general and to the progress of learning. If permanent tenure and automatic promotion may be presumed for all academics who are represented by trade unions, the selection which is necessary for creating, maintaining, and rewarding the highest levels of achievement in the leading universities—and not only in those—will be brought to an end. Every university will be condemned to live with the inevitable errors of its earlier decisions in matters of appointment.

There is another danger which the formation of academic trade unions brings to the maintenance of the solidarity of the academic staff formed around their own particular university and around the idea of the university in general.

If the trade union movement among university teachers takes the form which it has taken in the working class, it will harden the lines of cleavage in a dichotomized university, split between "we," the academic staff, and "they," the administrators. This is already an obstacle to the formation of corporate solidarity around intellectual values in universities.

Academics in Great Britain and in Israel have joined trade unions, which in their negotiations with their respective national ministries, have confined themselves to salary scales. There is a danger, which is however not inevitable, that academic trade unions will exceed this self-restriction. If the restriction to matters of salary scales is exceeded and the trade union unit within the university becomes a focus of loyalty, attachment to the idea of the university and to the particular university as a corporate entity concentrated on the pursuit and transmission of truth about serious things will be injured.

It is perfectly reasonable for the custodial staffs of universities, the electricians, plumbers, janitors, and other manual workers who are necessary to the maintenance of the physical plant of the university to join trade unions to improve their wages and conditions of work in the same way that workers in factories and offices do in liberal-democratic countries. Trade unions have generally not been concerned with the relative merits of the performance of individuals, they have traditionally been concerned to deflect attention from individually distinctive excellence and to conduct their arguments on behalf of comprehensive categories such as all the workers in a given plant or industry and in a given occupation. The aspirations of academic trade unions and the obligations of university teachers in matters of academic appointments are in principle antithetical to each other.

(It is also contradictory for university teachers to claim that they are employees under the authority of others and at the same time to assert that they have a right to share in the exercise of authority by the corporate bodies which govern the university and its subsidiary faculties and departments, but this is of secondary importance.)

There are several reasons why trade unions of the traditional sort are inappropriate to universities. The first is that in a university, there is no equivalent to the profit-seeking or profit-making employer whose profit depends in part on how little or much he must pay to his employees. The second and more important reason is that the idea of the free labor market, in which the possessors of labor power "sell" their labor power to the higher bidder, does not rest well with the idea of the university where teachers, although they must gain their livelihood as teachers, are in principle concerned with the acquisition of truth through research and with the transmission to students and colleagues of truths discovered by themselves and others. The establishment of a "closed shop" which makes the holding of an academic appointment dependent on membership in the trade union adds another obstacle to the strict application of academic criteria in decisions regarding appointments.

In the United States and to a smaller extent in Western Germany, there are, at the time of appointment, negotiations between individual teachers and heads of departments or administrative officers about salaries and certain conditions of work but in these cases, it is a matter of what the university authorities are willing to pay to a particular individual teacher, bearing in mind his standing as a scientist or scholar and as a teacher. Academic criteria are clearly involved. This is not the case in trade union negotiations about salary scales which are uniform for all persons within the given institution or system, and within particular ranks and grades of seniority. Trade union representations about the cases of individual university teachers, in the countries where the academic traditions concern themselves with individuals, seldom concern themselves with the intellectual and pedagogical achievements of the individuals. It is perhaps true that representations by trade unions or staff associations do serve to protect individual teachers from unfair discrimination or dismissal but questions of intellectual merit seldom are raised in such cases; at best it is contended that the minimal requirements of performance have been met or that the proper administrative procedures have not been followed in dealing with the individual in question.

These observations regarding academic trade unions need to be supplemented by the observation that the deleterious potentialities of trade unions for the functioning of the university as an intellectual institution are exacerbated when the academic trade union has a definite political cast and when it attempts to influence new appointments as well as reappointments and promotions of particular individuals.

Still, the fact of the unionization of university teachers remains and it is not likely to disappear, although for the moment the tide has ceased to rise—at least in the United States. It is necessary to affirm the obligation of academics who adhere to trade unions to support only negotiations about salary scales and to abstain from intervening in cases of the appointment, promotion, and discontinuance of individual teachers except in cases of patent procedural irregularities. Once a trade union becomes the rectifier of individual "grievances," it is likely to introduce extra-intellectual criteria for the determination of whether particular individuals should be appointed, reappointed, or granted promotion or permanent tenure. If the trade union presumes to deal with individual cases, it will tend to encroach upon the jurisdiction of appointive bodies which are intended to apply strictly academic criteria. By its very nature as a trade union, it is likely to try to obtain maximum security for its members, i.e., permanence of tenure from initial appointment onward. If the trade union of university teachers undertakes to define criteria to govern reappointment, promotion, and the granting of permanent tenure, it is likely to argue for criteria which will be antithetical to the criteria of intellectual excellence in teaching, research and academic citizenship.

The Obligation to Their Own University

University teachers owe obligations to the particular institutions in which they are holding appointments. This obligation is not a composite of obligations to their students and their colleagues. There is an obligation to sustain the particular university because it is a source of intellectual sustenance to its members. A university is of intellectual importance to its members through the immediate and specific stimulation of a new idea suggested or expounded by a colleague and through the critical and sympathetic response of a colleague or a student to an idea put forward by the individual teacher. But it also has an important intellectual function in presenting an environment of high standards of intellectual exertion and achievement. This environment of many intellectually active individuals is also fused into an anonymous, collective representative of the standards of intellectual activity. It is a constant reminder of the urgency of searching, studying, criticizing, reexamining old texts and data, seeking new data and putting them together with the old data. A university, in addition to its tangible, physical reality is a collectivity which stands over, in an impersonal way, all of its members who are sensitive to it. The university is an intellectual collectivity, and not just a collection of stimulating individuals and necessary services provided by the university; it is not just a legal construct and it is not an epiphenomenon. It is a general pattern of attitudes and activities which molds the activities of the individual members of the university. If this pattern is dissipated, it has a debilitating effect on the relation of teachers and students and of colleagues and colleagues. It is a pattern which is sustained by academic citizenship. By his own exertions, achievements, and bearing, each individual adds his own force to the strengthening of that impersonal intellectual collectivity, making it more apprehensible and more present to colleagues and pupils, present and future.

In addition to this strengthening of the university as an intellectual collectivity, there is a need to make it match the pride which those associated with it would like to have in it. Pride in an institution is not just the gratification drawn from its fame, from the esteem in which its accomplishments are held in the society outside the university. Individual academics are proud of their university when they see it as embodying the virtues espoused in the academic ethic. A university does not have to be the greatest university in the world in order for its members to be proud of it. Pride is, of course, sustained by achievement but not all achievement consists in the publication of ground-breaking scientific and scholarly papers and monographs or educating students who become Nobel Prize laureates or professors in leading universities. Pride in a university is a function of affectionate attachment to it and of its respect for the obligations of the academic ethic. This is quite compatible with interest in and responsiveness to the demands and standards of the larger community of scientists or scholars in the teacher's own field of special concentration far beyond the boundaries of any single university. Loyalty to the latter does not necessitate indifference towards the particular university in which an individual holds his appointment.

The good name of a particular university among other universities and in society at large maintains pride in the university and makes for its effectiveness as an intellectual environment. This is why university teachers have an obligation to do nothing which will bring their university into the contumely of the academic and the larger worlds by dishonorable conduct or frivolity or by pushing it into the infringement of the academic ethic.

In a university, there are very likely to be conflicts about intellectual matters; there may also be conflicts over individual status and the status of departments and groups of departments, about the allocations of resources and of influence within the university. The conflicts over intellectual matters not infrequently also become conflicts about nonintellectual matters. Not all conflicts in universities are conflicts over intellectual differences, although these conflicts over the exercise of power and resources are often put forward as intellectual conflicts. Whereas intellectual conflicts especially if conducted in a reasonable tone can be very fruitful for the growth of knowledge, the conflicts over power and resources are seldom helpful either intellectually or institutionally.

The obligation to one's university includes the obligation to try to check conflicts within the university, between the representatives of disciplines and of sets of disciplines, between individuals and between factions, between groups of students and groups of teachers, and between teachers and administrators. It is one of the vices of large universities—but not always confined to them—to foster animosity of teachers towards administrators, especially when they are full-time administrators, who are regarded as "they" in contrast to "we," the teachers. In universities where there were few full-time administrators, and where the higher administrators returned to their academic duties after limited periods of services as deans, rectors, and provosts, this was not such an acute issue because "they" were drawn from and returned to "us." In the very large universities of the type of which not so many existed before the Second World War and of which many came into existence after it, administrators became professional administrators to an increasing extent. This occurred even on the continent of Europe and in Great Britain. A large full-time administrative bureaucracy was a longer-established arrangement in the United States, and it has become larger since the Second World War. This administrative development has brought with it frictions and dissatisfactions with "their" actions. This, together with disciplinary boundaries and subdisciplinary specialization, the increased political interest and partisanship, and disappointment connected with failure to progress within the academic profession, have led to distrust—even hostility—not only towards the administration but towards "the university."

Severe cleavages between academics and their administrators weaken the academic ethos. They distract attention from teaching and research. They destroy the serenity and concentration of mind needed in universities. They precipitate and aggravate conflicts when there are political disorders within and outside the university and when the solidarity of the university should be reaffirmed.

It is right that the cleavage between university teachers and administrators should be diminished. It demands forbearance, patience, and the avoidance of arbitrariness on the part of both the academics and the administrators. An understanding of the necessities of the university as a whole is the minimal obligation of all individual academics; a respect for the requirements of courtesy, openness, and fair dealing with teachers and students is the minimal obligation of administrators.

Regardless of whether a university is a wholly self-governing and internally relatively "democratic" institution, much of the work of maintaining a university, apart from the actual performance of teaching and scientific and scholarly research and the details of administration is done by committees. The committees are almost invariably advisory to some higher authority in the university, whether that authority is the president or vice-chancellor, or rector, dean or chairman of a faculty or a faculty board or of a department or a department as a whole. Conscientious service on committees has become proportionately more necessary as universities have increased in size. Much that was previously accomplished in an informal manner has now to be done through formally called and conducted meetings.

Membership on committees is a burden except for those who have lost interest in the intellectual substance of academic life or who enjoy them as occasions for the struggle for power; such membership is in many ways a distraction for individual academics from the central tasks of teaching and research. Committees proliferate, unfortunately, sometimes fruitlessly, and much time can be taken up by them. They are also often very trying and tiresome because some of their members talk too much and because the chairman cannot keep control over the proceedings. Nevertheless, service on committees, and above all, the chairmanship of committees is indispensable to the government of a university as a corporate entity and as an intellectual collectivity. Unfortunately, it is often the best members of a university, those most fully imbued with its ethic and most outstanding in their intellectual achievements, who lose patience with the increase of work in committees. The belief that the reports of committees are disregarded by those to whom they are submitted is further discouragement to serious participants. One result of these views is that committees are left to "professional committeemen" whose interests are often not primarily academic. Academics have an obligation to prevent this from happening by accepting their responsibility for service on committees and by increasing the efficiency of committees.

The Obligations of the Academic Profession to Its Environing Society

Universities have dual obligations. On the one side, they are responsible for the maintenance and advancement of knowledge and on the other they are responsible for performing important functions for their societies. Emphases on these two obligations vary among universities; some universities lean more to the former, others more towards the latter, but no university can wholly divest itself of either of these obligations. University teachers are similarly under these dual obligations. Teaching at an advanced level and fundamental research are the most important of the activities through which universities meet both these obligations.

The Obligations of University Teachers to Their Society through Teaching

University teachers meet a paramount obligation in society through giving to their students the substantive knowledge and the methods of acquiring and assessing knowledge which will be valuable to them in their life after leaving university, in their occupational activities and outside them. They do this by teaching the students, up to the students' and their own utmost capacities, the most advanced knowledge in whatever the discipline in which their students are inscribed and do so in a manner appropriate to the student's level in his particular course of study. Teaching the students includes transmitting substantive knowledge to them and giving them an understanding of how such knowledge has been acquired or established. It involves teaching the student how to observe and reason about the phenomena with which his discipline deals. In giving him substantive knowledge and methods of thinking, it inducts the student or carries him further into some of the best elements of the intellectual and moral tradition of his civilization—and to some extent of other civilizations—and it enables him thereby to appreciate the dignity and the value of knowledge in human life. Students who have been successfully taught the substance, principles, and methods of a subject are simply by virtue of what they have gained from their teaching improved in their quality as human beings and hence as members of their society. What they should carry from this education into their life in society is a rational attitude, a respect for knowledge as a constituent of human action and as a constituent of the proper existence of a human being.

The teaching offered in a university also trains individuals for the practice of professions which require systematically studied knowledge for their practice and which are necessary for the well-being of society as a whole. Such professions include law, medicine, engineering, architecture, and the administration of private and public enterprises. At the same time, it should be emphasized that the university is not the same as a vocational school or a polytechnic college. Purely technical knowledge which rests primarily on practical experience and not on an understanding of theoretical or fundamental principles does not have a central place in the teaching programs of universities. The learning of manipulative skills is important for society. It is proper to have institutions for that purpose when "on the job training" is not enough. But that kind of training is not a task of the university. The tasks of the university are defined by the presence and necessity of advanced systematic, methodical, and fundamental knowledge. It is not the distinction between useful and unuseful knowledge which draws the line between forms of training appropriate to universities and forms of training which are not their province. Rather it is the distinction between, on the one hand, training requiring, primarily, manual dexterity in the performance of complicated operations and in which practical experience is the basis of learning, and on the other, knowledge which is centered around certain fundamental principles and procedures, the mastery of which is required both for the practice of the professions and for the advancement of knowledge. It is the latter kind of knowledge which must be taught in universities. Clearly there are marginal cases; there can be disputes about the precise boundaries. But in principle the distinction is reasonably clear. Universities which do teach this kind of fundamental knowledge necessary for the advancement of knowledge and the practice of the professions are conferring invaluable benefits on their societies. This in fact is exactly what many universities are already doing. This does not preclude the teaching of particular courses for mature and experienced persons, already engaged in their respective professions; it only means that such courses must have a scientific or intellectual content.

The idea of being useful to society is being badly misinterpreted at present. Some reformers think that being useful to society means that universities should give up their concern with fundamental knowledge and with the rationale of evidence, experience, and tradition and should concentrate on the training of young and middle-aged persons for the performance of the specific skilled operations which their society is willing to employ and pay for. These are, of course, perfectly legitimate educational activities, but not all of them must be taught in universities and they are certainly not all that universities should teach. Burdening universities with tasks which should be performed by other institutions hampers the universities in their performance of those tasks which are necessary for society and which the universities alone can perform. It has the consequence too that the young are trained only for occupations which exist here and now. In a rapidly changing society, such an education can easily produce future unemployables, quite incapable of adjusting to new techniques.

The enlightenment of the wider public through "extension" courses presented away from the campus or of lectures open to the public but delivered on the campus is a very desirable activity but it does not fall directly within the circle of the primary obligation of university teachers. The main achievement of the university in the furtherance of public enlightenment should be sought through the education of the university's students in the substance and methods of thought of the various academic disciplines and through arousing and maintaining in them intellectual curiosity and sensibility which will persist in their life long after they have completed their studies and which they will diffuse through its presence in their professional activities.

The Obligations of University Teachers to Their Society through Research

The only research which a university teacher should do is that in which he has an intellectual interest, since otherwise it is scarcely likely to be brought to a significant conclusion. He must consider whether his research will produce something of intellectual importance because it raises questions about a hitherto accepted theory, or supports a hitherto unsupported theory, or because it opens a way to a new theory. This motivation and expectation are, however, quite compatible with the intention that the results of the research should have practical value. This is indeed the case of much medical and agricultural research and much research in physics and chemistry. Intellectual significance and practical value are often intertwined in research.

There is one vital criterion to decide what kinds of research university teachers should undertake: this criterion is the probability that the research will contribute to fundamental knowledge. Although the conception of "fundamental" is not easy to formulate in a clear and comprehensive manner, some kinds of propositions are clearly of fundamental importance and others are clearly trivial and there is a large middle ground in which a judgment is more difficult to strike. Nevertheless, the idea provides a standard of assessment. It is a standard which each academic should apply when making a decision about what problems he will investigate. University teachers, except in cases of national emergency, should not undertake to do research of which they are not convinced that it might be a contribution to fundamental knowledge. The solution of strictly technical problems, which are of no scientific interest, for industry or government is not a part of the obligations of university teachers to their societies. If there were no other kinds of research institutions in society, there would be a justification for universities to undertake such research.

The criterion of the practical value of the results of the application of a piece of research is a supplementary one for academics. This does not mean that it need be secondary in the view of those bodies which support the research; for many of these it must be primary. Academics who seek to obtain funds from these bodies to enable them to do research which is scientifically interesting to them often incline towards the scientifically interesting research which is likely to have useful practical consequences; this enhances the likelihood of obtaining the financial support they seek. Sometimes indeed the prospective practical value might be so great as to outweigh the smaller scientific value of the research in the eyes of the patrons as well as the scientists. Like the boundary between fundamental and trivial research, that between research which will have practical as well as basic scientific value and research which will have only practical value is by no means entirely clear. Nevertheless, there is a real difference between these two kinds of research and it is incumbent on the academic scientists to choose the former whenever they can.

The investigations with strictly practical intentions and consequences can certainly be of great value but universities are not the places where their execution will be to the most general advantage. For one thing, universities do not always have the equipment or the resources or the practical experience to do them with the greatest effectiveness and universities have other things to do which are not less urgent and from which they can be diverted by preoccupation with primarily practical problems. There are bound to be differences among the faculties and scholars of a university with respect to their conduct of research with a practical technological intention. The professional schools of medicine, engineering, law, and architecture will naturally do a great deal more research with immediate and indirect practical intentions than will some of the social and natural sciences and the humanities. But even in fields like mathematics and economics a good deal of the research will be intended to have practical applications. In all these fields, faculties, and schools, however, the advancement of fundamental knowledge must be a concurrent intention. There is a wide variety of research institutions apart from universities in every modern society, and many of these exist for exactly the purpose of solving technological problems on the basis of existing fundamental and technological knowledge. There is a rough and reasonable division of labor between universities and these other research institutions and academic scientists should bear this in mind in making their choices.

It is by making contributions to fundamental knowledge, i.e., to a deeper understanding of nature, man, and his works, and society that universities meet their primary obligations to society through research. The production of fundamental knowledge serves both the practical and the intellectual values of society. Society is not only a set of arrangements for solving practical problems; it is also the occasion for and in certain respects an expression of an aspiration to a deeper understanding. It is one of the many humane tasks of the universities to serve this latter aspiration which is common to most of the societies of Western civilization.

A university which performs well the two basic tasks of teaching and research is going very far towards meeting its obligations to its society. It is producing educated, intellectually disciplined, and equipped young persons capable of carrying on some of the most central practical and intellectual tasks of their society and it is expanding the society's stock of knowledge and deepening its understanding. These are, to say the least, services of the highest value.

The proper audience of the results of research should not be conceived only as other scientists as specialized as the producers of those results or as the "users" of such results in industry, government, and other practically oriented organizations. The wider public should also be included in the audience. This public cannot be addressed in the same manner as scientifically qualified colleagues and "users" because it lacks the special training which would enable it to follow with full understanding the detailed technical accounts which appear in scientific and scholarly journals; nor do members of this wider public have the time needed to read all the papers and monographs in which these results are reported. There is therefore a necessity for the class of literature which may be called "popular science"; this "popular science" summarizes in generally intelligible form the results of a large body of research and it does so in relatively short compass such as an intelligent and generally educated layman can find the time to read with understanding.

There are many reasons why academic scientists should contribute to "popular science." In the first place, inasmuch as scientific and scholarly research is intended to enhance the understanding of the universe and of man and his works, that understanding should be shared, in the appropriate form, by the largest possible section of the population in each society. There is also a perhaps less immediately lofty reason for making the intellectual results of scientific and scholarly research intelligible to the laity; the willingness of the laity to support scientific and scholarly research through the taxes it pays and through private philanthropic patronage depends to some degree on its appreciation of the intellectual and practical achievements of research. The widest possible diffusion of scientific knowledge is necessary too for the creation or maintenance of the "scientific ambience," i.e. the general lay appreciation of the legitimacy and necessity of science. It is in such an ambience that children and adolescents become interested in scientific work so that some of them decide to devote themselves to it. Without this steady flow of boys and girls interested in science and scholarship, the growth of these kinds of knowledge would be hampered. Although university teachers are not to be expected to add teaching in primary and secondary schools to their obligation, the writing of textbooks for these purposes alone or in collaboration with experienced school teachers is a proper and desirable activity for those academics who can do it.

All of these grounds for the wider diffusion of scientific and scholarly research beyond the audience of specialized scientists and scholars, "users" and university students place an additional obligation on academics. The obligation is a less continuous one than teaching and research and it does not apply in the same way to all academic scientists and scholars in the way in which the obligations of teaching and research do. Nevertheless the writing of textbooks and popular surveys of the state of knowledge over a broad range is an obligation of the academic profession as a whole. It is something which the academic community as a whole owes to the wider public but only a small minority of its members can write such works. Because of this, such works may be written in collaboration with experienced textbook writers or "scientific journalists," who know enough about a field to be able to understand technical expositions and who can express their understanding in a way intelligible to the laity, both adult and youthful.

The Obligation of Academic Scientists in the Practical Application of the Results of Research

Academic scientists do much research which has the practical application of its results as an ulterior or immediate objective. To do research which is intended to have practical consequences assumes that those consequences can be foreseen and rationally striven for. In fact, however, this assumption is not always valid. Scientists often discover things which they did not foresee; in the same way, there are practical consequences which cannot be foreseen. To what extent therefore should academic scientists do research the practical consequences of which they cannot foresee? It would be an extraordinary, unnecessary, and illegitimate restriction on the freedom of scientific inquiry if scientists were required to predict with accuracy the practical consequences of their discoveries.

Nevertheless, in so far as practical consequences are, at least plausibly, foreseeable, and in so far as they disapprove of those foreseen practical consequences, academic scientists should be free to refuse to engage in the research which is thought to be necessary for the achievement of such consequences. As academic scientists, they are under an obligation to do research which will have intellectually significant or scientifically fundamental results. If they are as convinced as one can rationally be that the practical application of those results will be morally pernicious, without any compensating moral advantages, they should refuse to do that kind of research. They should abstain from performing experiments on human beings which have only slight scientific value and which will be foreseeably injurious to the particular persons on whom the experiments are performed or which can only result in injury to other persons.

The matter is, however, not as simple as it seems; unambiguous decisions are not easy to make. How can the possible benefits to many human beings be measured against the possible damage to the experimental subjects or animals? All that is possible is a very rough estimate of what is believed to be foreseeable; there can be no absolute guarantee that damaging consequences will not occur. It must be recognized that there are various degrees of risk in the assessment of possible damage and that there can be no unquestionable certainty in the prediction of outcomes.

It follows therefore that it is not reasonable to expect academic scientists to be held morally responsible for all the practical consequences of the application of the results of their research. It must be borne in mind that academic scientists who work on problems the solution of which is anticipated to be of practical importance are seldom the persons who undertake the application of those results; as long as the academic ethic of open publication is adhered to, the academic scientist is not in a position to prevent anyone who reads his account of his results from applying them if he can and wishes to do so. The only obligation laid on the academic scientist is to forbear from doing research which he is reasonably confident will have injurious effects on the persons involved in the research as members of the staff or as the subjects of experimentation. He is likewise under the obligation to forbear from performing research the results of which can clearly be applied only in a way injurious to the persons on whom they are applied and if these injurious effects are not substantially outweighed by the larger benefits of the application which are reasonably in prospect.

It will be seen that the obligation of openness of the communication of the results of research, an obligation which is central to the academic ethic, is incompatible with a demand that the academic scientist take on himself the responsibility for the application of the results of his research.

To assert that academic scientists are under an obligation to control the practical use of the results of their discoveries would require that they control access to those results. This amounts to the establishment of secrecy of the results of research already done or abstention from the investigation of certain subject matters or problems about which knowledge might be injuriously applied. Such secrecy and abstention are repugnant to the academic ethic. The freedom of inquiry is not simply a negative freedom from the constraints of church, state, and other earthly powers; it is a positive freedom to investigate whatever is adjudged to be intellectually significant.

One of the by-products of the intensified relationships of universities and governments and of universities and private business enterprises, arising from the capacity of university teachers to do research of practical value, has been the requirement of secrecy in connection with certain kinds of research. This is a new phenomenon in the history of universities. It is contrary to the tradition of science and scholarship to keep secret the results of research once the scientist or scholar has decided that his knowledge is reliable enough to lay before his colleagues. This problem does not arise for research done in governmental and industrial research institutions but it does appear in connection with research done in universities under contracts with governments and private firms.

(This assumes that these results meet prevailing intellectual standards. Editors of scientific journals might refuse to publish these results but they are justified in doing so only if they and their advisers regard them as too trivial or as insufficiently sound scientifically but this is another matter.)

What should be the relationship of academic scientists with research workers employed under those restrictive conditions? There can be no question about the access of these latter scientists to the published results of academic scientists; these are in the public arena and are available to anyone who wishes to see them. To what extent should an academic scientist make his still unpublished results available to scientists of these "secretive" institutions? There is no significant difference between transmitting still unpublished results and the publication of the same results which will shortly become available to anyone who wishes to and can read them. But what about situations in which scientists in universities, deliberately and by agreement with the authorities of the university, withhold their results from publication (or do not distribute preprints) for a stipulated period during which their application is considered by private business enterprise?

In practice, there is nothing amiss if academic scientists communicate their unpublished results to scientists in these secret zones just as they would to scientists in other universities as long as they make clear that they will and actually do publish their results in publicly available scientific journals when they think they are ready and if they are confident that their results will not be plagiarized or used for purposes which might be harmful to the laity. If the period of withholding is only about a few weeks or months, there is in fact little or no infringement on the obligation of open publication because the period between the date of submission to a journal and the date of publication is frequently much longer.

The practice of the openness of scientific and scholarly knowledge, except under conditions of extreme emergency, is one of the chief obligations of academic scientists and scholars. The principle of the autonomy of the university requires that decisions about what should be studied, how it should be studied, and whether the results should be published should be in the hands of academics and not in the hands of nonacademic persons in political organizations, churches, business firms, governments, and armies. It is because academics are best able to assess and decide about academic things that they may legitimately lay claim to the autonomy of universities. This autonomy is infringed when external institutions decide what research should be carried on in universities and assure themselves of this right to determine the choice of research problems in universities through provision in a contract made when the grant of financial support is given.

The matter is very complicated. Ever since academic scientific research began to exceed in cost what could be borne by the ordinary university budget, the carrying out of research projects conceived by academics in the natural sciences, and increasingly in the social sciences, has depended on the availability of external financial resources. If a patron, governmental, philanthropic, or industrial, did not wish to support a particular piece of research and if no alternative means could be found to provide the needed financial resources, the particular research could not be done. Since the middle of the nineteenth century, industrialists have approached individual scientists—as certain German chemicals manufacturers once approached Justus Liebig—with the request that they investigate certain topics of interest to those industrialists in return for which they would support the research, including provision for a certain number of graduate students, etc. This was a step towards the determination of the choice of research subjects by an external power. Arrangements such as have recently been established at the Massachusetts Institute of Technology might turn out to be an institutional establishment of such external determination of the choice of topics for research. Such an arrangement would probably also bring with it the restriction on the freedom to publish the results of research until they have been patented by the extra-academic patron. The arrangement about patents, however, continues an already existing practice in the patenting of processes, substances, and mechanisms discovered or invented in universities. Universities have been in the custom of patenting discoveries or inventions of members of their academic staffs. This has sometimes involved a short delay in the publication of the results of the particular research until the patent has been granted. There is nothing in this procedure contrary to the academic ethic, as long as the results of the research are published and thus made accessible to other scientists.

Recent developments also raise other questions. Certain discoveries and techniques of research in university laboratories—recombinant DNA is the most prominent—have in recent years turned out to have potentialities for ever greater commercial profitability. Numerous industrial enterprises are being envisaged for the development and production of substances discovered in this field by academic scientists. Should the individual academic scientist make his discoveries available to a particular firm and to no other in return for munificent support of his research and large honoraria? Should he establish a firm of his own through which he can exploit his discovery and which he will operate as an ordinary business enterprise? Should he simply publish his results in the established scientific journals, as scientists have always done ever since scientific journals came into existence, and allow his university to obtain a patent which will bring income to it? Should the university itself form an industrial corporation to develop and sell the knowledge of the processes, substances, or mechanisms discovered or invented in its laboratories and patented by it? Should the university take out the patent in its own name and then license it to industrial enterprises which wish to produce the substance or to use the process or mechanism for their own commercial profit? This is an unprecedented situation in the history of universities; it is difficult at present to promulgate the obligations of universities because the patterns and ramifications of the relationship of academic scientists and private business enterprises are still unclear. Certain things are indisputable: academic scientists, while holding full-time academic appointments, should not become the owners and managers of business enterprises which will take up most of their time and energy. Academic scientists furthermore should not be governed in their choice of research problems by the prospect of becoming rich from the commercial application of their discoveries. Recently there have been cases of university teachers who had created survey, statistical information, and economic advisory services. The founder and owner of one of these recently sold his institute for $10 million. Is there anything contrary to the academic ethic in such entrepreneurial activities?

In principle, this question is much like the question of the propriety of university teachers entering external nonacademic employment while holding full-time appointments at universities. There are precedents which would appear to justify the conduct of a private business enterprise by an academic who has a contract with his university for full-time teaching and research. Some professors of medicine have very lucrative private practices "on the side"; professors of law, accounting, and engineering and architecture have private practices or act in a private capacity in special cases and many serve as consultants and receive substantial incomes from these activities, in addition to their regular salaries from the university. There is a good argument for such activities to the extent that they infuse the knowledge gained by university teachers through such activities into their teaching and research. It might however also be a distraction from the primary responsibility of teaching and research.

External business activities are subject to criticism if the academics involved skimp on their service to the university in teaching and research in order to carry on with their "private practice." If it can be done without skimping, then it might be beneficial to the teaching, if not of the research, conducted at the university because it will enable the teacher to give the students knowledge of the most recent development in the practical activity for which the students are preparing themselves.

Association with commercial or industrial enterprises presents additional possibilities of diverting a university teacher from his obligations. The requirements of time and energy are not the only things which a university teacher owes to teaching, research, and other duties within the university; there might also be a conflict between the pecuniary interest of the firm with which the university teacher is associated and the pecuniary interest of his university. If, for example, an academic is the owner or a member of the board of directors of a firm manufacturing scientific instruments which seeks to sell its products to the department of which its owner or director is a member, the latter is obviously involved in a conflict of interest. It is necessary that such conflicts of interest be avoided by the university teacher.

The issue here is the extent to which the external activity hinders the performance of the primary obligations of the university teacher for teaching and research. If the business enterprises conducted by university teachers do not require their active and continuous management and require no more than about one day weekly and if they do not bring their owners into conflicts of interest or the exploitation of the resources placed at their disposal by the university for their own private profit, such activities are compatible with the academic obligations of university teachers.

The issues of whether academics may supplement their university salaries by income gained through consultation or the conduct of business enterprise or by any other means and whether such external earnings are to be reported to the administration of the university are to be resolved in accordance with the primary obligation of any academic who holds an appointment for full-time service in teaching, research, and other university duties. As long as a university teacher does not fail in his primary academic obligations, his income, assuming that it is legally gained, is entirely his own affair.

The Obligations of University Teachers to Their Societies through the Performance of Services

There are also more specific ways which university teachers are sometimes called upon or urged to serve their society. These services are of many kinds. One of the most common of these services in the English-speaking world used to be the conduct of extension courses for adults who were not regular students of the university; another has been the writing of articles in popular periodicals and newspapers and books for general circulation in which they set forth in relatively easily intelligible form the results of their research and their reflections. To these have been added in more recent years broadcasting on radio and television. Other services are the performance of special kinds of social welfare services, such as the provision of medical care and legal services for the poor, the conduct of mental health centers, the management of day nurseries for small children or the organization of educational and recreational activities for secondary schoolchildren of the neighborhood of the university; in some universities, departments of education have conducted primary and secondary schools. Others have entailed the performance of research including very descriptive kinds of quantitative social research or elementary soil analysis for farmers or the testing of materials for local industrial enterprises or municipal governments. Some universities have developed industrial research bureaus and survey research institutes, which, on a contractual basis, conduct surveys for governmental and private organizations. Still other services which universities sometimes have performed for nonacademic bodies are special training courses, e.g. for colonial administrators, Negro business enterprisers, or for policemen or civil servants of the middle or lower ranks, or for employees of private business firms desiring to be brought up to date in the knowledge which they need for their work. There are also services in management, for example, offered by universities against payment. (Athletic events and games are presented to the general public by many American state universities and other American higher educational institutions in anticipation of substantial income from television broadcasting firms in return for the privilege of presenting these very popular spectacles.)

Every one of these services has some justification. Some of them bring income to the university which is especially welcome when it is harder to obtain funds from other sources. Some are useful to the local community in which the university is located. Others are part of the "public relations" of the university which have the justification of causing taxpayers and the public at large to look with favor on the university. Some of these services are intellectual and are continuous in content with the activities which are central in the life of universities. Extension courses, special courses of lectures open to the wider public, popular accounts of specific projects and whole fields of research are made available to a wider public; some of the extension services sometimes also enable graduate students to acquire experience in teaching. The special training courses are built around the specialized knowledge of some of the teachers of the university, although sometimes more or less qualified persons are appointed specifically for the teaching of those courses. Some of the other services, such as the provision of staff for legal aid clinics, are also akin to the central activities of the universities in so far as they give students the opportunity to learn how to apply the knowledge they have been acquiring in their studies. Still other services have little to do with the intellectual tasks of universities but might be desirable as humanitarian undertakings or as a means of assuaging the animosity of "town" against "gown" or of maintaining the immediate social environment of the university and making life more attractive for students and teachers.

All of these services are however only of marginal significance in so far as they do not contribute to the main task of teaching and discovery. If research done on contract with industrial firms or government is also the kind of research which furthers the advancement of fundamental knowledge as well as serving the practical aims of firms or government, then it is acceptable for a member of the academic staff of the university to undertake it—assuming, of course, that he has an intellectual interest in it, that it does not distract him from more important research and teaching in which he was already engaged, and if the results can be published and shared with students and colleagues. If the training courses for police or civil servants or employees of business firms involves teaching at a level appropriate to a university and if they present fundamental social science knowledge in an applied form, that too is a service which it is acceptable for a university teacher to undertake. If it is less than that, then it should not be undertaken by university teachers, and their universities should not ask them to do so.

The line which divides services which have an advanced scientific or scholarly content in teaching or research from those which are no more than services which some other institution like a police training-college or a civil service staff-college or a municipal governmental statistical bureau or the census bureau of the central government performs as part of its routine activities, is not a very precisely definable line. Nevertheless, university teachers and those who represent them should ask themselves whether when they provide these services they are not stepping over that line. If they are over that line, they should not be undertaken.

The Obligations of University Teachers to Their Societies through Political and Publicistic Activities

It is in the nature of intellectual activities to make critical assessments of any received tradition. There would be no advancement of knowledge in any field by university teachers if they accepted unquestioningly the traditions of knowledge which were presented to them. The very advancement of knowledge rests on the discernment of gaps and insufficiencies in the tradition. The reception of and respect for the tradition of one's subject coupled simultaneously with a critical attitude towards those parts of it with which they are actively engaged are an obligation of the academic calling. This complex relationship to the tradition of knowledge is an essential feature of teaching as well as research in universities. Good teaching includes teaching how to be rationally critical towards what is taught and learned from the tradition.

This critical attitude has not been confined to the particular fields of specialized study and research. It has extended beyond the boundaries of any special field. This has been especially characteristic of university teachers—and students—in the nineteenth and twentieth centuries. It is in fact inseparable from the great achievements of universities. In some countries, it was the churches or rather traditional religious beliefs which first came under the critical study and evaluation of academic scholars. Since the latter part of the preceding century and through most of the present one, the critical attitudes of university teachers, especially in the social sciences, have been extended towards existing political, social, and economic arrangements in their societies.

One concomitant of this critical attitude has been the increased political interest and activity of academics. University teachers in the years since the Second World War have been drawn into political controversies and movements to a greater degree than ever before. University teachers have now become forces in the public and political life of their respective societies. The exercise of this critical disposition—unequally distributed among different disciplines—brings with it obligations.

University teachers are members of their larger society with the rights and obligations of all citizens. They also have additional obligations. These arise from their possession of special bodies of knowledge and their expertise on subjects which are very pertinent to problems of great importance to the wider public and its organizations and to government. The activity of university teachers, outside research, and university citizenship is addressed to laymen, i.e., persons who have less knowledge than they themselves possess. Just as in their capacity as teachers, they deal with students who know less than they do, as citizens engaging in a variety of political and publicistic activities, they are constantly in contact with other persons who do not have as much knowledge as the academics themselves about the particular subjects of which they possess complex knowledge. (In their domestic, convivial, and communal relationships, their large stock of complex knowledge has no bearing, although they are at times accorded a large measure of deference in recognition of this stock of knowledge regardless of its irrelevance to the situation in question.)

Academics have all sorts of interests and aspirations—just as do physicians and lawyers and engineers and factory workers. They are interested in higher salaries and security of tenure. They are often politically partisan. Neither their private desires nor their wishes for certain economic and social policies to be carried out nor their preference for particular economic, social, and political arrangements permit them to suspend the obligation of telling the truth about any particular subject as it has been arrived at by careful and critical study of the relevant evidence; this is the obligation which they have taken upon themselves by entry into the academic profession. This obligation is still valid, even though many infringe upon it. What should be thought of a physician who is careless in his diagnosis and treatment of a poor person, or of a person whose religion is different from his own; what should be thought of an engineer who neglects the principles of the strength of materials when designing a building for a person of whose political or religious views he disapproves? Or of a lawyer who having accepted a client, does not do his best to win the case because he disagrees with the client's political or religious views or disapproves of the client's moral qualities or temperament? As with physicians, lawyers, and engineers, so it is with the university teacher: he must not allow his political partisanship or any other predilections to influence his teaching or the collection and analysis of data in research. Admittedly it is more difficult for a teacher to control this tendency in the social sciences or some branches of the humanities than in the natural sciences but that only makes it more of an obligation to watch and discipline himself.

In his research, in addition to the control imposed by his own moral self-scrutiny and self-discipline, the academic is watched over by his colleagues. If he infringes on the obligations of painstakingness in observation, or of rigor in analysis, the editors of the journals to which he submits his papers and the referees selected by the editors and the reviewers of his monographs are likely to catch him out; even if he gets through their critical assessment, some of the scientists or scholars who read his published work are very likely to detect his factual mistakes and his misinterpretations and his work will be refuted or neglected. His reputation in his scientific or scholarly community will be damaged. External control within the community of his fellow scientists or fellow scholars reinforces the self-discipline which he learned as a student to exercise. These are all situations in which he is being observed and assessed by his peers. An equally demanding situation does not exist where his audience knows less about his subject than he does.

As a custodian of the best knowledge available through the best procedures of discovery and interpretation, respect for the truth is the unrenounceable obligation of the university teacher in all the public activities in which he engages. The difficulties lie in knowing just what is the truth about the particular subject matter under consideration; this very uncertainty about the validity of a particular proposition requires that it should not be asserted in a dogmatic way, as if it were unquestionable.

The obligation of an academic as a teacher to avoid as well as he can the assertion of his own political and ethical views in the guise of scientific or scholarly knowledge obtains also in his relations with individuals or institutions whom he serves as an expert adviser or consultant. Scrupulousness in adherence to the strictest standards of truthfulness are incumbent on him in all these situations. This entails, on the one hand, the avoidance of distortions impelled by political and moral ideals or partisanship on behalf of particular political movements and, on the other, a willingness to admit ignorance and insufficient knowledge. Even under the favorable conditions of presenting carefully prepared material in a classroom, this is a difficult requirement to meet. It is more difficult for an academic who engages in public debates, oral or written, in public meetings or on television or radio or in short articles or interviews in newspapers and periodicals.

Is an academic bound, in his publicistic and political activities and in activities as a consultant, by his academic obligations to adhere to the standards of intellectual integrity which he observes in his teaching and research? Does the fact that he is a university teacher impose any restraint on his freedom in the public sphere to which laymen are not equally subject? It does, in so far as his representations purport to be based on careful study and as long as they claim the authority of expertise gained through scientific and scholarly research. It certainly does, in so far as, in his public action, he allows himself to be identified by his academic connection and rank; in such cases, he is allowing himself to claim, or to have claimed on his behalf, the authority which is acknowledged to inhere in methodically acquired expert knowledge, disinterestedness and abstention from passionate partisanship. But even if he does not allow the name of his university to appear alongside his own name—in so far as he has any control over that—he is still under the obligation of intellectual scrupulousness which he accepted when he became a university teacher. He has also the obligation not to betray the trust which is given him when laymen look to him for objective knowledge and responsible judgment.

Academics who speak in public about the issues which engage public opinion almost always allow the presumption that they speak with the authority of scientific and scholarly study. Even where their sponsors have invited them on the assumption that the analyses and arguments of the academic person will support their own partisan position, they do so also on the assumption that the academic in question will enjoy special attention and respect because he will be presumed by the audience to speak with the authority conferred by intensive and scrupulous study of the issues involved. This gives special force to the duty of the university teacher to respect the obligations which are entailed in the custodianship and representation of scientific and scholarly knowledge. Even if they were to disregard the expectations of their audience, the obligation to speak the truth would still exist. Legally, an academic is entitled to tell as many half-truths and falsehoods in public as any lay politician, journalist, or agitator. He is legally entitled to be as demagogic and misleading as any other unscrupulous citizen. It might be claimed that a citizen should not be handicapped in his political conduct by his membership in the academic profession, that the political sphere is different from the academic sphere and that the obligations of the latter are not valid in the former. Such a claim would be wrong.

This claim to exemption of the academic from special obligations in the public sphere might be more acceptable if the two spheres were entirely disjoined from each other. They are, however, not so disjoined because knowledge of the kind which the academic represents as a teacher and scientist also enters or can enter into action in the political sphere and that is the reason why he is invited to speak and is listened to. Furthermore, the academic in the sphere of public discussion seldom divests himself of the appurtenances of his academic life, he uses his academic title or titles, and he allows his academic connections to be known; in doing so, he allows it to be believed that his detachment and his objectivity of judgment as a scientist or scholar are brought into play when he participates in controversy about political matters. In fact, he would not have such easy access to the public forum if he did not have these academic qualifications and if it were not believed that his assertions carried with them the authority of long and scrupulous study. The hearing which an academic receives from laymen, whether they be legislators, civil servants, or ordinary citizens, is more attentive and more deferential because of the laymen's belief that academics have a special qualification to speak truthfully about the issue at hand, because they have a detached cast of mind as well as a large stock of relevant and reliable knowledge on the subject at issue. For these reasons, an academic transmitting or intimating knowledge in the public and political sphere has the same obligations as are entailed in the quest for and the transmission of knowledge in the academic sphere.

Academics often do not have the same sense of obligation to their fellow citizens as they have to their pupils who come to them presumably to learn what the academics have acquired by their studies. The position of the pupil is also different from that of a political antagonist or of a potential supporter. The student has come presumably to have his mind furnished and guided and many teachers take seriously the responsibility arising from the fact that the student has entrusted himself to his teachers. Even though a lay audience might accord trust to an academic, that very fact, however, is sometimes regarded by academics as an advantage to be exploited rather than as imposing an obligation. The rules of the game are generally regarded as less exacting in the public sphere; there is more acceptance of a knockabout atmosphere, more of a tradition of the permissibility of overstatement and suppression. This is one of the reasons why academics, when they are politically engaged, regard themselves as absolved from the exigent obligations which many of them feel compelled to honor in their academic activities.

On the contrary, rather than being absolved, the academic in political and publicistic activity has a special obligation which is incumbent on him in consequence of his possession of an elaborate body of scientific or scholarly knowledge and more generally because the public standing which he is usually glad to accept is granted him by virtue of his presumed commitment to such knowledge. He can, it is true, be criticized for what he says in the public sphere but there are bound to be many persons in his audience who are not in a position to render an intellectually qualified criticism of his assertions and who are nonetheless citizens with the obligation to make up their minds about the general line of policy which public bodies should follow. These persons are entitled, when they open their minds or at least give their attention to an academic speaking in public, to have as truthful an account of the events about which they have to pass judgment as long and diligent study makes possible. The academics who participate in public political discussion have an obligation to these persons, not really different from that which they have to their students. In both cases, they are addressing themselves to persons who presumably know less about the subject under consideration than they themselves do. Academics who address themselves in speech or in writing to a larger public in the field of their expertise or in a field in which they are presumed to have expertise should regard themselves as bound by the trust which their audience grants them as scholars or scientists. But even if the audience has no special expectations, the academics themselves still have the obligations which they accepted when entering the academic career. Logically there is nothing in any proposition which requires that the person who knows it should avoid distorting it or suppressing it. Nonetheless, the ethical postulates of the high appreciation of the truths attained through systematic research and analysis and of the value of striving for them, which are entailed in the entry into and practice of an academic career, are incompatible with a cavalier attitude towards such truths and towards the evidence they require.

It has been said that the obligations of the academic acting in the public sphere are greater when he speaks with the authority of an expert in his own field of professional study than they are when he speaks outside his field of expertise. This is doubtful, regardless of whether he is speaking in his field of expertise or speaking outside it. He still receives attention because of his standing as an academic, as a member of a university, bearing the titles and degrees which are granted him for achievement as a scientist or scholar, and this attention carries with it these inescapable obligations. The moral limitations on the freedom of expression in the public sphere are therefore by no means entirely confined to social scientists and humanistic scholars; infringements on these limitations are, in fact, often committed by natural scientists too.

Many biochemists, physicists, and astronomers are certainly not experts on the matters on which they occasionally hold forth in the political arena. They are deferred to because it is thought that they are practising the same detachment and disinterestedness in their judgments about public matters that they evince in dealing with scientific problems. This deference should not be exploited although it often is exploited. If, as is frequently the case, their qualifications in substantive knowledge for receiving the attention of the public are not superior to those of any other citizen, they should not seek to enhance the persuasiveness of their arguments and analyses by alleging that the latter have been arrived at by strictly scientific methods and by allowing their academic connections and status to be adduced to fortify their authority.

For about eight decades, and to a much greater degree in recent years, academics have been conducting political activities through "open letters" in which the signatories list their universities, rank, and sometimes departments. This is an exploitation of public confidence in the integrity of scientists and scholars, but it is a very minor aspect of the problem. Even if this particular kind of exploitation were to cease and if academics were to throw themselves into politics as professional politicians do, they would still have the obligations arising from their professional acceptance of the custodianship of knowledge, not just of specific and factual knowledge in particular disciplines, but of the general rules of its acquisition and communication.

When one has entered voluntarily into the academic profession, one commits oneself to observance of the norms of disinterested scrutiny of evidence and of logical reasoning. It is an obligation to which one submits as a condition of entering the profession. Of course, this is not done in the form of an oath but that does not make the obligation less binding. This obligation extends to every sphere in which the academic acts in a capacity in which academic knowledge is involved and in which the academic intimates or asserts explicitly that his opinions carry the authority of disciplined study.

These obligations of the university teacher in political and publicistic activities are largely restrictive. They do not require that academics carry on political activities; they require only that when academics do so they should not play fast and loose with truths. There is however one object for which political activity is positively required by the academic ethic. It is an obligation of academic citizenship to look after the well-being of universities as intellectual institutions and not only the well-being of their own universities but of universities throughout their respective countries. Since universities are now so intimately dependent on governments, it is obligatory for academics to follow closely the activities of governments as they affect universities and to make representations to governments about existing and alternative policies. It goes without saying that the manner of these representations should conform with the stipulations of the academic ethic regarding other political and publicistic activities of university teachers. There is no obligation on academics to be supine or silent in the face of what they think to be wrong policies of governments, either about universities and scientific and scholarly research any more than there is for them to abstain from political and publicistic activities generally. But whereas there is no positive obligation on them as university teachers to engage actively in the latter, there is an obligation derived from the obligation of academic citizenship to concern themselves about the effects of governmental activities on academic things.

It is clear that all academics must engage equally in making representations for the protection and promotion of learning. It is undesirable that such representations should be left exclusively or primarily to the administrative officers of universities and to the professional officials of learned societies and academic associations.

The burden which is laid upon the academic of adhering to the required norms in his public and political activity is heavier than it is in the academic sphere proper; in the public and political spheres he bears it unaided by the disciplining and critical assessment of his academic colleagues. In the public and political spheres, he does not have the corrective protection which he receives in the academic sphere in the form of discriminating approval or disapproval of colleagues who are well qualified and who are the primary audience of scientific and scholarly works.

An academic in the public sphere does not have the same external constraints on him as he has when he is conducting research and presenting its results to his colleagues. In the public sphere, he is not subject to measured, painstaking assessment by persons who know as much as he does about the very things he is speaking or writing about. He does not even have the vaguely compelling discipline which sometimes comes from the physical presence or proximity of his colleagues. He may indeed be criticized for his statements by those academics who disagree with him, but, since the intellectual standard of public discourse is often regarded by academics as less exigent than that which should prevail within the academic community, their criticism of demagogic public statements by an academic colleague is often on the same level as the statements they criticize. Those who disagree with his political conclusions might censure them but more usually they will simply castigate him for being "radical" or "reactionary," according to their tastes.

In summary, it must be recognized that addressing an academic audience in a colloquium or at a scientific congress or in the pages of a journal or a monograph is different from addressing an audience of laymen, whether they are ordinary citizens at a public meeting or readers of a newspaper or a general magazine or whether they are legislators taking testimony before a legislative committee or civil servants reading a memorandum. In all the latter cases, the university teacher is not only addressing the laity, he is also having to make his scientific or scholarly knowledge intelligible to them. Because they are laymen, the knowledge given to them must be presented in an inevitably simplified form. It is true that in addressing undergraduates in a classroom at fairly elementary levels of the subject, allowances must be made which need not and generally are not made in addressing more advanced students. In simplifying for undergraduates, however, the teacher is aided by the tradition which is incorporated into textbooks; these embody an art of simplification for beginning students which has been developed over many years and this is a great aid to the teacher. Furthermore, the teacher is not expected to be omniscient about things which are still not known. Serious students do not expect a teacher to know things which no scientist or scholar has yet learned through research. The students know that they are attending an elementary course and they usually know that there is much that is still unknown to their teachers, even to the most distinguished ones.

A lay audience has different expectations. It listens to a scientist or a scholar because it believes that he is asserting definitive truths about the conditions or processes of which he is speaking. Such a lay audience appreciates less than an academic audience the imperfections of knowledge; it frequently assumes that a scientist or scholar "has the answers" to the problems under discussion. Furthermore, in his public activities, the academic is frequently constrained by the short time or small space which is allowed him; even before a legislative committee, he is not allowed the amplitude of a thirty-hour lecture course, or of a seminar running over a whole term. In addition to this, his exposition is frequently oral in mode, subject to interruptions and to his own feeling of the need to make his points strikingly to the audience which is not well informed and which he will not see again once his brief exposition is finished.

The university teacher in writing for a newspaper or a general periodical is under similar constraints. The audience and often the editor are not as qualified as his students are in their classes and seminars, they expect him to deliver a definitive answer and they require that he do it briefly. In the face of all difficulties, the problems of simplification are exacerbated. The simplification of scientific knowledge is a very demanding task. Most scientists and scholars are not skilful in it. It is sometimes done very effectively in magazines like *Scientific American, The New Scientist,* and *la Recherche,* but it is done in these journals with the aid of very experienced and knowledgeable editors and with the expectation that a good part of the readership already has considerable scientific knowledge.

The inherent difficulties of simplification of scientific knowledge and the plain fact that on many of the issues under contention in the public and political spheres there is no definitively demonstrable knowledge are additional obstacles. These obstacles are quite distinct from the temptations of partisan contention, but they add to the difficulties of fulfilling the obligations of university teachers when they engage in political and publicistic activities. They do not, however, invalidate the obligations of the university teacher who engages in such activities.

The Obligations of University Teachers to Government

University teachers have been turned to increasingly by governments as consultants and advisers. They have been invited increasingly to serve as members of commissions to prepare reports for both the legislative and executive branches and to appear as experts before committees of legislative bodies. They are also sometimes brought as experts into judicial proceedings. Their counsel is sought because they are presumed to know more about certain matters and to have more detached and better schooled judgment on those matters than the appointed civil servants in the higher ranks or than the elected legislators and their staffs or than ordinary witnesses. Academic advisers are not sought out by politicians and civil servants or lawyers because of their superior knowledge of moral truths; they are not chosen as moral guides and counselors but as experts who have studied and mastered certain subjects. They have been chosen because they can advise civil servants and others on the best, i.e., the most efficacious means of achieving their particular objectives or because they can analyze more reliably the ramifications and possible repercussions of a proposed policy or because they know more about the facts under contention. In the course of giving advice about prospective policies, they often do not confine themselves to the means of attaining given objectives; they also help to redefine the objectives by analyzing them more closely, by showing what their costs and benefits are likely to be. Sometimes they are explicitly invited to argue for a particular policy; sometimes they do so unavowedly in the course of making recommendations about the best means of attaining particular ends, with minimal costs with respect to other ends. They are also invited, especially by legislators, because of their known political sympathies and the prestige which their testimony will confer on the objectives the legislators wish to promote.

Academics are seldom invited to serve as consultants or advisers because of their "wisdom" in the delineation of the ultimate ends of policy. They are invited and given credence because they are thought to be in possession of more complex—and more reliable—knowledge of the subject in question than are the elected and appointed officials who are supposed to deal with those subjects. In some cases this might be so. But in many of those cases, the knowledge possessed by the academics in these subjects is too suppositious, too uncertain to provide an incontrovertible element in the discussion to which it purports to contribute exactly such an element. Often the research which has been done does not allow for a definitive and unambiguous answer to the questions which should be answered, if one alternative of policy is to be chosen over others. Even specially commissioned research seldom, if ever, produces indisputable answers to the questions which have been put to it.

What are the obligations of academic scientists and scholars in such circumstances? One obligation is not to abuse the trust which has been accorded to them on the presumption that they actually possess certain and definitive knowledge which can replace the ignorance and uncertainty of the laity. This implies the obligation to restrain themselves from overstating the degree of certainty of their knowledge and from contending for one alternative over others with a tone of conviction which the existing state of knowledge on the relevant subjects does not justify.

Since the politicians and civil servants know less about the relevant subjects than the scientists and scholars, however uncertain their knowledge is, should the latter be reluctant to press their own preferences? It could be said that, since after all, a decision must be made, and since the relevant facts have not been unambiguously established, the academic is as entitled as the legislator and civil servant or as any ordinary citizen to press his own preferences. This argument fails to recognize that the legislators were elected and the civil servants were appointed to make decisions under conditions of uncertainty and that ordinary citizens are not invited to do what scientific advisers and consultants are invited to do. The academic is called in, not in his capacity as an ordinary citizen for the purpose of making a decision under conditions of uncertainty, but rather because his knowledge puts him in a different position than that of an ordinary citizen and is thought to enable him to reduce or eliminate that uncertainty. If he cannot do that, it does not follow that he is entitled to attempt to usurp the powers and responsibilities assigned to elected and appointed officials.

A university teacher who is invited by a governmental or private body as an expert to advise about a matter in which a decision calls upon scientific knowledge is in a position not entirely unlike that of a teacher before his students or an academic addressing an audience which knows less about his subject than he does. A university teacher is under an exacting obligation to assess and disclose the reliability of the knowledge which he is transmitting to his students and to be as careful as possible to make sure that what he asserts as valid knowledge is not determined by his economic and political interests or desires. It is the same with respect to his activity in research. It is no different when he engages in public or political contention. It is no different when he serves as an adviser or consultant to government. It is not easy, especially in the social sciences, where methods of analysis are not so rigorous and where so many of the subjects studied are also the objects of political contention, to separate one's valid knowledge from what one's political and moral ends incline one to believe. Yet the distinction is a valid one and academics who are consultants or advisers on the basis of their "expertise" should attempt to observe it with the same conscientiousness that they exercise in their research.

Before the Second World War, there were usually relatively few opportunities available to tempt academics into excessive diversion of their time and energy into external activities. In Western Europe and North America, university appointments have mainly been appointments on full-time and by and large university teachers have conformed with expectations that most of their time would be spent on academic activities, with a very flexible allowance being made for the performance of various services and public and publicistic activities. In Italy, it was not rare for academics to be members of parliament while retaining their academic posts and looking after them as best they could. (In the countries of Latin America where university teaching was not a full-time occupation, it was expected that they would conduct private professional practices or would have some other sources of income such as governmental employment or private business.) After the Second World War, both the opportunities and inclinations of university teachers to engage in extra-academic pursuits have increased markedly.

The service of government in consultative or advisory capacities, like political and publicistic activities, presents problems in the fulfillment of the primary obligations of university teachers. All of these activities outside the university are usually undertaken while the person in question continues to hold a full-time academic post; they all require time and energy. Apart from conventions or regulations regarding the numbers of lectures or courses he is expected to give in an academic session, it has been generally accepted that the university teacher should be free to decide for himself how he will allocate his time among his various concerns. It has usually been assumed that, apart from his classes and seminars, he will spend his time primarily in research and study for the preparation of courses, with smaller amounts of time to be used for examinations and other tasks of university administration. University teachers who spend a great deal of time in the delivery of lectures to lay audiences, or who become "television stars" or who write a great deal for newspapers and general periodicals have sometimes caused eyebrows to be raised. Some universities have placed limits on the magnitude of income from nonacademic activities but it is not a widespread practice. Since there have been no precise stipulations as to how much time teachers should spend in such external activities, these cases of excessive participation in such activities have very seldom caused more than mild, informal disapproval.

As long as a university teacher holds an appointment on full-time at a university, the proportion of his time which he devotes to advice and consultation for government, like the proportion of his time which he devotes to consultation for private business firms or to the conduct of a private business firm or private professional practices of his own, must be limited. A reasonable rule would stipulate that not more than one day each week be used for external activities regardless of whether they are for political activities or consultation as an "expert" for private business firms or for government or for the conduct of a private professional practice.

What has been said about the special obligations of academics in political and publicistic activities or as consultants or advisers to adhere to the same standards of probity in the presentation of their knowledge that they observe in their research and teaching does not apply with the same force to those academics who cease to be academics by accepting elective or appointive office in government. It is right that many universities require that any of their members who accept such offices take a leave of absence of specified duration. These nonacademic activities must be carried on continuously and all the time and their practice is not compatible with the fulfillment of the obligations of an academic appointment.

It is, however, not only a matter of time. It is also a matter of the nature of the primary obligations and necessities of the life of a politician and civil servant. The scientific or scholarly validity of knowledge is not a primary concern of politicians and civil servants; they have moreover no obligation to add to the stock of fundamental knowledge by reliable methods nor have they any obligation to transmit the substance of that knowledge while training its recipients in the modes of acquiring and assessing knowledge. The practice of requiring that academics who become legislators or civil servants take leave of absence is necessitated not only by the incompatibility of the demands in time and energy of the two kinds of occupational activities. It is also a recognition that the obligations of the two are different from each other in substance. The recognition of the fundamental difference in the respective tasks of these two kinds of activity is an acknowledgment of the tension which is engendered when the academic engages in activities in the public sphere. As long as he is an academic and respects his obligations as an academic he cannot allow himself to act like any other nonacademic participant in political and publicistic activities or like any businessman or private or public administrator. The academic cannot "let himself go"; he is constrained by the obligations imposed by commitment to the life of scientific and scholarly knowledge, the rules of methodical observation, rational analysis, and critical assessment.

Note on Accountability to Government

In recent years, the issue of the accountability of scientists and scholars receiving grants from governments for research has been raised. This is a much more limited and special issue but it merits some attention in a discussion of the obligations of university teachers to their government. It is perfectly reasonable that scientists and scholars should be accountable for how they spend the money which governments make available to them for their research. There is no doubt that there is an obligation of accountability. The only issue is the extent of their accountability. They are certainly under the obligation which is required by law to show that the funds were expended only on legitimate objects directly connected with the research for which they were granted. They are also under obligation to work conscientiously on these projects; this is part of their obligation to knowledge. They should not however be regarded as under obligation to specify the exact amount of time in hours and minutes they spend on the project; they should also not be placed under obligation to conduct the research in precisely the manner which they specified on the application, if in the course of it, a new idea occurs to them as to how to do the research better than first occurred to them when they applied for the funds. This is in accordance with the freedom of investigation which is a part of the academic freedom to teach and to do research according to their best lights. The academic is accountable to governments for honest dealing in doing his research but nothing is gained by government or by knowledge if an academic scientist is forced to submit reports in an unrealistic degree of detail.

The Obligations of University Teachers to Their Societies Generally

Does a university teacher owe loyalty to the constitution and the central institutions of the society? In countries where university teachers are civil servants, this question is sometimes settled by the terms of appointment; the teachers have to take an oath to uphold the constitution. This does not, however, mean that a great measure of academic freedom and university autonomy does not exist in such countries. It only means that with the enjoyment of that freedom and that autonomy the university teacher has committed himself to be loyal to the constitution of his society. But these conditions do not obtain in countries in which university teachers are not civil servants. No oaths of loyalty are ordinarily exacted in such circumstances. This does not mean that the university teacher is exempted from the obligation of a minimal loyalty. The obligation is however that of any citizen and not that of a university teacher in particular. The obligation to abstain from subversive activities is the obligation of the citizen, just as is the obligation to abstain from criminal activities. Neither the right to academic freedom nor the autonomy of the university implies any privilege of academics to engage in subversive activities.

The individual owes no more loyalty to his society, its constitution, and its central institutions than does any other citizen and no less. To impose oaths of loyalty on teachers in universities—and other educational institutions—which are not demanded of all other citizens is invidious and unjust. The obligation of respect for the constitution and laws of his society is an obligation which does not derive from his role as a university teacher; it is an obligation inherent in citizenship. Within those limits, the university teacher should be as free as any other free citizen to espouse constitutional changes by constitutional methods.

Academic freedom in the sense of the freedom to perform the academic activities of teaching and research does not confer the freedom of subversion or terrorist activities any more than being a citizen confers such rights in the civil sphere. The autonomy of universities does not confer on individual university teachers immunities which no one else in society legally enjoys.

The autonomy of the university, the academic freedom and the civil freedom of the university teacher together exclude the use of the premises of the university for political purposes. The university teacher is not entitled to use them for any purposes not connected with the performance of his academic obligations of teaching, research, academic administration, and academic citizenship. If an academic is active politically, he should not use his office or other university premises for that activity, nor should he use his university address for any correspondence which is part of that activity. (These limitations are not intended to circumscribe the political activities of students which lie beyond the scope of these considerations.)

The university teacher has no obligation to be a conservative, or a liberal, or a social democrat or a radical or a revolutionary. Nor does he have any obligation not to be any one of these. He has, as a university teacher, only the obligations to seek the truth about the subjects he studies and teaches according to the best available methods, to respect and criticize the tradition of his subject and to transmit his knowledge to his students and colleagues with due regard to the criteria of reliability of evidence and of the logical coherence of interpretations and arguments. Some social and political attitudes might be more consistent with the obligations of the university teacher than others but the university teacher as such has no obligation to be consistent if there is a conflict between his academic obligations and the doctrines associated with his political attachment. But as a university teacher his first obligation is to the academic ethic and to what derives from that obligation when he engages in political or publicist activities.

Concluding Observations

The academic ethic is the sum of the obligations which are incumbent upon persons who hold academic appointments. These obligations are derived from the tasks of universities which are to extend and deepen scientific and scholarly knowledge, to educate young and not so young persons in that kind of knowledge, and to train them for the practical professions for which that kind of knowledge is required.

The obligations which constitute the academic ethic are not the same as a comprehensive code of conduct for university teachers in all spheres of life. University teachers are many other things as well as university teachers. They are citizens, members of churches, they are parents and spouses. The academic ethic touches only on the acquisition and transmission of scientific and scholarly knowledge within the university and among universities and on activities using that knowledge outside the universities.

Every teacher, whether in kindergarten or graduate school, bears certain moral obligations. Teachers at every level ought not to lie to their pupils, to be cruel to them, whether physically or mentally, ought not to destroy their curiosity, their imagination, their critical powers; they ought, on the other hand, to inform, to train, to develop the capacities of their pupils, to encourage them to face and to overcome their difficulties. These moral responsibilities flow from the very nature of the relationship between pupil and teacher. In dealing with the responsibilities of university teachers we are dealing with a very special class of teachers, working in an institution which is dedicated, which the kindergarten is not, to the advancement of knowledge as well as to its transmission.

In their concern with the advancement of knowledge, university teachers are also not unique in their obligations. A university teacher shares his obligations with the research worker who does his work in research institutes, in industry, or in his own residence—this last is a phenomenon still occasionally encountered in the humanities, if scarcely at all in the physical sciences. Like them, the university teacher engaged in research ought not to falsify his results; like them, he ought to be careful, assiduous, stringent in his criticism of his own work, fair in his criticism of the work done by other scientists and scholars, generous in his acknowledgment of the sources which he has drawn on. But unlike the kindergarten teacher, unlike the persons engaged exclusively in research, the university teacher's obligations arise not only out of his teaching, not only out of his research, but out of the need to conjoin the two within the framework of the university.

Towards the university to which he belongs and which supports him intellectually as well as financially and administratively, the teacher may feel a special loyalty to a degree which varies from time to time, from place to place. Such loyalty reaches its maximum, perhaps, in the fellows of an Oxford or Cambridge college which they help to administer in detail; it reaches its minimum in one of the huge "mass universities" in which the university is thought of, simply, as an institution which provides a living to the practitioners of certain learned professions, their loyalty being more to their professional discipline, and less to the university as such; they conceive of their duties to the university as differing in no vital respect from those of any employee to any employer. In this respect there has been a considerable change of attitude, at least in the Anglo-American world, during the postwar years, as mass universities have come to be the norm, as their administration has fallen more and more into the hands of professional administrators and as, on the other side, science and scholarship have been more and more extensively organized into professional societies, readily linked by rapid communications, so that a "colleague" is as likely to live thousands of miles away as to be a member of the same university. Loyalty to the university, not only to a particular university but to the very idea of a university, has probably diminished, loyalty to the profession has increased. Some of the problems which have beset our universities derive from that very fact.

The university teacher should recall that even in countries where the university teacher is a civil servant or where the attempt is made, by unionization, to force him into a confrontation of employee and employer, the university is no ordinary place of employment. It is unique in its devotion not to profit-making, not to administration as such, but to learning, in every sense of that word. Often, if by no means invariably, it is an institution which the teacher may be able to modify, or within which he can resist modifications imposed upon it from outside, whether in the name of equality or utility. The university sustains and nourishes the teacher intellectually; it does not simply house him and pay his salary. It is, indeed, an alma mater, not only to students but to teachers. Or at least it can be. Its capacity to be an intellectual home for its teachers may be greatly weakened if those teachers, professionally intent on "getting their own work done," disregard threats to its integrity, whether coming from outside its walls or from within, leaving the care for the university, in a scornful way, to "those who have the time for such things," except when they begin obviously to impinge on their own professional interests—when it is generally far too late to protest.

It is very tempting to think in terms of getting on with the job, to leave concern for one's university to others, until one day the peculiar characteristics of the university, and the job along with it, simply vanish. To act thus is to fail in respect to a special class of moral obligations, obligations towards the university as such.

If the degree to which the teacher can help to shape the future of his university, and of universities generally, varies from institution to institution, from society to society, two things characterize every university everywhere: the university teacher has students and he has colleagues and he has them within the setting of an institution. To his students, to his colleagues, and to his institution, the teacher has a variety of obligations but his central obligation is towards the truth. What does this amount to, in concrete terms?

This has been a hard century for the abstract values, not least for truth. Over two thousand years ago, of course, Plato already found it necessary to defend the concept of truth against the Sophists; at the purely philosophical level, the new skeptics are still employing the arguments of their Greek predecessors, Sophists like Protagoras, skeptics like Sextus Empiricus. Yet whatever view we finally take about that still-controverted question of what truth consists in and how it is to be recognized, it takes a hardy skeptic to deny that over the centuries human beings have built up a body of reliable information and that they have done so, in many cases, by those assiduous investigations we call science and scholarship. In the course of such investigations, too, they have developed habits, skills, and attitudes of mind which can be passed on to students, who can then employ them to add further to that body of information, whether it be about the physics of the stars, our own bodies, or the daily life of ancient Greece.

Even if we ignore the skeptic, as someone who cannot in practice help relying on exactly the same information as the rest of us rely on, two things have certainly to be admitted. The first is that in themselves facts are not necessarily of great interest. With no more developed resources than a telephone book and no more elaborate ability than sheer patience, any of us could construct a vast body of factual truths, relating, let us say, the number of persons in the telephone book whose name begins with "M" to the number of persons who live at an address which contains the number "3." But such truths bear on no problem and are entirely worthless. We would find it hard to rebut the charge that both science and scholarship sometimes present us with some truths which are of scarcely any greater value.

A second point is this: some of the things which even the most conscientious and studious teacher presents to his classes as truths will turn out to be false or at least to need correction. One can exaggerate the extent to which this is so. Most of what we learned at school still goes unchallenged, even if emphases have changed. Many different views have emerged about the causes and the effects of the French Revolution but the actual account of events remains as it was, unaffected by the varying spotlights which have played upon these events; most of what was taught at school half a century ago in chemistry or mechanics remains unaffected by the great changes which have occurred at the growing points of science since that time. At the university, however, the teacher is operating precisely at those growing points, as part of his function of helping knowledge to advance. The likelihood that what he tells his students will be in need of revision or correction is correspondingly enlarged.

Error, then, the university teacher cannot wholly avoid. But his first obligation is, at the barest minimum, not deliberately to falsify, not to mislead his students, even in the name of some cause to which he attaches great importance. Teachers, not only university teachers, are called upon, in this sense, to have a respect for the truth which admits of no exception. But that is by no means the final extent of the university teacher's obligation to truth. He ought to do what he can to avoid error, however unintentional; that is one reason why he must try to keep abreast of his subject. At all times, there have been university teachers who did not do this, who, even in rapidly changing fields of study, were content to use the same lectures year in and year out. The temptation to act in this way is now greater than it ever was. Pressed to do research, the university teacher may seek out some recondite field, quite remote from his teaching, and excuse the fact that his lectures remain unchanged by pointing to the necessities imposed upon him by his research to concentrate all his reading in that field. Again, the teacher may be simply overwhelmed by the sheer volume of new work. Or he may judge—he has to be careful that this is not an excuse—that the great body of new work is simply a passing fashion which he not only can, but ought to, ignore in his teaching. But whatever the problems which inevitably result, the university teacher has the obligation to ensure that his students are not left with the false impression that what they are being taught represents what is known at a given time, when that is clearly not so.

The situation in this respect will clearly differ from subject to subject. In the case of professional subjects like medicine and engineering, the responsibility is plain; to go on teaching what has been shown to be false is a gross dereliction of duty and a danger to society. In subjects where the conception of knowledge is more uncertain—philosophy, literary theory, and the more theoretical reaches of sociology are obvious examples—the teacher is more likely to expound his views, often with very little regard to what is going on elsewhere. And there is no great harm in that, provided that the situation is plain to his students, that it is apparent to them that what he is teaching his students as the truth has been subjected to criticism and to reservations, and which is not unanimously accepted as such. He can do this, for example, by being scrupulous to recommend reading which will make the idiosyncratic bent of his teaching obvious. (There are real problems here; some of the most influential teachers, some of those who are commonly regarded as "great teachers," Wittgenstein, for example, have not done this. But although we are glad to hear from their students what they were taught, we cannot feel that the influence of such teachers on those students was a wholly benign one. In any case, we have to take the ordinary teacher, a respectable scientist or scholar, as our norm, not the very rare genius.)

At a somewhat different level, where we are not concerned with high-level, necessarily controversial, theories but with supposed matters of fact which are nevertheless controversial, the situation is plainer. To take an extreme case: a teacher may be fully convinced that every dissident in the Soviet Union is either insane or in the pay of foreign powers or, on the other side, that there was no holocaust in Nazi Germany. But he ought not to proceed as if these were indisputable facts, of the same order as the date when Lenin entered the Soviet Union or as the original name of Joseph Stalin. He ought not to try to confine the reading of his students to that literature which shares his views; he ought to be prepared to face criticisms. So much, at least, follows from his obligation to the truth.

Of course, there are difficult marginal cases. We, all of us, dismiss certain views as not deserving serious attention. Is the biologist bound to warn his students that there are still creationists or the astronomer that there are still "flat-earthers"? But the general argument is reasonably plain, if not its precise force in marginal, difficult cases: the teacher ought not to pretend that what is controversial is not controversial. Of course, he can still be mistaken. What is apparently settled at one time may be highly controversial at another. The risk of error is part of the human condition. Like everyone else, the university teacher can only do his best to avoid misleading his students. His distinguishing mark lies in the fact that the standards of doing his best are in his case particularly rigorous. And those high standards flow from his special obligations in relation to the truth.

One can light on truths, of course, in many different ways. The university teacher has no monopoly in respect to the discovery of truths. Before he goes to school any child has lit on a great many myths, as a result of his own experience and his communication with his fellows. Not only that, the poet and the sage can light on truths. Then why suppose that the university teacher has distinctive moral obligations arising out of a unique relationship with the truth? In a university such truths, formed by systematically ordered experience and imagination and rational reflection, are brought to the test. Claimants to truth have to make their claims good. The university teacher is dedicated, not only to the truth as such and already established truths but to the spirit of inquiry, curiosity, and criticism. Many of his students, to be sure, will never catch that spirit; many will fail to communicate it. Some teachers see themselves, some students see their teachers, simply as purveyors of information, of facts, of unquestionably settled propositions. The greater the degree to which university courses are crammed with facts, as a result of the "knowledge explosion," the less leisure the student has to think and to work for himself, as a result of the time it takes to cram him with the facts, the less likely it is that this spirit will be communicated and implanted or aroused.

The spirit of inquiry begins from serious problems and tries to solve them within the traditions of science and scholarship. To participate in those traditions one has to be disciplined or trained. More and more, universities take the professions as their model; the scientist and the scholar are anxious to win the support of what they now unselfconsciously refer to as "the profession," a phrase which, not so long ago, would certainly not in the English-speaking world, have been applied to their pursuits by philosophers, scholars, and scientists. (The idea of learning as a profession arose in Germany and from there was translated institutionally into the American graduate school.) Two by-products of this idea are the production of much research on trivial problems, in relation to which professional skills can most readily be demonstrated, rather than fundamental problems where the method of proceeding is more uncertain, and passing judgment on what is one in terms of professional standards rather than on its actual intellectual value—as when, let us say, an edition of an important philosopher prides itself on its adherence to professional bibliographical standards and brushes aside the objection that it is going to tell philosophers a great deal that there is no point in their knowing and will make inaccessible, or wholly ignore, what would really help them. In these circumstances the spirit of inquiry can fly out of the classroom window.

The student disorders of the 1960s were intellectually antinomian; one of the targets of the rebellion was any sort of training or discipline. The rebellious students were confused, too, in their notions of what constituted "relevance." Yet, in their confused way, some of the students were rebelling against the conception of the university as a place for turning out thoroughly drilled professionals rather than as a place for study and reflection on fundamental problems, arousing intellectual curiosity and assimilating the spirit of inquiry. One of the major problems for the university teacher is to train, without, in the process, narrowing the vision. He has to give expression to a certain kind of deep seriousness, which is not the same thing as solemnity; he must have a "sense of relevance," not as that was understood by those students who meant by it relevance to current social and political issues, but as relevance to those central problems which distinguish an intellectual tradition and which constitute its reason for being.

What the university teacher must not do is to acquiesce in that onslaught on science and scholarship, on disciplined thinking of every kind, so characteristic of the 1960s and still exerting an influence, if now somewhat submerged, beneath a new wave of vocationally minded professionalism. A university teacher who succumbs to that onslaught, who is content to say whatever comes into his mind, without respect for evidence and argument, and who encourages his students to proceed in the same way, is committing the ultimate treason against the university. Systematic, disciplined investigation is its lifeblood. Those who reject it as a governing principle have no more place in a university than an atheist has in a church. They are, of course, entitled to attack the universities as an atheist is entitled to attack the churches. But they are lacking in a sense of moral intellectual obligation if they remain within the university, seeking to retain the advantage of membership in it after they have lost faith in the ideals which can alone make sense of it as an institution. The situation of such a university teacher is like that of a priest turned atheist or skeptic and who continues to preach in church. They are both lacking a sense of moral and intellectual obligation. If it is really true that one opinion is as good as another, that there is no such thing as objectivity, then the universities have no function and no justification for their continued existence.

The nature of rational argument, the force of evidence, the extent and character of objectivity—these are topics which can properly be analyzed and serious questions may be raised about each of them. Without being skeptical about the value of disciplined inquiry in science and scholarship, one can ask fundamental questions about the way in which it is being conducted and reject as extravagant some of the claims which have been made on its behalf, e.g., the claim that it offers us absolute certainty or the assumption that scientists and scholars are more than human in their ability utterly to cast aside all inherited beliefs or the belief that scientific knowledge alone can provide proper and exhaustive guidance in moral and political decisions. To raise such issues is by no means to be morally irresponsible; nothing can so readily provoke cynicism and scepticism as the making of extravagant claims and the refusal to discuss the postulates of one's position. But such criticisms must themselves, in the context of the university, be propounded and developed in a rationally disciplined way. Moral obligation is rejected only when the teacher is content to make dogmatic pronouncements, to fulminate in a manner which may be perfectly proper in a seer or a prophet, but which has no place in a university.

By developing in his students the capacity to participate in the great traditions of science and scholarship, in however minor a way, by getting them to understand, at the very least, the modes of imagination and the characteristic forms of criticism which they exhibit, a teacher demonstrates his reverence for truth and fulfils the consequential moral obligations, in a manner specific to him as a university teacher. His obligations in relation to truth automatically generate a sense of obligation to his students. If he leaves them with the impression that everything is settled and that there are no longer any but minor problems, or with the belief that when problems were settled in the past it was always either by deduction from dogma or by the application of established methods, then he has failed not only in respect to those students as individuals but in respect to the maintenance of the spirit of inquiry, which is at once rational and reflective. And he is also failing his colleagues in so far as he is neither himself participating in inquiry into fundamental questions nor encouraging his students to do so.

This is connected with the fact that both science and scholarship are collaborative inquiries. Even the most solitary scholar stands, in Newton's famous phrase, on the shoulders of his predecessors. Scientists, natural or social, are far from solitary; they often work as members of teams. Even in the humanities, even in philosophy, the book or article with several authors has become commonplace. This, however, is less important than the collaboration which takes place across the boundaries of research teams and of single institutions and across the boundaries of countries. Scientists build on the work of other scientists, most frequently outside their own universities and very often in other countries; their publications are read and drawn upon by scientists in other parts of the world. It is approximately similar in the humanistic and social science disciplines, particularly the more abstract ones like linguistics and economics. A scientist or a scholar is a member of an international group with shared assumptions engaged in a common enterprise of exploring a particular class of problems by using particular methods, immediately communicating their results to one another. It is one of a university teacher's responsibilities to arouse and guide his abler students to participation in such groups, disciplining them in the methodical procedures, developing in them the substantive knowledge and the skills, and introducing them to the ideals which make collaboration possible. He does not do this by preaching to his students but rather by teaching them with seriousness and devotion and by having some of them participate in his research, as members of his particular group and with some of these becoming, as they move further in their studies, research assistants or junior members of the teaching staff.

What of the ordinary student, not working at a level at which he can expect to be invited to join his teacher's research team? There is a familiar way of referring to universities—as a "community of scholars"—which seems to suggest that every student is automatically a scholar, and some students demand the right to be regarded as such, from the beginning of their university days. But, of course, even the best of them—the rare precocious genius apart—is in fact a learner. A teacher is failing in his obligations if he treats his students as scholars when they are not, if he does not insist that they have to learn. A university, it is more correct to say, is a community of discoverers, teachers, and learners. Yet one should not lightly dismiss the feeling which underlies the older designation of the university as a "community of scholars." It suggests that a university teacher should try to do what he can to try to bring home to his students what it is like to be a scholar or a scientist, as distinct from encouraging them to treat some textbook as sacred. He will not treat his students as if they were children, even if he cannot treat them as scholars. Otherwise he forgets his obligations to the advancement of knowledge, an advancement which depends in the long run on the sympathetic understanding of a great many persons who are not themselves scientists and scholars but have at least some appreciation of what it is like to be one.

These are the essentials of the academic ethic. There are universities in which it is relatively easy to adhere to it and there are those in which it is more difficult. In universities where there is a tradition of its observance, new members and aspirants among the students who aspire to academic careers will quite readily assimilate it. There are, however, universities in which the conception of the functions of the institution, promulgated by their higher administrators and accepted by teachers, old and young, is inimical to the academic ethic. Institutions of higher education whose governing members regard them as vocational training schools or as institutions the main task of which is to serve the local community will be less congenial to observance of the academic ethic.

The academic ethos survives through the respect which academics give to their obligations and by the exemplification of it in their own actions before their colleagues, senior and junior, and their students. Students who aspire to academic careers learn the academic ethic by seeing it being practised by their elders. The academic ethic is supported by the conscience of individual academics and their consciousness that their colleagues are adhering to it. Its effective practice by individuals is sustained by the support which it receives in the conduct of colleagues.

Even in the universities in which the academic ethic is best observed, there are many defections and infringements. Quite distinguished scientists and scholars are often self-seeking; some of them are eager to use the power which they exercise in appointments to confer patronage, pay off personal debts or advance the interests of friends and protégés with little consideration for their intellectual and academic merits. Many care only for their own departments, their own special field within their own discipline, and their own conception of the best methods and their own line of substantive interpretation. If it were not so, there would be no need to elaborate and affirm the academic ethic.

The fundamental obligations of university teachers for teaching, research, and academic citizenship are the same for all academics. All these activities are necessary for the university to perform its indispensable tasks for modern societies and modern intellectual culture and it falls to the individual academic to contribute up to the best of his capacity to the performance of those tasks. Not all academics are equally endowed or equally inclined, for whatever reason, to the activities needed to meet these obligations. Some are much more inclined and much better endowed for research, others more clearly for teaching and some are better equipped for academic citizenship than others. Nevertheless, to abstain from any of these totally and to show no respect for them is contrary to the obligations of an academic career.

The Criteria of Academic Appointment

I Introduction

The existence of the University of Chicago is justified if it achieves and maintains superior quality in its performance of the three major functions of universities in the modern world. These functions are (1) the discovery of important new knowledge; (2) the communication of that knowledge to students and the cultivation in them of the understanding and skills which enable them to engage in the further pursuit of knowledge; and (3) the training of students for entry into professions which require for their practice a systematic body of specialized knowledge.

In intellectual matters, at least, the whole amounts to more than the sum of the parts in isolation. A university faculty is not merely an assemblage of individual scientists and scholars; it must possess a corporate life and an atmosphere created by the research, teaching, and conversation of individual scientists and scholars which stimulates and sustains the work of colleagues and students at the highest possible level. Research, teaching, and training are the work of individuals. These individuals depend for their effectiveness, at least in part, on the university's provision of material and administrative services which enable their work to go on; they depend also on the maintenance in the university of an atmosphere of stimulation, tolerance, and critical openness to new ideas. The function of appointive bodies is to bring to the academic staff of the university individuals who will perform at the highest level the functions of research, teaching, and training and the maintenance of the intellectual community of the university. A university which does not perform at this level will lose its standing in the world and therewith its power to attract outstanding faculty members and outstanding students. Its failure to attract them will in turn reduce the quality of its performance. Every appointment of a mediocre candidate makes it more difficult to appoint a distinguished candidate later and it makes it more

Reprinted from *The University of Chicago Record* IV/6 (17 December 1970): 1–15.

difficult to bring outstanding students to the university. This is why scrupulous insistence on the most demanding criteria in the act of appointment is so decisive for the university.

The conception of the proper tasks of the university determines the criteria which should govern the appointment, retention, and promotion of members of the academic staff. The criteria which are to be applied in the case of appointments to the University of Chicago should, therefore, be criteria which give preference above all to actual and prospective scholarly and scientific accomplishment of the highest order, actual and prospective teaching accomplishment of the highest order, and actual and prospective contribution to the intellectual quality of the university through critical stimulation of others within the university to produce work of the highest quality.

The University of Chicago should not aim to be a pantheon of dead or dying gods. Appointments to the university should not be made solely on the basis of past achievements but only to the degree that past achievements promise future achievement.

The tradition of the University of Chicago has defined it, primarily but not exclusively, as a research university of the highest international standing. The University of Chicago is, by its tradition, an institution where research is done by academic staff and where students are trained to do research, by induction into the state of mind and disposition to do research on important subjects and with original results. Undergraduate teaching at the University of Chicago has been and must be conducted in a way which arouses in students their capacity for discrimination and disciplined curiosity so that upon reaching the latter years of their training they will have the skills, knowledge, discrimination and motivation to make original discoveries or will begin to be ready for the effective performance of roles in society where these qualities will bear fruit.

In the performance of its functions in research and in professional training, it becomes necessary to appoint supporting staff who are indispensable to the performance of these functions but who are not qualified for appointment to the university faculty. This raises serious problems for the university in its effort to keep to its major tasks at the level its traditions and aspirations demand.

II Procedural Matters

Criteria

Any appointive body must have a standard by which it assesses the merits of the alternative candidates before it. Academic appointive bodies in general, and at the University of Chicago in particular, must have clearly perceived standards which they seek to apply to particular cases. They must seek to choose candidates who can conform most closely with these standards in their most exigent application. The standards to be applied by any appointive body should be those which assess the quality of performance in (1) research; (2) teaching and training, including the supervision of graduate students; (3) contribution to intellectual community; and (4) services.[1] Distinguished performance in any one of these categories does not automatically entail distinguished performance in the others. For this reason, weighting of the various criteria cannot be avoided by appointive bodies. The committee thinks that the criterion of distinction in research should be given the greatest weight.

The Application of Criteria

All academic appointments to university faculties must be treated with great seriousness. They should, wherever it is at all possible, be made on the basis of careful study by members of the appointive body of the publications and other written work of the candidate, and of written assessments, where desirable, by outside referees or consultants which assess originality, rigor, and fundamental significance of the work and which estimate the likelihood that the candidate is or will become a leading figure in his field. They also should be made on the most careful consideration of his teaching ability which includes the ability to contribute effectively to the research of graduate students. Appointive bodies should take into account the observations and written opinions of those who have observed or experienced the candidate's teaching or who have observed its results in the accomplishments of his students. They should be made on the basis of the best available information about the candidate's contribution to the intellectual activity of the university where he has worked previously in addition to his publications and his success with his students in their doctoral and subsequent research, as attested by their dissertations and publications.

All appointments, whether they are first appointments to instructorships or assistant professorships, or reappointments to assistant professorships, or promotions to permanent tenure at the level of associate professorship, or promotions from the rank of associate professor to that of professor, or appointments from outside the university to associate

1. The criteria for academic appointments sometimes are distorted or degraded by pressures from the faculty or administration as a result of the need for special talent to carry out supporting services of the university or to fulfill a commitment made by the university to perform certain services.

professorship, or extension beyond the age of normal retirement, must be conducted with the same thorough deliberation, the same careful study of relevant documentation and other evidence, and the same process of consultation. No decisions to appoint, retain, or promote between any grades should under any circumstances be regarded as "automatic."

Junior appointments of candidates who have just finished graduate work to instructorships or assistant professorships do, however, have a character of their own. The candidate's written work is likely to be scanty and may not even be available. There may be little or no evidence of his teaching, and it may be difficult to disentangle his originality from that of his professors. In such cases, all available evidence must be examined just as in other cases, but there cannot be the same certitude of judgment. For this reason, appointive bodies must always be quite explicit in stating that such an initial appointment is for a limited term.

There must be no consideration of sex, ethnic or national characteristics, or political or religious beliefs or affiliations in any decision regarding appointment, promotion, or reappointment at any level of the academic staff.

Particular care must be taken to keep "inbreeding" at a minimum. "Inbreeding" at the level of appointment to the rank of instructor and assistant professor is a temptation because the internal candidate is already known to the appointive body. The arguments against "inbreeding" are (1) the dangers of relaxation of standards; (2) the dangers of narrowing and stereotyping the intellectual focus of the department in question; and (3) the dangers of appointing candidates who are excessively dependent intellectually on their former teachers' ideas and even presence. These are arguments to be taken seriously by appointive bodies. Nonetheless, the barrier against "inbreeding" should not be insuperable. Whenever an "inbred" candidate is considered, great pains must be taken to identify and examine with the utmost care the credentials of external candidates of high quality so that internal candidates can be properly compared with external candidates. Special emphasis should be given to external assessments in decisions which entail "inbreeding." Where, after severe scrutiny, the internal candidate is very clearly superior in his estimated potentiality as an original scientist or scholar to any of the external candidates, and if he is not only superior to his immediate competitors but is deemed likely to become an outstanding figure in his subject, the objections to "inbreeding" should be overcome in that instance.

Decisions regarding retention or promotion must deliberately eschew considerations of convenience, friendship, or congeniality. No decision to retain or promote should permit the entry of considerations of the avoidance of hardship which might confront the candidate if a favorable decision is not made. Similarly, favorable decisions to retain or promote should not be rendered on the grounds that evidence is not sufficient for a negative or positive estimate of future accomplishment. The insufficiency of such evidence is in such cases indicative of the candidate's insufficient productivity.

No appointments should ever be made in which the chief or major argument is that "outside" funds would accompany the appointment sufficient to relieve the regular budget of the cost of the appointment. Similarly, no appointment should ever be made on the initiative of a person or body from outside the university who offers to defray all expenses, salary, etc. on condition of a particular person's appointment.

Care must be taken to avoid undue regard for the rights of seniority in promotion. Consideration should be given only to quality of performance, and age should be disregarded. Thus the fact that an older member of a department or one with a longer period of service remains an associate professor should not be permitted to inhibit the promotion of a younger person to full professorship; similarly, in promotions of assistant professors the age of the candidate in relation to the age of his colleagues at the same rank should not be considered in any decision.

Great caution must be exercised by appointive committees themselves to prevent their being "stampeded" by the prestige or influence of contemporaneity. There has for some years been an increasing tendency for universities to concern themselves in their teaching and research with contemporary events—especially in the social sciences and humanities—and it is perfectly understandable that this should occur. With this focus of attention, however, there has also been a corresponding tendency to regard participants in the contemporary events as qualified to become academic staff members on the ground that their presence in the university will bring to the university the immediate experience of those events. Appointive bodies must remember that universities are, in so far as their major intellectual functions are concerned, places for scientific and scholarly analysis and training in such analysis, not theaters for the acquisition of vicarious experiences. Proposals to appointive bodies urging them to consider present or recent public notables for academic appointments must be responded to by strict adherence to the criteria of academic appointment. Where rare exceptions to this rule are permissible, such appointments must not be classified as appointments to the faculty.

These observations should not be interpreted to mean that a candidate who hitherto has not been wholly or at all in the academic profession should be automatically excluded from consideration. It means only that appointive bodies must be certain to apply the same high standards of distinction of scholarly and scientific performance to these candidates as they would to any others.

Mode of Arriving at Decisions

At present there is a wide variation among the various schools and departments of the university in the composition of their appointive bodies and in the sequence of stages of the appointive process. There is no need for uniformity, other than that recommendations for appointment (retention, promotion, extension) should originate within departments and schools, pass to the dean of the division or school and thence to the provost and president for approval or rejection or reference back for further consideration.

The committee recommends that departments, schools, and committees in the university make arrangements whereby all faculty members, irrespective of rank within the department,[2] possess a voice in the appointment of new members. When it is a matter involving reappointment or promotion of existing faculty members, e.g., the reappointment or promotion of assistant professors, it is reasonable for those at the same level or below not to have a voice in the decision. The same documentation on prospective appointments which is available to senior members and external assessors should normally be available to junior members of the academic staff.

The committee recommends that the various departments and schools of the university should establish rules which they regard as appropriate in inviting and considering the assessments of candidates for appointment made in a consultative capacity by students. The committee is of the view that advisory student assessment of candidates for appointment should be taken seriously, particularly with regard to teaching performance and graduate supervision. The *Statutes* of the university and the obligations of the departments and schools in the performance of the three main functions of universities preclude the membership of students with voting powers on appointive bodies.

2. Not necessarily including those persons on expressly terminal appointments.

External assessors should be selected very meticulously. They should not be chosen perfunctorily or in anticipation of an assessment favoring a particular candidate. The committee does not recommend that external assessors be invited to become formal members of appointive bodies or that they be invited to be present at interviews of candidates. It does recommend that the external assessors be provided with full documentation such as bibliographies, offprints, etc., just as provision should be made for all members of appointive bodies. At the same time, it points out that external assessors are sometimes more indulgent in their view of candidates for appointments at other universities than they are at their own. One procedure which might be followed is to request the external assessor to indicate whether he would support the appointment of the candidate at his own university to the same rank for which he is being considered at the University of Chicago. Supplementary oral consultation with assessors by telephone would be useful.

The committee suggests that some designated members of appointive bodies, whenever an appointment is to be recommended, present their assessments of competing candidates in independently written statements as well as orally. These written assessments, together with the vote taken in the appointive body, should be sent to the dean of the division together with the recommendation.

Appointive committees should not consider only one candidate at any one time for a given appointment. It should be a firm rule, followed as frequently as possible when there is an appointment to be made, that several alternative candidates be considered. Although difficulties might be encountered because not all the candidates considered might be willing to accept appointment, this practice would lend rigor to appointive procedures. This same procedure should always be followed when an assistant professor is being considered for reappointment for a second term or for promotion to an associate professorship. At this point, he should be considered as if it were a new appointment. It should be made clear that no appointments carry with them the assurance of reappointment or promotion.

The decision to appoint an assistant professor for a second term (of two or three years) should be made only if there is reasonable confidence that at the end of that period he is likely to be qualified for promotion to the rank of associate professorship. In considering internal candidates for retention or promotion (or extension), members of appointive bodies must be willing to recognize that their earlier assessments might have been wrong. The effectiveness of the university in the performance of its intellectual functions would be diminished by the repetition of earlier erroneous assessments.

Special Situations

The foregoing remarks accept the principle that the power of formal recommendation of appointment rests with the faculty members of departments and committees and schools. This is the general practice, established by tradition and convention, and it should be adhered to. There are, however, occasionally special situations where deviation from this practice is necessary.

Where the quality of work of a department, school, or committee has declined over the years, special weight should be given to the views of external assessors regarding any candidate whose appointment has been internally proposed. Where a field, subject, or department is expiring because first-class intellects are not available to constitute its staff, the discontinuation or suspension of the department should be considered.

One way to deal with the situation of a deteriorated department or, what is quite a different situation, of a department which has too few professors to make the necessary judgment about optimal lines of development is for the dean of the division to appoint an ad hoc committee of distinguished persons from other universities and from adjacent departments in the University of Chicago to canvass the field and make recommendations for appointments and promotions. Another way is for the president or provost to appoint a new chairman with powers greater than those ordinarily enjoyed by chairmen.

Terms of Appointment

Initial appointments to the rank of instructor or assistant professor should be treated variously. In some cases the evidence at hand may be strong enough to indicate that the candidate may well be a strong prospect for permanent tenure. In this case an initial appointment as assistant professor for a term of four years is advantageous. (This is within the present provision of the university *Statutes.*)[3] This would have the advantage that the next decision would be taken after a period of three years rather than the present period of two years for a three-year term

3. *Statutes*—13 (a) (2), p. 41: "(2) *Assistant Professors:* The appointment of an assistant professor normally shall be for a term of either three or four years of full-time service in one or more Faculties of the Departments, College, and Schools, provided that no person shall be appointed to serve in this rank for (*a*) a total of more than seven years, nor (*b*) a total of more than six years if he previously had an appointment for full-time service in the rank of instructor for as long as four years. . . ."

of appointment. The latter term is often too short for the accumulation of sufficient evidence on the intellectual promise of the candidate.

In other cases, an initial appointment is based largely on recommendations of the candidates from outside graduate schools so that an initial appointment for two or three years, given the possibility of reappointment, may be most appropriate. In some departments it should be possible as a matter of general practice to offer junior appointments with the explicit understanding that the appointment is strictly a terminal appointment and that most or all of those so appointed will leave the university at the end of that term. Such arrangements have certain advantages in promoting a flow of young talent, in taking care of certain teaching and service obligations, in training young postdoctoral students here, and in assisting the flow of scholarly information. Moreover, the university remains free to appoint the very best of such persons in more permanent ways.

In many ways, the promotion to rank of associate professor and to permanent tenure is the one requiring greatest care and consideration.

Promotion to the rank of professorship from associate professorship should not be automatic either on the basis of seniority or after the lapse of a specified period of time. Promotion to professorship within the university should be made on the basis of the same procedures as appointments to full professorship from outside the university.

The committee believes that on approaching the age of sixty-five, members of the academic staff might be considered for reappointment for a three-year period. Each case should be considered by essentially the same procedures and with the same intensive and rigorous scrutiny as appointments at earlier ages and at lower ranks. The main criteria in the assessment of the faculty member in question should be teaching, research, and contribution to the intellectual accomplishment of his colleagues. Once a faculty member has reached the age of sixty-eight, he may be considered for subsequent reappointments of one year. Each such appointment should be considered in the light of the same criteria which are applied to earlier appointments. If the age of retirement should ever be raised to sixty-eight, postretirement appointments should be made for one year at a time. Each reappointment should be subjected to the same criteria and procedures as other appointments.

In this connection, it is sometimes important to take into account the effect of retirement upon the general strength of the department. If, for example, several retirements are scheduled to take place concurrently and prospects for adequate replacement are not favorable, the department involved might be threatened by serious depletion of its staff within a single year. In such cases, it may be desirable to "stagger" the retirement of senior faculty members by appropriate extension of their appointment.

In view of the fact that academic members of the university sometimes make arrangements several years before the age of normal retirement to resign in order to go to another university where the age of retirement is later, it might be desirable for the university that such decisions regarding extension may be made as many as two years prior to the age of normal retirement. (The arrangement for the supervision of dissertations also counsels a decision prior to the last year of normal tenure.)

The committee discussed the possibility of an age of "early retirement" with modified pension provisions. It also discussed instances in which, for various reasons, a faculty member's association with the university should be terminated before the statutory age of retirement. The committee noted precedents for such a procedure in other universities and recommends that where a faculty member on permanent tenure shows no promise of continuing usefulness to the university, the termination of his appointment be given serious consideration. Such "early retirement" may be made possible through either modified pension provisions or the "commutation" of full-term appointment by a lump-sum payment of anticipated future salary.

The committee recommends that there should be a category of strictly temporary appointment for which there is not only the usual terminal contract of appointment but explicit statement to the appointee that the appointment will not extend past a particular date. These short-term appointments should be used only on special occasions, such as emergencies where there is no regular member of the academic staff available to teach a particular subject which must be taught. If a person is on an emergency short-term appointment and is considered for regular appointment at the end of the period of his emergency appointment, his candidacy should be treated like any outside candidacy. (These observations do not apply to the short-term appointments of visiting professors and lecturers. To these appointments the same criteria apply as to normal appointments.)

Conditions of Appointment

All academic appointments, when confirmed by the provost, president, and Board of Trustees, should be notified by letter to the appointee, stipulating that his acceptance of the appointment places him under obligation to "conduct and supervise research, teach, and contribute to the intellectual life of the university."

Uniformity of Application of Criteria

A question has repeatedly been raised concerning the differing standards which seem to be applied to faculty members whose primary duties are in the college and those whose primary duties are in the divisions. Those in the latter category are judged primarily by their research accomplishments. The application of these same criteria for promotion and permanent tenure to those who are burdened with teaching does not seem to be fair. The existence of dual standards cannot be avoided as long as these two categories exist. The only way to abolish the dual standard is to abolish one of the categories by abolishing the differences in the kinds of tasks performed by members of the faculty.

The three criteria for appointment to the University of Chicago—distinction in research, distinction in teaching, distinction in intellectual contribution to the university as an intellectual community—should be applied in all situations in which appointments must be made. In general, as has already been stated, the criterion of distinction in research should be weighted most heavily. The University of Chicago faces a peculiar dilemma, however. It arises from the fact that at least since the 1930s, and more acutely over the past quarter of a century, there have been integrated into the structure of the university, two not wholly harmonious modes of weighting the criteria of research and teaching. Appointees to the university faculty posts in divisional departments, schools, and committees have been selected primarily according to the criterion of distinction in research; the other criterion was applied but given secondary significance. Appointees to the college have in certain fields been selected primarily according to the criterion of prospective teaching performance and promoted in accordance with evidence of distinction in teaching. The research criterion has not been disregarded, but it has not been given primacy or even equal weight.

These divergent weightings of the criteria have resulted in a degree of stratification in the university which is injurious, and various efforts have been made to overcome this stratification by various departments. Some of these efforts have apparently been successful; in others they have introduced an unassimilated mass of persons who do not share the intellectual aims of their colleagues and who believe they have no future in the university. In still others, stratification has been contained with good grace on both sides, but even in such fortunate outcomes, the fact remains the same: the criteria have been applied with different weightings and they have, therefore, constituted two different sets of criteria.

The committee believes that normally appointment should involve both teaching and research and that candidates should be judged on both qualities. Appointive bodies should discourage appointments for research alone or for teaching alone. In particular, college appointments should not carry teaching loads so heavy as to preclude productive research activity.

Joint Appointments

It is one of the merits of the University of Chicago that it has often led in the development of new subjects through the freedom of its members to conduct interdisciplinary research and teaching. "Joint appointments" have been one of the devices by which this kind of work has been fostered, and the committee views such arrangements with favor. These joint appointments have, however, sometimes led to grave difficulties for both the individual holding the appointment and for the university. Primarily because of administrative problems and faculty politics, there have been cases where persons have held appointments with full privileges in one department but were denied the privileges associated with the appointment in another department. Joint appointments should enjoy the full privileges of the respective organizations, according to the level of appointment. Appointments initiated by institutes, interdisciplinary committees, etc. should be made as joint appointments with one of the teaching departments, and no members of the faculty should be able to find shelter from teaching by virtue of institute or committee appointments alone.

Joint appointments often present difficulties for junior members at the time of their reappointment or promotion. They find themselves in "double jeopardy." Each department applies the criteria for advancement in its own way, and each exacts its own full set of demands independently of the other. Hence it is important to protect the joint appointee by not demanding twice the commitment of service on committees, examinations, etc., expected of normal appointments in a single department.

The committee wishes to emphasize that when such appointments are made, each department participating should treat the appointment, whether it is from within or outside the university, with the same stringency as it would treat an appointment entirely within its own jurisdiction. The committee is especially concerned that the fact that a department's share of a joint appointee's services in research and teaching is not paid for from its own budget should not cause the appointive process to be treated perfunctorily. Agreements to share in a joint appointment of a candidate wholly paid for from another unit's budget should not encourage its treatment as a matter of "courtesy." Research associates are not members of the university faculty entitled to the prerogatives of faculty members, except where as holders of joint appointments, they enjoy the title of "research associate (with rank of . . .)" in one of the departments.[4] Research associateships do, however, fall into the category of academic appointments. For this reason, the committee believes that their appointments should be reviewed periodically by the appointive bodies of departments, to ensure that the criterion of distinction in research is strictly adhered to. This would also render less likely the possibility that a research associate will become so "embedded" in the department that he is retained until the age of retirement or until he is recommended for faculty appointment.

III Criteria

Research

The criteria of appointment are implicit in the definition of the aims of the University of Chicago. The traditions of the University of Chicago in which these aims are contained place it under the obligation to be in the first rank of the universities of the world in all those subjects and fields in which it is active. This means that appointive bodies must seek to recruit to its staff and to retain on its staff persons whose accomplishments and potentialities are adjudged to be of the very highest order in research and in teaching and in the creation of an intellectual environment in which research of the highest order is done and in which students of distinguished intellectual potentiality are formed and guided.

The committee regards distinction in research accomplishment and promise as the sine qua non of academic appointment. Even where a candidate offers promise of being a classroom teacher of outstanding merit, evidence should be sought as to the promise of distinction in his research capacity. Even if his research production is small in amount, no compromise should be made regarding the quality of the research done.

The appointment of academic staff members must, therefore, place in the forefront the criteria which will populate the university with persons capable of research at the most advanced level and of the highest quality.

It is imperative that in every case the appointive body ask itself

4. The university *Statutes*—13 (b) (1), p. 43—state: "The normal period of appointment of research associates shall be one year, and reappointments may be made without limitation as to number of reappointments in any rank."

whether the candidate proposed, if young, is likely in a decade to be among the most distinguished scientists or scholars of his generation; if middle-aged whether he is already in that position and whether the work which he is likely to do in the remainder of his career will be of at least the same quality.

In the recruitment of new staff members, emphasis should be placed upon the recruitment of younger persons who have not yet reached the height of their potentialities.

Young staff members should be encouraged to do research in spite of the importance and pressure of their teaching. At the same time, appointive bodies must be on the alert against the dangers of appointing young persons in a way which forces them into research projects in which they have no genuine interest.

To offset the handicaps which might arise from concentration on undergraduate teaching, university departments should make a more determined effort to rotate their undergraduate teaching responsibilities so that junior members of the faculty can be provided with more time for research, especially when it is requested.

When older, very distinguished persons outside the university are considered for appointment, the major emphasis should be on their prospective intellectual influence in the university through teaching and informal contact with colleagues and students, as well as on the likelihood of a continued high quality of their own research. These same observations apply in general to candidacy of any person well past his middle age.

While stressing the preponderant importance of the appointment of young persons, the committee recognizes that exceptions must sometimes be allowed. Thus, sometimes if there has been a disproportionate number of retirements or resignations by eminent senior members of a department, candidates at the same level of seniority and eminence might be sought by the appointive body. The need to maintain the prestige of the department and to render it attractive to outstanding younger persons would justify making this exception to the recommended emphasis on the appointment of younger persons.

It is obvious that sheer quantity of scholarly or scientific production, if of indifferent quality, must never be permitted to be counted in favor of any appointment. In assessing the research accomplishments of a particular candidate, adequate regard should be given to the extent to which his original intellectual or research accomplishments are contained in the work of research students and junior colleagues. Nonetheless, it is the quality of the actual publications, or the likelihood of such, which must be given the primary weight in assessment of research accomplishment and potentiality.

Appointive committees, in seeking out candidates and in making their decisions, should bear in mind the prospective development of the subjects on which the candidates have been working. They must seek to appoint a sufficient number of members of the department whose interests and skills are complementary to each other's, so that students will obtain a well-rounded training in their respective fields and so that there will be sufficient mutual stimulation within the department. At the same time, the appointive committees must be alert to the dangers of narrowing the range of intellectual interests represented in their respective departments.

Appointive committees in considering candidates should reflect not only on the candidate's capacity for development to eminence in his subject but the prospective vitality and continued significance of the candidate's main interest. It is important that departments should not become graveyards for subjects which have lost their importance. Thus, appointive committees in seeking out and considering candidates should, while regarding present or prospective distinction as indispensable, attend to the needs of the department in the various subfields within the discipline or subject and the capacity of those subfields for further scientific or scholarly development. Just as research projects should not be undertaken simply because money is available for them in substantial amounts, so there should be no academic appointments simply to staff a particular project.

Teaching

Teaching at various levels and in various forms is one of the central functions of the university. No person, however famous, should be appointed to the university faculty with the understanding that he will do no teaching of any sort. Considerations regarding appointment should include the requirement that a candidate be willing to teach regularly and the expectation that he will teach effectively. Appointive bodies must bear in mind that teaching takes numerous forms. It occurs in lecture rooms, in small discussion groups, in research seminars, at the bedside in medical school, in laboratories, in reading courses, in the supervision of dissertations, and in the guidance of research assistants, postdoctoral students, and residents in hospitals. It should be borne in mind by appointive bodies seeking to assess the teaching accomplishment of candidates that no one is likely to be equally competent or outstanding in all the different forms of teaching.

The committee regards the success of the student in learning his subject and in going on with it to an accomplishment of intellectual significance as the best test of effective teaching. Assessment of performance in teaching should not be unduly influenced by reports, accidentally or systematically obtained, about the popularity of a candidate with students or his "being an exciting teacher." Other evidence of teaching effectiveness such as arousing students' interest in a problem, stimulating them to work independently, clarifying certain problems in the student's mind, etc., must be sought by appointive bodies. The assessment of teaching should include accomplishments in curriculum planning, the design of particular courses, and other teaching activities which go beyond the direct face-to-face teaching of students. The teaching of introductory courses should count to a candidate's credit no less than the teaching of advanced courses. (The responsibility of teaching an elementary course should be recognized by reduced teaching schedules as compensation.)

There should be no appointment in which the appointed person is expected to spend most of his time on classroom teaching.

Contribution to the Intellectual Community

The university is not just an aggregate of individuals performing research or a collection of teachers instructing students at various levels and in various fields. It is an institution which provides the services, auxiliary services, and facilities for research and teaching. The university must be administered and it must have financial resources to enable its academic staff to perform the functions for which they have been appointed.

In addition to being an institution with an administration and financial resources which provide the framework and facilities for research and teaching by academic staff members and students, it is also an intellectual community and a constellation of overlapping intellectual subcommunities built around, but not bounded by, committees and schools. It is an intellectual community in which interaction is about intellectual matters. The contribution which a member of the academic staff makes to the work of his colleagues and students by his own work, by his conversation in informal situations and by his criticizing and reading of their manuscripts, by his discussion of their research and of problems in their own and related fields is of great importance in creating and maintaining the intellectual quality of the university. He also contributes through his role in devising and revising courses of study (curricula) and other activities which go beyond his own teaching.

To what extent should these contributions be considered by appointive bodies?

First, regarding administration, members of the academic staff are not appointed to fill administrative roles. The fact that a candidate for appointment has been an excellent dean or is a good "committee man" or willingly serves on departmental committees or has been or might be an excellent department chairman adds to the merit of a member of the academic staff. But it is a "gift of grace" and it is not pertinent to discussions about appointments, which must concentrate on intellectual performance, actual and prospective.

Although in principle younger members of the academic staff should be enabled to serve on committees and perform departmental duties other than their teaching and research, the decision regarding their reappointment or promotion should not be affected by their having or not having done so. The performance of some of these departmental chores often being at the expense of research, an appointments policy which accords importance to accomplishments of this sort might be injurious to the young staff member's development as a scholar or scientist.

Universities require financial resources to support research, teaching, and administration of the university. Nonetheless, the capacity or incapacity of a candidate to attract financial resources or to "bring them with him" should not be a criterion for appointment. The acquisition of financial resources should be a task of the administration and a derivative function of the distinguished scientific or scholarly accomplishments and capacities of the members of the university faculty. If this rule is not observed, the university will be in danger of becoming an aggregate of affluent mediocrities.

The intellectual contribution of the academic staff member to his colleagues and students is a different matter. It is partly a function of his research and teaching accomplishments, but it also goes far beyond them. If a candidate is known to greatly stimulate his colleagues and students by his conversation and his criticism of their work, so that their individual performances are thereby improved, this should weigh in the consideration of a candidate for appointment.

Influence on the intellectual life of the university as an institution can be negative as well as positive. A member of the academic staff might be an impediment to the university's performance of its intellectual functions, quite apart from his own performance as a research worker and teacher.

It should go without saying, therefore, that all appointees to the academic staff of the university should possess the requisite "academic citizenship." By this the committee means that appointive bodies are entitled to expect that persons whom they appoint to the academic staff will contribute what they can to the intellectual life of the university through their research, teaching, and intellectual intercourse in the university, and that they will abstain from deliberate disruption of the regular operations of the university.

The university must operate as an institution in order for its individual members to pursue their research and teaching. Deliberate obstruction of the work of the university through participation in disruptive activities cannot claim the protection of academic freedom, which is the freedom of the individual to investigate, publish, and teach in accordance with his intellectual convictions. Indeed, the only connection between disruptive actions within the university and academic freedom is that the disruptive actions interfere with the very action which academic freedom is intended to protect. Appointive committees, concerned with the maintenance or improvement of the intellectual quality of research and teaching in the university, must expect that those whom they appoint will enjoy the protection of academic freedom and that they will also be the guardians of that freedom. It is pertinent at this point to affirm what was said above about the irrelevance of political or religious beliefs and affiliations to decisions regarding appointment.

Services

1. University Services

(a) Services integral to research and training outside medicine. There are various kinds of services performed by members of the university. The first of these is the service which is indispensable for the performance of the central functions of the university in research and training. For example, faculty members in the physical sciences often require the collaboration of engineers for the conduct of their research. Such persons are normally highly qualified and could hold senior posts in engineering faculties or in industry. Their contribution is integral to research and although not members of the faculty they must therefore be accorded emoluments and privileges comparable to members of the university faculty of similar accomplishments and professional standing. Similarly, the training of social workers requires that supervisors be provided for their training in field work. Those performing these services are not defined by the university *Statutes* as members of the university faculty.[5]

5. See *Statutes* of the university, 13 (b) (2), p. 43.

(b) Health care and the medical school. University service functions in the medical realm are those which do not ipso facto serve the primary functions of the university, viz., research and teaching. They include the provision of health care by the medical school to both the community at large and the student body. The staff who deliver these services are university faculty members in clinical departments, other academic personnel,[6] and perhaps additional persons not specified in the *Statutes.*

It must be emphasized that though delivery of health care may be solely a service function (as in student and employee health clinics) more frequently it is an integral part of the university as an academic institution. It is such when it involves the teaching and training of medical students, interns, residents, and fellows. Of fundamental importance is the fact that teaching and care at the bedside on the one hand and medical research on the other are mutually interdependent and continuous activities, both of which provide intellectual tasks of the highest order. The commitments of members of the university faculty in the clinical departments (unlike those of members of the faculty in the basic medical and biological sciences) are therefore threefold. The training of outstanding physicians requires that faculty members deliver the best of medical care in addition to their research and teaching activities. For many reasons, it is practically impossible to ensure that every appointment in clinical departments reflects a similarly balanced excellence in all three areas. Thus, appointments to various academic faculty ranks in the clinical disciplines usually embrace a wide range of personnel, ranging from research workers of acknowledged excellence whose contributions to patient care may be outstanding, good, or slight; physicians whose respective contributions are equally meritorious but not of the very first rank; and clinicians whose dedication to research is modest. Some clinical departments also appoint a relatively small number of distinguished investigators who may or may not have a medical degree and who do not participate at all in clinical care.

The committee believes that a great university medical school rapidly loses its eminence if it ceases to have a considerable number of outstanding investigators on the faculty of its clinical departments. Nevertheless, a medical school which cannot provide excellent care to the patients in its wards and clinics will produce only poor physicians and will fail to attract students, interns, and residents of high intellectual potentiality.

Physicians engaged in purely clinical work, who make no serious contributions to research or teaching, should under no circumstances be

6. Ibid., 13 (b) (1), pp. 42–43.

given any form of faculty rank or have any formal voice in recommendations for academic appointments. Many such clinicians who are not members of the university faculty are at present given the title of "research associate."[7] This term may be a misnomer inasmuch as these persons are not engaged in research and the title is also used as an additional designation for bona fide faculty members who hold joint appointments in two or more departments. The title of "clinical associate" might better describe persons involved in purely clinical service functions.

In situations where the financial competitiveness of private (or nonacademic) medicine has helped to deplete the academic pool of a clinical department, its resuscitation should depend more on attractive competitive stipends than on lowering the standards for academic appointments.

(c) Concluding observations on university services. The likelihood of appointments for purely "service" purposes is increased whenever the university undertakes, for whatever reason, the extension of services not related to its research and teaching functions. Such enterprises by definition require expertise and performance of a different kind from those expected of regular faculty members, and appointments to meet such needs should never be appointments to the faculty (as defined by the university *Statutes*). Decisions to extend medical and other services which do not involve either teaching or research or both should be made in the awareness that whatever persons who are appointed will not be granted the status of members of the university faculty.

2. External Services[8]

(a) Public services. There is a second type of service in which members of the academic staff become involved. This is public service, i.e., service for the federal, state, and municipal governments and for civic and voluntary associations. To what extent should appointive bodies consider accomplishments in such services as qualifications for appointment? The committee is of the view that such services should not be considered as qualifications for academic appointment unless the service has a significant intellectual or research component. Thus, membership in a govern-

7. Ibid.

8. The *Statutes* of the university (Statute 16, p. 61) state that "A member of the Faculty during the quarters of his residence may not engage in consultation, teaching at other universities, regular compensated lecturing, compensated editorial activities, or other substantial outside employment, unless such activity is consistent with his obligations to the university, is not inimical to the fullest development of his scholarly activities, and meets with the approval of his Chairman and Dean."

mental body which does not perform research or make decisions regarding the promotion of research should not be regarded as a qualification for appointment. Membership in an advisory body which organizes, supports, and oversees research should be regarded as a positive qualification. Proximity to the design and execution of the research program and its quality must be taken into account.

Incumbency in elective or political office, whether it be the presidency of the United States or the prime ministry of a country, should not be regarded as a qualification for appointment to the academic staff of the university.

Participation in the "delivery" of services for the nonuniversity community should be considered in decisions regarding academic appointment only when there is an increment to knowledge or a valuable function in instruction or training arising from the "delivery." Certain of these "deliveries" are undertaken as part of the "public relations" of the university or because government or civic bodies have not taken the initiative or responsibility which are properly theirs.

Nothing in the foregoing paragraphs should be interpreted as a judgment on the merit of the various public services or the appropriateness of their performance by members of the academic staff in their capacity as citizens. On the contrary, such services are often very important for society—local, national, and international. They must not, however, be counted as qualifications for academic appointment.

(b) Academic services. Among the service activities sometimes performed by members of the academic staff are those performed on behalf of learned and scientific societies which the committee designates as "academic services." A threefold distinction can be made between (1) honorific services, e.g., presidency of a learned or scientific society; (2) intellectual services, such as editorship of a learned or scientific journal; and (3) administrative services, e.g., secretaryship of a learned or scientific society.

The first is a distinction conferred on persons who by their research have made and are making valuable contributions to their subjects. In most instances, such honorific offices represent a confirmation of the major criteria of academic appointment, namely distinction in research, and they may therefore be taken into positive account by appointive bodies.

The second, the editorship of a learned or scientific journal, is a contribution to the intellectual community in a particular discipline beyond the confines of the university. It is a contribution to the maintenance of standards of excellence in the discipline. It too should be taken into positive account by appointive bodies. Membership on advisory panels, e.g., National Institutes of Health (NIH) "study sections," is an intellectual service; it is similar to editorship of a learned or scientific journal and is a contribution to the national and international learned and scientific communities. It should, accordingly, be taken into positive account by appointive bodies.

The third academic service, the secretaryship or a similar administrative function on behalf of a learned or scientific society, on the other hand, is a time-consuming activity which does not entail contributions to teaching or research; this type of service should not be taken into positive account by appointive bodies.

(c) Private services. Consultative services for private industry are admissible as considerations in academic appointments only if they entail an enhancement of the scientific accomplishments of the person involved. This is the aspect which should concern appointive bodies.

IV Conclusion

The positive task of appointive bodies, i.e., the appointment of persons of the highest abilities, has been the main focus of attention in this report. There are, however, also negative tasks; these are the refusal to make appointments. These negative tasks fall under three headings. The first is relatively simple; it is to refuse to make appointments when there are no available candidates of sufficiently high quality. The only excuse for appointing a candidate of acknowledgedly undistinguished qualifications is that certain necessary teaching must be done if students are to be prepared for their degrees. This necessity can be met by the expedient, referred to in the body of the report, of explicitly temporary appointments for particular teaching tasks. This irregular situation should be under constant review so that it can be restored to a regular condition through appointments of the proper quality.

Where there is no particular teaching task of great urgency, in situations where there are no candidates of sufficiently high quality, actual or prospective, no appointments should be made. It is better for the university to allow a field to lie fallow than to allow it to be poorly cultivated. Appointments should not be made just because there is a list of candidates and funds to pay their salaries.

Appointive bodies have a second negative function, and this is to exercise a stern scrutiny over expansion. This responsibility, of course, they cannot exercise alone; they depend heavily here on the support and cooperation of the dean of the relevant division, the provost, and the president of the university.

Great care must be exercised in expanding the staff in established fields or in reaching into new fields of academic work. One of the great advantages of the University of Chicago in the present situation of universities in the world is that it is relatively small. There are many things which universities do, some of which are useful and admirable, but which need not be done by the University of Chicago. There is a great temptation, both when financial support is plenteous and when it is scarce, to take on new members, new fields of study and research, and new service functions because financial support is available. Some of these might be properly done by the University of Chicago where the university has a tradition which would enable them to be very well done or where there are clear and important intellectual and institutional benefits to be obtained from doing them. But to allow expansion and new appointments simply because financial resources are available to support them would be an error which would be wasteful of resources and damaging to the university.

The judicious performance of this negative task must not, however, be permitted to prevent the taking up of important new fields of study and research about which there are genuine and well-based intellectual convictions in the university and outstanding intellectual capacities to do them outstandingly well. Even where a field is intellectually important, the university, and this also means appointive bodies, should not venture into them simply because other outstanding universities are working in them. The expansion into the important new field should be undertaken only if appointments at a high level of quality can be made to provide the necessary staff.

There is a third negative function, already referred to in the body of this report. This is the problem of dealing with fields in decline because the subject has become exhausted within the country or in the world at large or because not enough young persons of sufficient potentiality for distinguished accomplishment wish to enter them.

The last three tasks are negative only in the sense that they involve the refusal to make appointments when the quality of the candidates is not sufficiently high. In fact, however, these negative functions, if properly performed, are as positive in their outcome as the more obviously positive tasks. It is indeed only if equal attention is paid to both—i.e., to the need for adamant refusal to be tempted into making appointments just because appointments can be made, as well as to the firm insistence on appointing only candidates of actually or potentially great merit—that the University of Chicago will be what it ought to be. Only by an undeviating adherence to the criteria set forth in this report can the University of Chicago maintain and enhance its reputation among the universities of the world as a university of the first rank in certain fields, regain that position in others in which it has declined, and open up important new fields which no other universities have yet entered.

Do We Still Need Academic Freedom?

I

Sidney Hook once told me of an observation made by John Dewey in his last years. Dewey, according to Hook, remarked rather wryly that, when the American Association of University Professors was formed in 1916, a committee A and a committee B were established. One was intended to deal with academic freedom and tenure and the other with academic obligation. The activities of the committee on academic freedom and tenure made up most of the agenda of activities of the Association; the committee on academic obligations had never once met, according to Dewey's recollection. The American Association of University Professors was a product of the situation in which some of the leading university teachers in the country thought that, because the academic profession was entitled to respect as a calling, they were entitled to academic freedom. Even in the second decade of the twentieth century, powerful persons outside the universities, and within the universities—trustees, presidents, and deans, or heads of departments—still regarded their academic staffs as hired hands to be appointed and dismissed at will. Such persons were regarded as the enemies of academic freedom. Although there are still some rough-handed presidents and deans in back-country colleges and state universities, on the whole these traditional enemies of academic freedom are seldom any longer to be seen.

In the minds of the American academics who were active in the early years of the Association, academic freedom and permanence of tenure were indissolubly associated with each other. At that time, it was said that the latter was needed to guarantee the former.

Academic freedom was declared to be an assurance that new ideas would be discovered, that sound old ideas would be appreciated in a more critical way, and that unsound ones would be discarded. The argument for academic freedom was roughly the argument for liberty in general put forth by John Stuart Mill in *On Liberty*. It was also assumed by

Reprinted from *The American Scholar* LXII (Spring 1993): 187–209.

their proponents that academics, even if they did not discover new ideas, should be free, in their teaching and writing, to say what they believed. It was further assumed that they would not be arbitrary in what they believed and taught; it was accepted that they would try to tell the truth as it was understood by them from their study and rational reflection.

Since the chief sanction against academics who honestly spoke their beliefs in teaching was dismissal, the best protection for their academic freedom seemed to be the guarantee that such a sanction would not be exercised against them. Permanent tenure seemed to be that guarantee.

Permanent tenure now has gone off on a career of its own. It has become a self-evident good in itself; it has become "job security." Permanent tenure—or plain "tenure," as it is now called—is an object of great desire among academics, especially the younger generation who are preoccupied by it. I seldom hear it mentioned as an assurance of freedom. Yet whenever some modification of the current practice of providing permanent tenure after a probationary period or on the attainment of a particular rank is proposed, the argument that it is necessary for academic freedom is brought to life again. In those circumstances it is restored to its former status as the main argument for permanent tenure. This, however, is rather infrequent since the institution of permanent tenure is nowadays rather firmly established in American universities and colleges.

Academic freedom, too, has taken a path of its own. It is no longer thought that it has any close relationship to the search for or the affirmation of truths discovered by study and reflection. It has become part of the more general right of the freedom of expression. Expression is not confined to the expression of reasoned and logically and empirically supported statements; it now pretty much extends to the expression of any desire, any sentiment, any impulse.

II

University teachers in American society, since the Second World War, have become privileged persons. In the leading universities at least, they have a rather light stint of teaching. They have long vacations, they often have interesting young persons as students and friends, they sometimes have interesting colleagues. They can usually, in most universities much of the time, teach courses in which they are interested and not teach courses in which they are not interested. They are usually allowed, with or without the consent of their colleagues and administrators, to shift their academic interests within their fields, and they can vary their teaching and research accordingly. They are generally free to choose their subjects or research in accordance with their intellectual interests, within the limits imposed by financial resources, equipment, and the like. Compared with persons in many other occupations, they have immense privileges. Academic freedom is one of these privileges.

Academic freedom is not a universal or human right, enjoyed in consequence of being a member of the human race. It is not entirely a civil right of participation in the political activities of a liberal democratic society. It is not identical with the freedom of the citizen to act in the political sphere. The American university is an institution of the civil sphere; whether a private or state university, it is an autonomous institution with its own rules and standards of decision with respect to its characteristic activities—namely, academic activities. Academic freedom is a qualified right; it is a privilege enjoyed in consequence of incumbency in a special role, an academic role, and it is enjoyed conditionally on conformity with certain obligations to the academic institution and its rules and standards. It is an immunity from decisions about academic matters taken on other than academic or intellectual grounds, by academic, governmental, ecclesiastical, or political authorities.

Academic freedom has two parts. One, the most important, is the freedom to do academic things without the threat of sanctions for doing them. The sanctions may range from arrest, imprisonment, torture, dismissal, withdrawal of the right to teach, expulsion from learned societies or refusal of admission to learned societies, censure by academic administrators, refusal of due promotion, and imposition of exceptional or onerous tasks, to personal abuse and the disruption of classes.

Academic freedom, in this first sense, is the freedom to do academic things, to express beliefs which have been arrived at by the prolonged and intensive study of nature, human beings, and societies and of the best works of art, literature, etc., created by human beings, and by the reasoned analysis of the results of those prolonged and intensive studies. These beliefs, arrived at by careful study and reflection, must be made as true as they can be. Thus, academic freedom is the freedom to seek and transmit the truth. Academic freedom postulates the possibility of arriving at truthful statements and of discriminating among statements as to their truthfulness in the light of the evidence which is available to assess them.

The criterion of truthfulness is inherent in the activities of teaching and research. This means the freedom to teach according to the teacher's convictions about the matter taught, arrived at by careful study and with due respect to what is thought by qualified colleagues, without any of the sanctions mentioned above or others. It certainly includes the freedom to disagree with colleagues about matters of substance and to do so in accordance with reasonable evidence and arguments. It means the freedom to teach in ways which the teacher regards as effective as long as respect is shown for the rules of reasonable discourse, for the dignity of the student, and for general rules of propriety. It means the freedom to choose one's problems for research, to use the methods one thinks best, to analyze one's data by the methods and theories one thinks best, and to publish one's results. Academic freedom, in its specific sense, is the freedom to do academic things within the university.

Academic freedom is also the right of the academic to participate in those activities within the university which affect directly the performance of academic things. The right to participate in these activities also carries with it the obligation to do so. The privilege of academic freedom confers the rights and imposes the obligations of academic citizenship. In the first instance, this includes the right and obligation of the academic to participate in the decisions regarding the appointment of teachers and research workers who will work in his or her own department. It also includes the right and obligation to participate in decisions regarding the substance and form of courses of study, examinations, the marking of examinations, and the awarding of degrees. At this point, academic freedom becomes the right and obligation to participate in academic self-government.

In all cases, this freedom is hedged about by academic and intellectual traditions. These traditions, which are difficult to delineate, include not only the substantive intellectual traditions of disciplines and of fields of study and research, but also rules of conduct toward colleagues and students. These traditions must not, however, be so interpreted that they restrict the intellectual freedom of the academic; at the same time, their imprecision is not a license according to which anything goes.

Academic freedom is thus not an unlimited freedom of teachers to do anything they want in their classrooms or in their relations with their students or to work on just anything in their research by whatever methods they wish and to assert whatever they wish in their publications. There has to be, above all, concern to teach the truth, to attain the truth, and to publish the truth.

In matters of academic appointment, the decisive and overriding criterion must be the candidate's mastery of established truths, his achievements in discovering new truths, his respect for truth in teaching. The traditions regarding what is true, what are the best methods, and the rest, are not absolutely and unquestionably precise. They have to be interpreted, but they must be interpreted with respect for truth—and reliability—as the chief value of academic life.

The provision of academic freedom does not provide for the right to publish the results of one's research in any particular journal, regardless of the assessments of the editor and his referees about the scientific or scholarly merit of those results. Academic freedom does not include the right to obtain financial support for one's research regardless of the assessment of the intellectual merit of the proposed investigation rendered by qualified referees or peers. At the same time, the refusal of publication or of financial support on political, sexual, racial, or religious grounds is an infringement on academic freedom. It introduces other than intellectual criteria—that is, criteria derived from the central academic value of truthfulness—into decisions about academic matters.

The protection of the academic engaged in the performance of academic actions from sanctions imposed on him or her on the basis of political, religious, or sexual criteria is the central function or justification of the guarantee of academic freedom.

There is another set of activities which are to be protected from sanctions by the guarantee of the freedom of academics. This is the right of academics to the performance of legal political actions, to be members of or otherwise associated with legal political parties or societies; to participate in the activities of these bodies as freely as any other citizen of a liberal democratic society. Political activities such as the practice of terrorism, kidnapping, or assassination are not to be protected by the invocation of the principle of academic freedom, any more than they are assured by the right to political freedom of any citizen, academic or nonacademic. The polemical justification or praise of terroristic activities in a liberal, democratic constitutional order is a marginal case.

Thus, there are the two sides of academic freedom. The first is obviously the most important for the pursuit of the values of academic life. The second—the civil freedom of academics—is of great importance to academics because it frees them from special burdens which are not imposed on other citizens. In that respect, it might also contribute to academic freedom in the first sense in that, by freeing the academic from a degrading discrimination, it allows him to perform his academic obligations with his mind untroubled by anxiety.

The civil freedom of academics does not extend to the conduct of political propaganda in teaching. It is easy enough to avoid this in the teaching of mathematics and the physical sciences. It is more difficult in the disciplines dealing with human beings and their works. In courses of political science, anthropology, economics, and sociology, the subject matter of which overlaps with the objects of political activity, the avoidance of political propaganda is more difficult; it is certainly not impracticable. The university or college teacher must strive to discipline himself in this matter. This is not because academics may properly be restricted in their political beliefs and in the expression of those beliefs but because the university is not an institution for the pursuit of partisan political objectives.

There are marginal phenomena which are close to academic freedom to which reference should be made. These include the freedom of individual students or associations of students or of senior members to invite nonacademic persons to speak at nonacademic assemblies on the premises of the university or college; they include the freedom of those speakers to express their views without obstruction or disruption. They include also the freedom of individual students or associations of students to express their views on political topics outside of classes but on the physical premises of the university.

These rights to freedom of expression of members of universities and colleges are not part of academic freedom. The right to discuss, outside the classroom in meetings open to the public on a university campus and in a rational way, differences between ethnic or sexual groups, or between religious groups, and so forth, is a civil right as much as the right to vote in elections or to stand for political office. Although the discussion takes place on the premises of the university or college, if it is "extracurricular"—if it takes place in a public meeting or in a conversation between two or three individuals—infringement on that right is not an infringement on academic freedom in the specific sense. But it is nevertheless an infringement on the freedom of the citizen, just as is the dismissal of a teacher who, outside the university in his capacity as a citizen, declares his support for one legal political party or another.

Historically, there have been other restraints on the actions of teachers in colleges and universities which, although infringements on their freedom, have not been infringements on academic freedom. The actions which they restrained were those which contravened primarily sexual morality. Adultery, for example, if exposed, was often followed by dismissal; homosexuality likewise. Unmarried cohabitation, the same. "Keeping bad company," giving or attending "wild parties" at which alcohol was consumed and women smoked cigarettes might not alone be grounds for dismissal but, coupled with other infringements on conventional rules of conduct, could be grounds for dismissal or at least for the withholding of promotion or raises in salary. Nevertheless, those restraints on the freedom of conduct of academics were not regarded as infringements on academic freedom. The American Association of University Professors did not enter the lists on behalf of their victims. In recent decades the performances of such actions by academics scarcely cause an eyebrow to be raised, to say nothing of not calling forth substantial sanctions. In any case, they have never been seriously regarded as falling under the protection of the right to academic freedom.

III

It is possible, if John Dewey's recollection was correct, that the reason for the inactivity of the committee B—the committee on academic obligations—lay in the assumption of the leaders of the American Association of University Professors that academics were, on the whole, fairly strict in their observance of their obligations in teaching and research and that this was generally understood by university administrators. It was assumed that academics were, by and large, dutiful with regard to the tasks of teaching—it was mainly teaching at that time—and in meeting the obligations of academic citizenship in the sense of the observance of the rules of academic life.

In most colleges and universities a moderate conservatism prevailed. The American Association of University Professors accepted that there might be reasons for dismissal; it did not come to the rescue of professors dismissed for adultery or homosexuality. Its concern was with the freedom of belief in political and religious matters, mainly political; it did not gainsay the right of colleges ruled by churches or sects to demand religious conformity. It was interested in the security of tenure, less because security of tenure was its main concern than because dismissal was the most frequently exercised sanction for the expression of political beliefs. The objectives sought were the academic freedom and the civil freedom of the academic; security of tenure was the chief means of protecting that freedom.

As long as it was concerned with the protection of the civil freedom of academics, the Association did not venture to limit the powers of the administrators of universities to require their teachers to do their academic duty and to conduct themselves in what were believed to be morally respectable ways.

It did not attempt to define the substance of teaching. It understood teaching to require that teachers teach their subjects or disciplines as these were laid out in the best literature of the field and to add to and improve on that literature in their research and teaching. It was recognized that knowledge about some topics was not always certain, and for that reason, such topics were to be presented so that the student would be enabled to distinguish the certain from the uncertain, the more probable from the less probable. Teachers were not to be interfered with or threatened with any penalty by any authorities within or outside the university, as long as they conscientiously taught the subjects which they were appointed to teach. They were, above all, not to be interfered with on political or religious grounds—that is, on grounds of political or religious statements outside the classroom.

The committee on academic freedom and tenure was not unmindful of the obligation of the teachers, whose academic freedom was to be assured, to teach their subject up to the level to which it had been raised by the work of the best scientists and scholars in their fields, up to the level of their own abilities, conscientiously exercised, and up to the level of the students' capacities and level of attainment. The teachers were to be assured of freedom of conscience or judgment, but they were not, without good reasons growing out of their own study and research, to wander far from the consensus of the respected authorities in their own branches of science and scholarship. Their freedom to diverge from the prevailing consensus in their subjects was to be guaranteed as long as the divergence was based on conscientious study, research, and reflection, and their own understanding and appreciation of the traditions of their disciplines.

Academic freedom certainly extended to intellectual originality. It was for the departmental colleagues of their own university and their peers outside their own university, when one of them departed from that consensus, to decide whether the individual in question was being original, or divergent within reasonable limits, or eccentric to the point of mental incapacity, or impermissibly arbitrary, indolent, or otherwise irresponsible. Sanctions for their failure to conform with accepted intellectual standards could not be denounced on the grounds that they infringed on the right of academic freedom. Nor could frequently recurrent and unexcused absences from scheduled classes fall under the prerogatives to be assured by academic freedom.

Academic freedom did not include freedom to substitute a subject or topic for another subject or topic which had nothing to do with the subject or topic a teacher had been appointed or assigned or had agreed to teach. If a teacher were not reappointed—tantamount to dismissal—or not promoted on grounds of intellectual eccentricity, mental incapacity, or intellectual irresponsibility, that was not to be regarded as an infringement on academic freedom.

In other words, the protection afforded by academic freedom did not extend to the point of protecting the teachers in their derelictions from their obligation to seek and respect the truth in their teaching and research, according to their best lights and capacities. Similarly, if teachers fabricated, falsified, or plagiarized the results of their research, they could not claim the protection of academic freedom. Nor could they claim the protection of academic freedom for statements for which they had no evidence or which were flagrantly and arbitrarily contrary to the prevailing interpretation of the available evidence.

There are sometimes genuine difficulties in the way of deciding whether the departure of a teacher from the consensus of the best workers in the field or discipline is an original discovery or an arbitrary and baseless assertion. Furthermore, if the originality of thought is presented in teaching, then it is not easy for colleagues or superiors to discover what has in fact been said in the classroom. Of course, the difficulty of discovering what really goes on in the classroom has certainly afforded freedom, de facto, to academic malpractices which were, in principle, certainly not entitled to that freedom.

There was, I think, general consensus between university administrators and trustees, most academics and the American Association of University Professors that teachers were not entitled to claim the protection of academic freedom for the attempt to persuade students in classrooms to accept the teacher's own points of view on political or parochial religious topics which were not germane to the subject matter of the courses being taught.

IV

The American Association of University Professors sought the immunity of the individual academic from actions which would drive him from the path of the discovery and disclosure of truth or, in a more humble formulation, truths about things about which truth can be discovered. The American Association of University Professors seems to have thought that if individual academics could be protected, then all would be well. But a university as a collective undertaking to find and transmit the truth must not only be concerned to protect in their pursuit of the truth those persons who are already in it; it must be no less concerned to bring into itself persons who are zealous to discover the truth. If it does not do so, academic freedom will lose its justification.

For this reason, the process of selecting teachers who are going to be serious scientists and scholars is a precondition for the continued existence of the university as a corporation in pursuit of the truth. Life within the university—if it is a good university and is more than a technical or professional training college—strengthens the desire of the individual for the truth. But that strengthening can occur only in those who already possess the disciplined propensity and who have given evidence of it. The process of appointment must discover such persons; they are the persons who merit appointment to the university as teachers, scientists, and scholars.

Many American universities have not been as attentive to the process of appointment as they should have been, and the quality of the universities has suffered accordingly. In excuse for this slipshoddiness it can be said that there was a need for more teachers than there were well-qualified persons. This is probably true, but it was not an excuse for disregarding the criteria of achievement and promise of achievement. It may also be said that the capacity of assessors on appointment for accurate and reliable assessment is not as good as it ought to be and that mistaken assessments are inevitable. This is true, but it, too, is no excuse for acting contrarily or for being indifferent to the proper criteria of academic appointment.

It must be said, furthermore, that university and college teachers, where they are the assessors, and administrators—deans, provosts, and presidents, when they must assess the assessment—are often not as scrupulous as they ought to be. Nevertheless, all these things being said, the fact remains that in the leading American universities in the first two-thirds of the present century, considerable progress was made against the adduction of criteria of religious, political, and ethnic congeniality and of original social status in academic appointments, and parallel progress was made in the strict application of academically relevant criteria.

Appointments are not matters to which the category of academic freedom in the specific sense applies directly. But they are intimately connected with academic freedom because they are determinants of the concern for the attainment of the truths at which academic activity must aim and which academic freedom must protect. If persons who do not care deeply for truth are appointed, the university enlarges the part played by persons who care little for the objectives which merit the protections provided by academic freedom.

V

The situation of academic freedom in the United States is now very different from what it was three-quarters of a century ago, even half a century ago. Boards of trustees have become more refined; they are not as puritanical and self-righteous as they used to be and they are not as arrogant; they no longer regard their trusteeship as a police function or as a moral custodianship of the institution which they must protect from political radicalism or sexual impropriety. Presidents no longer act like headmasters of private secondary schools before the First World War. They do not watch their academic staff so closely and distrustfully, and, if they do, they are very reluctant to do anything which would cause the academics to complain against them. They have largely transferred their responsibilities for the internal affairs of universities to provosts and academic vice presidents, and these, too, are very reluctant to do anything to arouse the disapproval of their academics.

Churchmen, especially when they sat on the boards of trustees or when their sects, denominations, or churches had a statutory and financial relationship with the particular college or university, were often instigators of infringements on academic freedom. Now, except for the colleges ruled by fundamentalist religious sects, they no longer tamper with the freedom of their teachers. They are too skeptical, too liberal, and too fearful of being called illiberal to exert themselves as they once did to keep university teachers on the straight and narrow path of orthodox political and religious belief and puritanical sexual conduct.

The small-town press as well as the popular metropolitan press used to be among the institutions, external to the college or university, which from time to time raised a stir about the radicalism of a teacher in the local college or university. Now, to the extent that these small-town newspapers still exist, they practically never express the view that a teacher who criticizes any of the existing institutions of society should be removed from his post. Small-town editors are nowadays not very different from the writers of editorials and columnists and other journalists of the metropolitan press, which is far more sympathetic with collectivistic liberalism and antinomianism than it used to be.

More important is the fact that there has been a rather fundamental change in opinion in the United States, so that what was once a ground for disapproval is not even noticed anymore. In the days when American academics were moved to found the American Association of University Professors, to denounce the state government or the government of the United States, to accuse it of being a "tool of the interests," and above all, to assert such criticisms in time of war, to proclaim oneself as, in one way or another, a socialist, and—from 1917 until about a decade after the end of the Second World War—to praise or justify or apologize for or exculpate the Soviet Union could land a college or university teacher in trouble. The trouble might culminate, from time to time, in abrupt and unseemly dismissal, sometimes in a more patient biding of time so that a teacher could discredit himself by a scandal in his private life and therefore be dismissed with good conscience, or he could be encouraged to leave by denial of promotion.

University administrators are nowadays very reluctant to dismiss, suspend, or take any other action against teachers whose conduct falls short of the traditional expectations of morality or respectability. Dereliction of duty in teaching, always difficult to prove, is likewise viewed with a blind eye. More important for the matter under discussion here is the abstention of administrators from any sanctions against academics for radical political views or for political agitation in their classrooms. Administrators are, it is true, concerned to prevent "hate language"—usually by students—but this has little to do with the traditional occasions for the application of sanctions against academics. Where administrators do attempt to impose restrictions on verbal or graphic expression, it is usually on behalf of aggrieved and demanding groups of homosexuals, feminists, blacks, and Hispanics in the student body. The sanctions are not of the conventional sort; the imposition of attendance at a course of "sensitivity training" is a common sanction, sometimes imposed on teachers. Sometimes the provision of another course in the same subject is ordained by administrators who receive complaints from students that a particular teacher is insufficiently compliant with their demands or holds views of strictly academic subjects expressed in conventional academic journals that are contrary to the plaintive students' views on racial or sexual matters.

The point of these observations is that administrators are nowadays very fearful of taking actions of a sort which were, until about a quarter of a century ago, regarded as infringements on academic freedom proper or on the civil freedom of academics. Indeed, they lean over backward to avoid such infringements. Having broken down first in the face of the policies of affirmative action of the federal government, they have now often become pawns in the hands of "minorities" in their student bodies. It goes without saying that many teachers now enjoy a high degree of freedom to infringe on the obligations of academic life, such as conscientious teaching, respect for evidence, etc.

Even on issues which are intellectual or academic in the narrow sense—having to do with substance of teaching and research—university administrators have tended to avoid drastic action which would appear to be an intrusion into the academic side of the university. This has been evident in the way in which universities have responded to the discoveries of dishonesty in research. The falsification of evidence is surely one of the most dastardly actions in which an academic can engage. It is admittedly difficult to determine with complete finality that falsification has been committed, but even when the evidence has appeared to be conclusive, university administrators have been inhibited in their response. Is this because they have been persuaded over the course of many decades to abstain from intrusion into any academic matters? If that is so, then the inhibition is a gain for academic freedom, but it might still be a damage to the university. Perhaps it shows a deficiency in academic freedom, which is supposed to protect the search for truth but which, in these cases, protects the promotion of untruths.

The passivity of senior university administrators in the face of actions which would have called forth from their predecessors severe sanctions has moved hand in hand with the greatly increased frequency of the performance on the part of academics of actions which their predecessors would, out of fear of such sanctions, have abstained from or concealed. In other words, on the one side, there are more actions which were once proceeded against by administrators, and on the other, there is more indifference or timidity among administrators when confronting such actions.

VI

About 1960 the American Association of University Professors changed the order of its agenda by placing security of appointment and other matters related to the terms of appointment (salaries, requirements of the amount of teaching, and promotions) on the first part in its agenda. This was an indication that the threats to the civil freedom of academics and to the freedom of academics in sexual and political matters had diminished—almost to the vanishing point. The civil freedom of academics was never deleted, but it took second place in the concerns of the Association, which in fact became a trade union claiming the legal right of collective bargaining on behalf of its academic members.

This was an acknowledgment—unacknowledged in any explicit statement—that the civil freedom of academics, and of course the more specific substantive academic freedom, was now so well established that the academic profession and the officers of the American Association of University Professors could cease to be anxious about its protection.

The decision of the American Association of University Professors to become a trade union might also have been a response to the fact that many American college and university teachers had come to regard their academic appointments as "jobs" for which they were "hired" and from which they could be "fired," rather than as a calling or profession with its own proper moral and intellectual dignities and obligations. There certainly has been such a development. But most important in this shift in the view of the Association has been the fact that by the 1960s and 1970s, academic freedom and, above all, the civil freedom of academics had ceased to be the pressing issues that they had been in the first half of the century. Academics are certainly concerned about "tenure" or "job security," but they do not fear the abridgment of their academic freedom in any of the traditional senses conveyed by that term. In fact, they now take its existence very much for granted.

Another indication of how much the situation has changed in American universities in recent years has been the acceptance of the notion that a person who regards his or her task as a university teacher to make propaganda for socialism or for revolution among the students is not being unfaithful to his academic obligations and is therefore entitled to the protection of academic freedom. Nowadays, some teachers even think that the necessity and desirability of the destruction of the existing society and its cultural traditions should be incorporated into the syllabuses which they prepare for their students. They think that, as university teachers, they have a unique opportunity as well as a moral obligation to further the cause of revolution. Naturally they think that such activities should be carried on with all the guarantees afforded by the rule of a full academic freedom.

This conception of the obligation of a university teacher is a far cry from the original intention of the American Association of University Professors to protect academics from dismissal or from other penalties for the expression, outside the university, of political or religious views of an even moderately unconventional sort. The American Association of University Professors never contended that teachers should be assured of a right to conduct political propaganda before their students in class.

After the flurry of Senator McCarthy's hearings, academics, at first intimidated and humiliated, discovered during the agitation about the war in Vietnam that their academic freedom was as extensive as they wished to have it. They gained courage from the example of the students who affronted, mostly with impunity, the authorities of their universities and the government. But even without the agitation about Vietnam, a change had been taking place over a long period in the attitudes of university and college administrators. The antinomian inclination of the change was accentuated by the silent fear of injury arising from Senator McCarthy's menacing investigations. Intended to curb the radicalism and pro-Communist sympathies of many academics, McCarthy's activities, in the end, aggravated them. They came out all the more strongly once it became safe to abuse their own government and their own universities.

VII

The movement of university presidents away from the domineering, imperious attitudes which they had previously expressed toward their academic staffs has been a part of the weakened position of institutional authority in Western countries over the past half century and particularly in the United States. This has gone hand in hand with a quite separate tendency toward the elevation of the status of the academic profession in the United States and the elevation in its self-esteem. This has been neither a unilinear trend nor a homogeneous one. It reached its peak several decades ago and has either stood still or declined since then.

Ever since the formation of the three new universities—Johns Hopkins, Clark, and Chicago—in the last quarter of the nineteenth century on the model of German universities, a new type of university teacher appeared in the United States. Energetic in the determination to discover new truths by research, the professors of this type insisted on facilities for research and for independence from authorities outside the universities. They would not accept a status of inferiority to a person who was not himself a scholar or scientist. They were on the whole not opposed to businessmen, but they would not be bullied by them either.

This change in the regard in which academics held themselves was probably relatively rare at the turn of the century. It was not found in many universities. It occurred first in those that sought to appoint persons of outstanding intellectual achievement or promise of achievement. They were in many instances persons who had studied abroad, particularly in German universities. The proud German professor was their model. Service on the sufferance of the president was not compatible with that ideal.

The change in attitude toward their own status was not a movement initiated or borne by radical university teachers. In fact, there were very few radical teachers at that time. The increased unwillingness to be subordinated by administrators was related to pride in being a scientist, especially, but also in being a scholar. Academics were aware that they were members of an international community of learning. They felt akin to the great Germans whom they regarded as among the greatest figures of living generations, and as such they would no longer be treated as "hired hands." The movement went very slowly until even as late as the 1930s. Most academics, however, quietly accepted their subordinate status.

University presidents gradually understood the message communicated by the spoken attitudes and unspoken bearing of their professors. Gradually the real constitution of the universities began to change. The statutes and bylaws probably did not change in written form until the second half of the present century, but in fact the "real constitution" began to change in the leading universities by the 1920s. The greatest change occurred when new appointments to departments began gradually to be made by the professors in the departments and were no longer made by presidents and deans. There has never been a legally self-governing university in the United States in the sense of the self-government of Oxford or Cambridge colleges, in which the governing body consisted of the master and the fellows. Nevertheless, although very unevenly, the leading American universities moved toward department and university-wide self-government in academic appointments and in other academic matters.

With this, they also moved, in the leading universities, into a period of greatly increased academic freedom. University teachers gained civil academic freedom. They gained it at a time when, given their growing interest in politics and the prevalence of the earlier pattern of the concentration of authority in the university, they would have been on a collision course. The course, even when the administrators showed willingness to withdraw, still was by no means one of perfectly safe navigation. It has not been an unswervingly unilinear movement.

American academics became more interested in politics around the beginning of the fourth decade of the present century. There had been little interest in politics before that. There had been a few radicals, but they were relatively isolated in their universities. In the 1930s, such radical attitudes became more common among academics, but they were still relatively scant in number. Many were swept into the wake of the New Deal, yet even they were a minority of the academic profession, concentrated among younger teachers and primarily in the humanities, social sciences, and theoretical subjects. There began to develop a hostile attitude toward the traditional economic, political, and cultural orders in the United States.

With that hostility, the situation of academic freedom also changed. A new category was added to the justification for infringement on the civil freedom of academics. Whereas before the First World War, radical "political" academics were charged with being inimical to private capitalism, to puritanical individualism and its sexual morality, and with being sympathetic to socialism, they were now, additionally, or instead, charged with loyalty to the Soviet Union and to the communistic social system which was even more abhorrent than its socialist variant.

The character of the infringers also changed. Coalitions of trustees of the colleges or universities, local businessmen, and newspaper editors had once been the chief agents of infringement. The presidents of the colleges or universities had been their agents. Sometimes they were not their agents but acted independently, perhaps in anticipation of the prospective reactions of the external persecutors, perhaps in accordance with the dictates of their own rectitude.

Before the Great Depression, federal politicians paid practically no attention to universities. State politicians had hitherto taken little notice of universities, except to vote generous appropriations for them. Sometimes a legislator might be aroused to action against a state university by an angry constituent, but, by and large, universities were esteemed by state legislators and they forbore to intrude. There were other reasons, too, for the good relations between state legislators and their state universities. The state universities stood high in popular esteem, and, by their training and services, they served the governments and the people of their respective states well.

Populistic political radicalism was relatively acceptable in certain states—although not always or uniformly so. Xenophilic radicalism, bohemian radicalism, radicalism which extolled the working classes over farmers and businessmen did not go down so well. The decades between the two great wars saw an increase, at first very slight, in xenophilic—particularly Russophilic—radicalism in the universities. So slight was it that at the beginning of the 1920s, the xenophobic Lutz Committee of the New York state legislature—passionately hostile to radicalism—left the universities practically unnoticed in its quest for subversive intentions and actions. Ten years later, when the marked increase in political interest began in the universities, antiradical investigative committees of state legislatures proliferated, and they gave considerable attention to the universities. The epidemic lasted for about twenty years; then it lost its force.

The decade before the Second World War and the first postwar decade were years of menace to the civil freedom of academics. The number of academics brought before these investigative committees was fairly small. There were some dismissals and much anxiety among some of the academics who had been fellow travelers or members of the Communist party in the 1930s. There is no evidence that academic freedom in the more exact sense—freedom in teaching and research—was affected by the harassment conducted by the investigative committees. Nevertheless, their consequences were very significant.

At first, they had a very intimidating effect. Even at a university where academic freedom was as assured as it was at the University of Chicago, and where there was so little sympathy with communism, some of the teachers thought that they should step carefully lest they be attacked. It was a period when academics were rather prudent and tried to avoid doing anything which might arouse the curiosity of Senator McCarthy. This was a period when the word "fascist" as a description of a major feature of American society came readily to the minds of academics. The inquisitorial senators and congressmen and state legislators and their unwholesome informants and junior persecutors were regarded as forerunners of a fascist regime in the United States. The congressional hearings confirmed apprehensive academics in their collectivistic liberalism and in their admiration for the Soviet Union, where they thought honest men were not persecuted. The intimidation was accompanied by severe alienation from American political, economic, and social institutions. The intimidation lasted only until the latter part of the 1950s. The alienation still persists and expands. A polymorphous alienation has taken hold in departments of the modern humanities and in the "soft" social sciences. Antinomianism runs through them all.

VIII

In the face of the far-flung expansion of the new forms of radicalism and, above all, of emancipationism, college and university presidents, provosts, and deans have been very complaisant. Many of them approve of the new trends of antinomianism, either because they think that emancipation from all traditional norms is right or because they are fearful of the angry criticism of the minority of their teachers and students who are enthusiasts for emancipation. They combine autocracy with supineness.

The situation is of a mixed complexion at present. There are still colleges and universities where the president acts as college and university presidents acted a century ago, although their number has been decreasing. They and their deans and vice presidents frequently do as they wish; they appoint, promote, refuse to promote, and dismiss as they wish. But most of them, including many who are tyrants in other respects, also accommodate themselves to the emancipationists. Hence, in such universities and colleges the imperious actions of the administrators are not directed against radicals and bohemians and others who were previously the object of the restriction of the civil freedom of academics. As far as academic freedom proper—the freedom of the academic in academic matters—has been concerned, the administrators have seldom interfered except in denominational colleges where the biblical accounts of cosmogony and geology and the history of ancient Judaism were contradicted by the achievements of geochronology, geophysics, paleontology, the "higher criticism," and evolutionary biology.

IX

The concern about academic freedom on the part of the teaching staffs of the American colleges and universities well into the 1950s was not by any means shared by most of their colleagues. The fact is that even in the time of its greatest prosperity, the American Association of University Professors never attracted to its membership more than a minority—often only a very small minority—of the teachers in any college or university. Most academics have not and do not give much thought to academic freedom. For many of them, it has not been an issue at all. They did not dream of doing any of the things which might have been the object of sanctions and for which the protection of academic freedom would have been adduced. They have usually been indifferent when sanctions were visited on a colleague in some remote department for having expressed himself outside the university on some political or social issue.

Some teachers, especially in schools of medicine, business, engineering, and agriculture, think that the persons whose academic freedom is being infringed upon are in fact being given their just desserts. Many are simply indifferent. Only a minority has become exercised about infringements on academic freedom. They have become extremely indignant that some of their colleagues have been deprived of academic freedom or have been threatened with such deprivation; they have usually insisted that those colleagues were blameless. But of those who thought that way, many were usually too intimidated to complain in public. They were simply cowardly.

It has sometimes been thought that university teachers are bound to be fervent in their devotion to academic freedom. It has been thought that even those who are not impassioned for it in principle would not look with favor on the restriction of the academic freedom of their colleagues. In fact, however, the situation has been quite otherwise.

There are many academics who disapprove of those who rock the boat, who cause commotion, who instigate external criticism of the university, who attract the disfavor of prominent persons outside the university. They are often unsympathetic with colleagues who become the objects of restrictions on their academic freedom. There are many reasons for this: they might not like their political views; they might dislike them personally; they might not like to have the reputation of their college or university darkened by criticism of government, and so on.

I mention in passing what happened at Columbia University about two decades ago. The department of the history of art would not turn over to the agents of the United States Department of Labor charged with the enforcement of the policy of affirmative action the records of its deliberations and other documents bearing on the appointment of teachers in the department. Thereupon the federal government, at the behest of the Department of Labor, ceased or threatened to cease all payments on grants or contracts with the university or grants to it. Naturally, this was bound to affect severely the medical school and the departments of physical and biological sciences. There was much resentment in the latter sections of Columbia University against the department of the history of art for insisting on the autonomy of the university; they wanted to get on with their research and they did not want to be hampered by the obstinacy of the department of the history of art in refusing to yield to the federal government. When, about two decades before that, a small group of brave academics, led by Edward Tolman of the University of California at Berkeley, refused to subscribe to a loyalty oath to be imposed on university teachers by the state government because they regarded it as an infringement on academic freedom, they were bitterly castigated by many of their colleagues for "creating a fuss" and for endangering the position of the University of California before public and political opinion in California.

The situation is a paradoxical one. The academic profession, taken as a whole—all fields, departments, and disciplines included—is not especially concerned with academic freedom. A small number of persons of high principle, such as John Dewey, Arthur Lovejoy, and Glenn Morrow, and others, were very concerned with it. Those whose academic or civil freedom was threatened, or who were in danger of sanctions for having acted in ways in which they were reproved, or who had already suffered such sanctions, invoked academic freedom as a means of protecting themselves. How much they cared for academic freedom in principle is unclear. Academic Communist party members or admirers of the Soviet Union never concerned themselves about the academic or civil freedom of university teachers in the Soviet Union. Yet many of them were the first to invoke the protection of academic freedom when they were being harassed or when sanctions were in prospect against them and their kind.

The freedom of academics to do the things for which sanctions were in the past inflicted on them has, in the past several decades, never been in a more impregnable position. Academics in the United States enjoy unprecedented freedom to say and do things which fifty and seventy-five years ago were the objects of severe sanctions by academic administrators, supported or pressed by businessmen, politicians, clergymen, and others. In that sense, the founders of the American Association of University Professors have been nearly completely successful. Seldom has an ideal been so nearly attained as that of academic freedom. The particular freedoms which they sought are now, at least for the time being, secure.

Nevertheless, in some respects, academic freedom is more infringed on now than it has been for several decades. These latter infringements are not unilaterally imposed by university administrators or instigated by the old external custodians—often self-appointed—of the university. They are imposed by incumbent academics, encouraged by the policies of the federal government, which is a relative newcomer on the academic scene. Infringements on academic freedom are nowadays, to a greater extent, infringements imposed from within the university and even from within the teaching staff. But these internal enemies of academic freedom do it with confidence in their external support.

X

The executive branch of the federal government of the United States had never, until the 1960s, sought to enter into the heart of the university. It is true that, since the Second World War, it had become the chief patron of scientific research in universities. This patronage gave it great power over the choice of research projects and over decisions as to which fields of research are to be cultivated. On the whole, it has exercised these powers with as much tact and consideration for academic interests as its financial power and its interest in the practical application of scientific discovery have permitted. At various times, it has gone a little astray, but on the whole these deviations have been rare. As for the conduct of research, once undertaken, it has let investigators be very free to follow their own lights.

This regard for the primacy of intellectual interests in academic institutions has, however, not been a uniform policy of the federal government. In its desire to guarantee that discrimination against blacks be brought to a halt, it has adhered to a policy of what has been called "affirmative action." In the execution of this policy, the executive branch of the federal government has for two decades intruded into the process of academic appointment through its insistence that the universities follow the stipulations of the Equal Employment Opportunity Commission in the appointment of "minorities," meaning blacks, women, Hispanic-Americans, etc. In a variety of ways, a steady pressure has been exercised on universities to appoint individuals of the categories previously discriminated against. The threat of withholding grants and contracts for research and for scholarships on which the universities have become dependent has compelled the universities to accept the policy of affirmative action as their own. The incumbency of Republican, reputedly conservative, presidents has not diminished or attenuated the pressure for affirmative action in academic appointments.

As evidence of good faith, universities have appointed affirmative action officers to see to it that the policy of affirmative action is followed. These administrators have frequently been a goad to those who appointed them to use their authority to press for more appointments of "minority teachers." A consensus among senior administrators, with or without the representations of the affirmative action officer, puts the burden on departments to carry out this policy. Within each department in the modern humanistic and in the "softer" social sciences (that is, the social sciences other than economics), it is commonly understood that the higher administrators will look favorably on recommendations for appointments of candidates from "minorities."

Now there would be no reasonable objection if this policy were intended to suppress discrimination against "minority" candidates. The fulfillment of the policy goes much further. Departments and whole divisions of distinguished universities make commitments that a determinate proportion of all their appointments will be made from among candidates of the groups hitherto discriminated against.

This policy is inimical to the ideal which is to be served by academic freedom. To put it simply, the decision to give precedence to appointments of persons from "minorities," hitherto discriminated against, very frequently entails disregard for the criteria of intellectual achievement and promise of intellectual achievement. This means that the criteria of the candidates' determination and capacity to pursue and transmit truths about the matters taught, investigated, and studied in universities are given a secondary position in the making of appointive decisions.

Such decisions have a self-accentuating tendency. Once one such appointment is made, it is a precedent for other such appointments. Such appointments become the normal thing. They also generate within a department a group of proponents of more such appointments.

The governmental policies of affirmative action and "positive discrimination" have an expansive tendency. They are accepted as self-evidently right by university administrators and teachers. Recently, the Middle Atlantic States Association, one of the accrediting associations which has been assigned the task of testifying to the educational genuineness of institutions seeking financial aid from the federal government, has sought to compel colleges and universities which wish to be accredited to comply with its demand for diversity. "Diversity" is a euphemism for the appointment of more African-Americans, women, and Hispanic-Americans, for offering more courses in black studies, women's studies, gay/lesbian studies, and for reducing the preponderance in the syllabuses of the cultural achievements of older, white, male persons of heterosexual orientation. The investigative teams of the accrediting association which have wished to impose this standard of "diversity" on colleges and universities are also academics and academic administrators. Their conduct is evidence of how compliant university and college administrators are to the governmentally required, or encouraged, suspension of academic criteria. The United States Department of Education, in a reversal of federal governmental policy, refused to renew the accreditation of the accrediting body. This was a momentary check on the drive toward enforced "diversity." The demand for "diversity," at the expense of academic freedom traditionally understood, continues nonetheless.

There is something else to be said about the policies of affirmative action and "positive discrimination." These policies have been put forward and adopted at a time when the traditions of ethnic discrimination were already being discarded. These policies have greatly accelerated the movement. This improvement of civility in the United States has, however, coincided with and also contributed to a more general turning against American society and Western civilization among academics in the humanistic subjects and in certain of the social sciences. This does not mean that all the beneficiaries of the policy of "positive discrimination" have become exponents of this hostile attitude toward the traditions of American society and of Western civilization in general.

The confluence of the valiant and long overdue, if misguided, effort to eliminate discrimination against blacks and women with the emancipationist attitudes which were latent in collectivistic liberalism, and with an uprooted and disillusioned Marxism, has touched the foundations of academic freedom. It has touched the most crucial point in the justification of academic freedom. Academic freedom is only justified if it serves the causes of the discovery and transmission of truth by scientific and scholarly procedures.

XI

An aggressive and intimidating body of antinomian academic opinion has gained in strength. It has objectives very different from those which the American Association of University Professors once sought to protect.

In its view the equality of "genders," the equality of "races," the equality of "cultures," the normality of homosexuality are the only real values, while the criteria of truthfulness are illusory, deceptive, and fundamentally intended to exploit women, people of color, homosexuals, and the poor. The value of academic freedom is denied; it counts for nothing alongside these other values, since the truth which it would protect is declared to be an illusion.

The theory of academic freedom rests on the view that the truth can be achieved and that it can never be attained by coercion or by fear that the political, economic, or religious powers will inflict sanctions for any view which is contrary to their own. If there are no criteria of validity or truthfulness, because no statement can ever be truer than any other statements, then it is useless to attempt to assess the validity of the achievements of scholars and scientists. It is useless to attempt to assess the scientific or scholarly achievements of candidates for appointment or to decide which students have done well or poorly in their dissertations and examinations. What is there for academic freedom to protect except security of tenure and the prerogative of frivolity? That is not what the founders of the American Association of University Professors had in mind when they took in hand the strengthening of academic freedom in American colleges and universities.

The Eighth Jefferson Lecture in the Humanities

"Render unto Caesar . . ."

Government, Society, and the Universities in Their Reciprocal Rights and Duties

I

THE CLAIMS OF CAESAR AND THEIR LIMITS

The Pharisees wished, according to Matthew 22, to "entangle" Jesus "in his talk" so "they sent out unto him their disciples with the Herodians" to ask him: "'Is it lawful to give tribute unto Caesar, or not?' But Jesus perceived their wickedness, and said, 'Why tempt ye me, ye hypocrites?' "Jesus showed them evidence of Caesar's earthly sovereignty by pointing to the "image and superscription" of Caesar on a coin, saying, "'Render therefore unto Caesar the things which are Caesar's; and unto God the things that are God's'. When they heard these words, they marveled, and left him, and went their way."

I am an heir of the Pharisees in the sense that I still marvel at these words. I still ponder on these pregnant words which assert a profound general rule. Like all profound general rules, it is enigmatic and does not provide ready unambiguous answers. It is a rule which guides but does not clearly specify. In what follows I shall attempt to set forth my interpretation of what things are Caesar's and what things belong, if not to God, then to that sphere of human striving in which the ideal of intellectual contact with the ultimate order of existence is cultivated. The effort to achieve understanding of the order or pattern of existence constitutes a sphere which is as close as many of us can come to the

Reprinted with permission of Kluwer Academic Publishers from *Minerva* XVII/2 (Summer 1979): 129–77. In *Minerva,* these essays appeared under the general heading "Government and Universities in the United States," as well as the title used in the present edition.

sphere of the divine. The relationship between the sphere of science and learning and the sphere in which Caesar acts is my theme.

I do not presume to speak on behalf of God or of the realm of the contemplation of God's will and of life in accordance with His will. That is beyond my powers and beyond the task which I have undertaken here. I do presume to speak on behalf of that realm which is the secular counterpart of God's realm, namely the realm in which human beings devote themselves to the systematic, disciplined effort to understand the universe, the earth, society, and man and his works. This is the realm which in our modern societies falls properly under the jurisdiction of the institutions of higher education, of universities and colleges, which I shall refer to simply as universities.

The realm of science and learning is a realm or sphere of life which has its own necessities; they are intellectual and moral necessities as well as material ones. It is also a realm which impinges at many points and in many ways on the world of practical affairs, on the world of society and government. Society and government also have their own necessities. Various parts of society pursue objectives which lay claim to moral obligations and material resources; government, on behalf of society and of its own maintenance, also has its objectives and necessities.

It would be a world unlike the one we know or are likely to know, if these ideals, objectives, and necessities were all completely harmonious with each other.

If one believes that the state, the political authority exercised by government, is the highest form of social life, because the world-spirit has come to rest in it or because it is the instrument of a party chosen by God, history, or itself for the complete subjugation of all of its society and all of its culture to its own purpose, then there is no problem of determining just how far government may go. If one takes an anarchist standpoint and insists that the state can and should be abolished because there is no need for it and that only harm can arise from it, then there is no problem of deciding just what the state should do or be allowed to do. It should do practically nothing, according to this latter view. Caesar would have everything or nothing if these were the alternatives from which we had to choose. But they are not. The alternative which I have chosen is a compromise among alternatives. It is difficult to define in any precise way and accordingly is bound to be difficult to realize.

In these three lectures, I want to explore the following questions: In the first: what does the federal government—to whom I shall refer as Caesar from time to time—have a right to demand of the universities; what does it not have the right to demand and what does it owe to them?

In the second lecture my task will be to inquire into the obligations to government—and society—and the obligations to the spirit, i.e., to the ideal of learning in science and scholarship to which the universities must attend. What must they render unto Caesar and what must they render unto the ideal which is inherent in their undertaking; and what do they have a right to expect from government? Finally, in my third lecture, I shall try to lay down the terms by which the universities and government can live at peace with each other for the benefit of their respective responsibilities.

I should add that my reason for choosing this problem is the unsatisfactoriness of the present situation in certain important respects. Caesar is distrustful of the universities and the universities are distrustful of Caesar. Not in every respect but in some important ones. The situation needs to be repaired.

I

Everyone knows what the plain facts are. Before the Second World War the federal government contributed practically nothing to the universities. It gave them practically no money, it demanded nothing from them in return. The courts very seldom intervened in the affairs of the universities. *In the Matter of the Trustees of Dartmouth College v. Woodward* in 1819 was one of the few times that the Supreme Court dealt in an important way with a case concerning an institution of higher education and its decision was that the government of a state could not intrude into the affairs or the possessions of a private institution. Later the federal government provided land and modest sums for agricultural teaching and research in universities. So it went until the First World War when, in a prefiguration of events a quarter of a century later, university chemical laboratories were used to conduct research which was proposed by the Bureau of Mines. Then came another period of federal indifference and restraint towards the universities.

The relationship of the state governments to the universities was quite different. As in most federal systems, education in the United States was a provincial matter. The state governments issued charters to all universities and colleges; sometimes they appropriated small sums of money or provided other sources of income to the private ones. Nearly every state had a state university; if it did not, it had a state agricultural and engineering college. The state universities enjoyed much of the autonomy which the private universities had. They had approximately the same internal system of university government; they had a lay board of trustees, generally not chosen by co-optation like the lay boards of trustees of private institutions, but appointed by the governor or elected by the citizens of the state or both. By and large, they had more freedom of action in regulating and setting their standards for admission than the European universities had. They—or rather their presidents, deans, and heads of departments—appointed their own staff or teachers and research workers without having to submit their recommendations to a final decision of the state department of education. They could determine the requirements for degrees, set their own examinations and mark them according to standards which they prescribed for themselves—although naturally influenced by the standards which were expected by the professions for which they trained their students. It was legally provided that they should maintain certain professional schools alongside the college of arts and sciences. These usually included engineering, medicine, agriculture and law, veterinary medicine, and other fields of the sciences which were regarded as bearing on the prosperity and health of the people of the state. In Wisconsin, but not in Wisconsin alone, teachers were asked to help to draft legislation and to advise the legislature and the executive. By and large there was a good understanding between the executive and the legislative of the state on the one side and the universities on the other. Each recognized and respected the jurisdiction of the other.

There were, it is true, cases of infringement on academic freedom in the state universities. Without attempting either to shrug them off or to deny that they were occasionally disfiguring blemishes on the generally good relations between the states and the state universities, they were not unique to the relationship of the American states and their state universities. There were a few cases in Germany in the nineteenth century, e.g., in Göttingen in 1837 and in Berlin in 1898; there was the dismissal of Ernest Renan from the professorship to which he had been appointed in the Collège de France in 1863. Even in one of those universities which were financially and legally independent of the state—as were Oxford and Cambridge for most of their history—there was an attempt also in 1863 by theologically conservative churchmen to have Benjamin Jowett deprived of his post. It is not intended to be a minimization of the infringements on academic freedom if I say that before the Second World War private universities were at least as susceptible to privately instigated infringements on academic freedom as the state universities were to restrictions arising from their legislatures; sometimes state legislatures also intruded into the affairs of private universities, as did a committee of the legislature of the State of Illinois in 1935 into the affairs of the University of Chicago. The governing bodies of the private universities were not behind in infringing on the freedom of university teachers, as Leland Stanford University in the Ross case, the University of Pennsylvania in the Nearing case, and Columbia University in dealing with McKeen Cattell demonstrated.

One should really speak of the actions of individual legislators or small groups of legislators rather than of the legislature as such. I think that until the legislature of the State of California enacted the "loyalty oath law" after the Second World War, no state government ever enacted legislation which specifically restricted the civil freedom of university teachers in its state. Governmental interferences with academic freedom were sporadic, they were frequently initiated against particular individuals rather than against a category of individuals or institutions and they acted through harassment, mainly offensive publicity, and not through legislation. They practically never concerned themselves with what went on within the university—although the reading of the *Communist Manifesto* as a set-book in an undergraduate course in the social sciences was the point of origin of the Illinois state legislative committee's investigation of the University of Chicago in 1935. These sporadic infringements were usually directed against individuals for the extra-academic expression of their opinions about economic and social affairs. This was generally true of the "academic freedom cases" in the private universities too. They involved the expression of opinions outside the university. What went on inside the university was not taken as a legitimate concern of the state governments. It was generally assumed that, provided with necessary funds, the universities could be left to do what was right. They were left to appoint and promote teachers according to their own criteria, to set syllabuses according to what they thought necessary for the students, to examine and mark according to their own standards. It was thought that they would do research which would turn out sooner or later to be of beneficial application.

II

The situation has changed since the Second World War in several important respects. The state governments have relatively remained unchanged in their relations with their universities except to provide much more money for them. The federal government began to attend to the universities by improvisation. It did so sometimes benevolently, often munificently. The federal government in the course of these improvisations acquired a superficial conception of universities. Since it had very little to do with universities except to call upon their teachers for services during two world wars and during the Great Depression, and occasionally for special services—as the Industrial Commission of 1908 had called on John R. Commons—it did not have any tradition within itself which could guide its action when it became interested in them.

What it acquired instead was a mode of "using" universities, developed during the Second World War when it decided that it would use the laboratories of the universities for the performance of needed research, and would have specialized training for certain types of military functions provided there by academic experts. Thus it entered upon its more intense and active relationship with universities, knowing them primarily as institutions to which it could turn in order to have particular and clearly defined jobs carried out. As the federal government became increasingly active, it added to the "use" of the university as an instrument of its policy demands that the university itself become an object of some of those policies. Some of these latter policies imposed heavy financial burdens on the universities, burdens which it could not shift to the students as business firms can shift additional costs to their customers. Others of these policies imposed demands incompatible with the university's proper performance of its functions.

In an incoherent and improvised way the actions of the government reached deeply and startlingly into the universities. They reached as deeply and more startlingly into certain internal affairs of the universities than had been the case on the continent of Europe, where universities were state institutions legally under the control of the ministries of education and where their constitutions were enacted by the state legislature, or by the central government in countries like France and Italy which were not federal in structure.

The new view taken by the federal government, indeed assumed by it without closer observation or deeper understanding, accepted the existence of the universities as already existing entities, as something like an inexhaustible natural resource, a free good which need not be replaced and which required no more capital investment than the machinery needed to pump it out of the ground. Much—not all—of the government's action towards the universities presupposed their prior existence as institutions which could effectively perform the functions of teaching, training, and research because each of its parts and its past provided an indispensable matrix for every separate and discrete activity. Every particular activity of each part of a university has been performed in the setting of a tradition carried forward by the university as a whole. As the universities extended their activities beyond their older tasks, and added certain new functions such as the provision of direct services and training for occupations which were not of the same standing as the older learned professions, these additions at the periphery did not erode the central tradition of the university, even though they were not fully absorbed into that tradition.

There had already been a widespread acceptance in the United States that the universities should not be aloof from practical life. The establishment of business schools and engineering schools within the universities was an expression of this belief. Neither the state universities nor private universities allowed this conviction to obliterate the fundamental idea that the universities were centers of disinterested learning, permeated by the ethos of devotion to the task of discovery and transmission of truths which are of intrinsic value. It was generally accepted that this task was the heart and soul of the university. In certain fields such as the biomedical sciences, the two functions were fused. Devotion to the ideal and to the pursuit of truth was harmonious with the belief in its ultimate beneficent application. The peripheral functions, the training for the minor professions, accrued to the universities because their proponents thought that they would benefit in substance and prestige through association with a center of disinterested fundamental learning where objective knowledge could be acquired. The universities were respected because they were associated in the public mind with objective, fundamental knowledge; universities were thought to be the repositories and creators of this objective, fundamental knowledge.

III

These additional functions were only extensions of the central intellectual traditions of universities. They drew upon its quality as a place where intellectual discoveries were sought, where intellectual achievements were interpreted and transmitted. The degrees which universities awarded testified, in principle, to accomplishment in the mastery of some part of an intellectual tradition; advanced degrees certified achievements in adding to and improving the tradition.

Those who received degrees acquired more prestige and income than they might otherwise have had; entry to certain occupations depended on having received a degree. Awareness of these advantages led some students to disregard as much as they dared the intellectual content of what they were required to study and to think primarily, if not exclusively, of the degree rather than what it was supposed to certify. In the United States, many ambitious young men of lower-middle-class origins and some of lower-class origins interested themselves in the degree; the intellectual aspect was of relatively little interest to them. Universities became channels of social mobility; they provided opportunities for ascent to higher status which were otherwise not available to impecunious, ambitious, and talented young men. In the United States, where ambition used to be highly regarded, the state universities and the City College of New York were praised because they made it possible for ambitious young persons to rise in society. One of the great virtues of the American state university system for which it was appreciated all over the world, was that it provided "equality of opportunity" for these ambitious young persons, regardless of the social position of their parents, to gain a higher education with minimal financial cost to themselves. Scholarships or grants to the more talented, i.e., the intellectually more promising, helped to confirm this standing of the American state universities as avenues of social ascent for the talented, ambitious, and self-disciplined, at least for those who were white. On all this the federal Caesar looked with a coldly indifferent eye, until . . . until he became interested in promoting equality!

It was inevitable that this should be so. The possession of knowledge about fundamental or charismatic things has always been an object of deference in societies. There is no society in which knowledge of sacred or ultimate things does not entitle its possessor to deference. Authority too is esteemed in society and certification by a university of the possession of a certain stock of the tradition of fundamental knowledge qualifies its possessor to enter into certain roles in which authority is exercised. Thus attendance at a university had a function in the system of stratification of deference, income, and authority in society. In the twentieth century, society became more open to the effective exercise of talent; criteria of achievement slowly and partially displaced descent from particular families and membership in particular ethnic groups and religious communities, and they became more significant in determining access to desired occupational positions. Before 1945, Caesar was willing to allow all this to happen because he did not think that it had anything to do with him. He was, in any case, disqualified from acting in such matters on constitutional grounds and by his own conception of his obligations, which did not include the active promotion of equality.

Universities had always been means of social ascent, just as the priesthood had in Western Europe enabled young men of relatively humble familial origins to rise to more esteemed and relatively well-remunerated positions. Those who were well-born attended universities because this was necessary for them to remain in the positions to which they were born. As the improvement of one's position through "working one's way up," through starting business enterprises or through being apprenticed to learn a trade, became more difficult or lost attractiveness, ascent through higher education was all the more desired.

It was not thought in the past that everyone should have a higher education; it was not thought that most of the young persons in any generation would want it. Indeed it probably did not occur to most of them that such a thing lay within the bounds of possibility. No one believed, moreover, that there would be any advantage to society in the steady multiplication of the number of university graduates. It was not until the administration of Lyndon Johnson that such an idea was taken seriously. In the 1930s, at the end of the remarkable century which began with the opening of Liebig's chemical laboratory at the University of Giessen in 1831, there was an increasing unease about the growing number of unemployed university graduates in Germany, France, and Japan. Anyone who proposed universal higher education at that time would have been suspected of frivolity. It seemed economically impossible, economically useless, inhumane, and contrary to sound sense and good policy. The idea that universities could create social equality had not yet been conceived. The most that was demanded of them by those concerned to improve society in this regard was that they should be more open to the sons and daughters of the poorer classes, if they had the necessary talent and the ambition.

IV

After the Second World War, the federal government gratefully provided the "GI Bill of Rights" to the former soldiers who had suffered the danger and discomfort of military service. It was not as a policy of egalitarianism that the GI Bill was enacted. It was primarily to help in resettling young men whose careers had been disrupted; it was an act of gratitude that offered a prize which had in the past been restricted to a very small proportion of each generation. This generous policy coincided with the greatly enhanced prestige of science.

The prominent place taken by new industries which entailed the use of complicated, scientifically contrived equipment—and particularly the development of electronics and computers—and the prestige of the natural sciences, carried over from their important achievements in the war, launched Western societies onto the fantasy of a "knowledge-based" society. Scientific knowledge such as is created and transmitted in universities became indispensable to economic growth, which took the place of the idea of progress as the standard for measuring the merit of a society. The realm of Caesar began to expand; he took by common acclaim the responsibility for the promotion of scientific research. The range of occupations which were "knowledge-based" widened and the universities were obviously the places where this kind of knowledge could be acquired. The universities expanded through the risen tide of students supported by the GI Bill, the increased governmental support to scientific research, and various special programs. There seemed to be a natural harmony between the interest of Caesar and the interests of the secular church of scientific knowledge. The universities were happy to render unto Caesar what was Caesar's while at the same time rendering unto their god what was his.

Caesar for his part could be content with his actions. He was helping multitudes of former soldiers to avail themselves of a means of "self-improvement" to which many young persons had aspired without fulfillment in the past; he was also discharging his newly assumed responsibility for promoting economic growth and his old one for assuring the military security of the country by the financial support of scientific research. To do these two things, so generally applauded, he used whatever instrumentalities were at hand. The universities happened to be one of those instrumentalities. Caesar was little concerned with how they had come to be there or what enabled them to be there. He shirked responsibilities for their maintenance; he was unaware of the unarticulated traditions and the institutional attachments which are essential to their maintenance.

V

Caesar was encouraged to move further on his new path of exploitation of the universities by the good conscience which came from the contemplation of his own munificence; he was also encouraged by the eagerness with which the universities received his munificence. He was further encouraged along that path by the widespread belief that there was an unlimited need for "high-level manpower" and by the economists' discovery that education was the "residual factor in economic growth." Hitherto, higher education had been regarded as an advantage to the individual seeking to "improve" his condition; this was now confirmed by the economists' analysis which showed that total earnings over an entire lifetime were closely correlated with the number of years of education. The economists now went further and showed that economies grew better and their societies benefited more from growth if they invested more in education. The implications of this analysis were perfectly clear. More was to be spent on the education of individuals. There was no primary intention to spend money on the universities.

For a time, every new inspiration of Caesar seemed to bring benefit to the universities. Some of the inspiration indeed came from the universities. The economists who made those self-serving analyses were university professors, the scientists who did the research were university teachers and graduate students. The universities were the recipients of the payments for these services. The universities sometimes forgot their own *lares* and *penates* and their own high god in order to serve Caesar. Their very enjoyment of their service to Caesar's purposes confirmed him in his expectations.

When it was pointed out to Caesar at the end of the 1950s that there was poverty in the country, what was more natural than to see education as a remedy for and as an insurance against poverty? The larger the amount of education, the better the protection. Higher education thus offered the means to enable the ambitious and talented to go ahead and to provide the knowledge-bearing persons, the "high-level manpower," needed to enable society to grow economically and to be militarily secure; it could also free human beings, regardless of their talents and virtues, from the stigma and discomfort of poverty.

The agitation for the civil rights of blacks and the heightened awareness of the disabilities which the black population of the United States had imposed on them by their exclusion from occupational and other opportunities led to additional demands of the same sort on the universities. The universities ceased to be regarded as the ladder through which the ambitious and the talented could rise higher in a society which accepted inequality. They became instead mechanisms by which it was hoped that groups of the lowest status could be made equal to everyone else so that all the American people could be made equal with one another. After the blacks came other more or less colored ethnic groups and groups which were colored only by virtue of not having had ancestors present in significant numbers in the country fifty or a hundred years ago.[1] There was a certain amount of arbitrariness in drawing the lines between those who were to be raised to equality and those who were "already equal." Then the women's movement entered the battle for the equality of women. The crippled came later. All these demands for equality were translated into demands on the universities to educate

1. The Poles, Italians, Slovaks, Serbs, Croatians, Czechs, and others like them were excluded by the trade unions and ethnic purists when restrictions were placed on immigration a half-century ago; now they are passed over as not falling into the category of "minorities." Of the various victims of the ethnic discrimination of the earlier decades of the century, only the Chinese and Japanese have managed to enter into the favored category of "minorities."

them, to provide facilities for them and to appoint them to their staffs. These demands for equality as conceived by the government have done damage to the universities and threaten to do more damage in the future.

University education had become important in Caesar's view and in that of his advisers, not because learning elevates the spirit of its possessors but because its degrees are the tickets of entry unto a plateau of comfort, deference, and freedom. When Caesar interested himself in equality, institutions of higher education were confirmed as the most crucial instruments of that transformation. They were to be made just as useful for the attainment of equality in American society as they had been for the conduct of research, the training of specialists, and enabling the ambitious and talented to rise in society. The difference was that in the conduct of research and in the training of specialists the universities were allowed to go on applying criteria of intellectual merit as they had in the past. In pursuit of the ideal of equality, Caesar came to believe that his objectives could not be attained if the universities insisted on the exclusive application of the intellectual criteria in appointment and admission, which were integral to their effectiveness in the pursuit and transmission of systematically acquired knowledge.

VI

The confluence of faith in education and science as the solvent of poverty, as the means of economic growth and military security of a "science-based" society, and as the means of establishing an egalitarian society, together with the belief in the emancipation of the individual and in the competence of governmental action to achieve ends never achieved before, has greatly altered the relationship between the universities and Caesar. Within a quarter of a century, Caesar, whose experience of universities was very slight, who had not mingled with them and had had very little understanding of them, discovered that they could be useful to his multifarious ends. He had no tradition to restrain him in his relations with the universities. The universities seemed to him to be wonderfully malleable material.

By now Caesar has had nearly forty years of experience of universities. Yet he still does not know what they are. He knows what they produce; he knows that they produce knowledge and graduates. He is a little like a person who knows if he puts a coin into a slot of a certain machine a tin of Coca-Cola will appear. What goes on inside the machine, how the Coca-Cola tin got into the machine, how the Coca-Cola is made—all this escapes him. He pays his money and he gets his Coca-Cola. He is also unlike the person who receives Coca-Cola for a coin. The purchaser of Coca-Cola does not just pay for the water, syrup and metal, he pays for the plant, the dividends to stockholders, he pays those who hold the patent for the syrup, the machine and so on. He may be ignorant but he pays up; otherwise he would not be able to have the Coca-Cola. If he refused to pay for the interest on the capital which maintains the Coca-Cola plant, there would be no Coca-Cola for him. Either the firm would cease to operate or it would live from other consumers of Coca-Cola.

When Caesar turns from Coca-Cola to universities, he gets a better bargain. Universities are not profit-making enterprises; this makes it more profitable for government to deal with them. The fact that they sell to the government things for which there are no traditionally established market mechanisms to set prices improves Caesar's position. Many of the monetary costs of Caesar's demands on the universities cannot be passed on to the purchasers, and this places the universities in a difficult position. Caesar had placed himself in a monopolistic position; this gives him another advantage. Even better for Caesar is the fact that his "purchases" from the universities—it is he who insists on the language of commerce—are subsidized by the universities, who in turn are subsidized by the taxpayers of their respective states and by their private patrons, for whose generosity Caesar nowadays likes to claim the honor by calling the gifts of private patrons "tax credits."

The fees paid by students do not match the costs of providing them with instruction. However high the tuition fees and other charges at private universities, the cost of providing for the student—admittedly a very ambiguous figure—is greater than what he himself pays. The overhead is already there so a university gains by having more students. Still the generosity of Caesar requires supplementary subsidy by private patrons and state governments. Caesar is very self-righteous in scrutinizing the conduct of his contractors to make certain that he gets what he is paying for. In fact he is not paying for much of what he demands and receives.

This readiness of Caesar to live from the bounty of others, to avoid full payment for what he likes to think is a purchase of a service, is characteristic of Caesar's frivolity in dealing with the stock which his society and its institutions have inherited from their forebears. So much for the material side of the matter.

A university is more than its stock of capital, its buildings, books, machines and instruments, and its monetary endowment. Nor does a university consist just of highly trained individual scientists, scholars, and teachers together with the physical plant and monetary endowment. It is a capital of institutional traditions as well as of intellectual traditions; every member and every action of discovery, interpretation, and transmission benefits from these traditions. The intellectual traditions are the accomplishments of scientists and scholars, scattered over many places in the United States and in the world and located at numerous points in the recent and remoter past. It is a state of sensitivity of the intellect to problems and to standards which depend on the existence of each university as an academic community and of most universities taken together as an academic community. The government has the advantage of the use of this capital of the academic ethos. But instead of protecting it and sustaining it, Caesar harasses, suspects, and regulates it and supports it at less than cost-price. Caesar receives an unrequited subsidy from the academic ethos. The government's policies pay little enough attention to the maintenance of capital in the material sense for the support of libraries, laboratories, heating plants, the upkeep of buildings; its fiscal policies by fostering inflation reduce the value of the endowments of the universities and increase their costs. Its policies towards the universities pay even less attention to the maintenance of the nonmaterial capital of the universities.

VII

Jesus asserted no elaborate criteria for deciding what should rightly be given unto Caesar and what should be reserved from him because God is entitled to it. Nonetheless, the position was clear; there was God and there was Caesar; each had a realm of his own, the one earthly or secular, the other divine. Jesus thought poorly of the secular realm but he acknowledged its existence and its power. To concede obedience to it was a recognition of its indifference when weighed in the scale with the realm of the divine on the other side.

We are in a different situation. The tension between God and Caesar is not quite what it was. We take Caesar more seriously, not just as an inescapable power to which we must submit—as one interpretation of Jesus' view might have it—and we are not so devoted to God. We regard Caesar as part of a legitimate order of society of which we and all other members of this society must recognize that we too are parts. Caesar is part of ourselves. Furthermore, despite close affinities, the realm of intellectual things is not wholly identical with God's realm. Nevertheless, the parable of Caesar's and God's realms contains much truth and is no less important than it was nearly two thousand years ago.

In Jesus' lifetime, Caesar had not taken on the lineaments of Leviathan as he has increasingly done in the present century. Caesar did not purport to control all of society. Jesus was living in a tradition in which the earthly power of the priesthood was still a fresh memory in His audience. Although the House of Herod had attempted to gain dominion over it, it demanded no services other than the assurance of its legitimacy and incumbency by its favorites or at least by those who would be subservient to it. The Maccabees had fought a bitter war to put an end to the subversion of the Ark of the Covenant by renegades in the service of the earthly power. Generally, many ancient rulers did not care about the religious beliefs of the peoples they conquered as long as they acknowledged the supremacy and even the divinity of the ruler. Our present Caesar demands much more, just as he also does much more than his ancient predecessors.

The present situation is more complicated than it was in Jesus' time. Caesar now pursues ideal ends. This is something which the Caesar of Jesus' time did not aspire to do—certainly not on the same scale or with the same persistence. He wanted loyalty and subservience mainly to assure his own power and not to serve an ideal. This would seem to place our present Caesar in a more honorable position than his predecessors. The earthly power which Caesar desires now is alleged to serve the realization of ideals which many persons would affirm in a very general form. The ideal ends Caesar seeks involve changing the society and thus forcing some parts to perform actions which are alien to their nature and their traditions. The ideals pursued are those of equality of status and condition even more than the equality of opportunity, the ideal of material well-being for all individuals, of the right of self-expression for all individuals, and of the security of the national community. These are worthy ideals but they are certainly not the only ones which must be respected by individual human beings and human societies.

There is the ideal of the understanding of the cosmos and of what goes on within it, the ideal of the understanding of the patterns of the world-system, from the solar system to the smallest particles, and the understanding of the life of organisms of all sorts and of human beings among the organisms; the understanding of the course of human life on earth, and of human beings in their societies, and of the works created by the human mind. This is an ideal with at least as strong a claim to reverence as the other ideals sought by Caesar. It is an ideal the pursuit of which is at least as essential to the dignity of human beings as equality of status or material comfort and convenience and an extended life span of relatively little pain and misery. Let us simply ask ourselves whether these things sought by Caesar—assuming that Caesar had the ability to bring them about—would, if they were granted to us, constitute a good life.

Let us assume that we could live a long time relatively painlessly, that we ate well, were not cold, that we could all work for our comfortable livelihood, and were not forced to be idle when we wanted to work. Let us assume that we were free to express our opinions and to try to persuade our fellow citizens of the correctness of those opinions so that they would agree with us. Let us assume that everyone could have any employment he wished and that ancestral class and ethnic connection did not influence the chance of entering into such employment. Let us assume that no one was disparaged because of his ancestral class and ethnic connections. Would that be enough?

It would not. Human beings with all their lapses are aware that there is more to life than individual pleasure. Even though their own conduct falls short, they know that some things are better than others, that those better things include some which transcend individual pleasure. The understanding of the world is one of these. There are many things which many individuals do not understand but the understanding of these things by some persons in their society, and the availability to others of the same and subsequent generations of the growing and accumulating body of understanding, are regarded as measures of the merit of the society in which they live.

The very fact of the existence of the National Science Foundation and of the National Endowment for the Humanities is evidence that even Caesar, whose defective appreciation of what he has to deal with I am criticizing here, is not entirely insensate to the value of the disinterested understanding of fundamental things. They are evidence that Caesar himself recognizes that there is a realm which is not that of earthly power; that there is a realm which he does not create and which he cannot create; but which he can help or hinder.

But the National Science Foundation and the National Endowment for the Humanities, with all my esteem for them, have not created the institutions to the support of which they contribute substantially. They have not created, and they could not create, the traditions which its beneficiaries draw upon in order to fructify the financial resources which are given to them by these patrons. Those institutions and those traditions are the products of the striving for the ideals of understanding, of cognitive penetration and appreciation over many centuries, going back for millenia deep into the past of our own civilization which began in the Middle East and on the shores of the Mediterranean and which has been elaborated over several thousand years by intensive and disciplined devotion to the ideal.

What does Caesar owe to this ideal? He owes it at a minimum the respect which is expressed in not damaging it and in not doing anything which will undermine its continued existence. I am less sure that he owes it money than that he owes it self-restraint. He is in any case under obligation not to take away with one hand what he gives it with the other. What good will be done by money however munificently given, if the recipients are so crippled that they cannot use it effectively?

To what extent is Caesar entitled to what has been created in the past by individual and collective private efforts? To what extent is he entitled to use up the traditions created by collective efforts and entrusted to new generations for their care? To what extent is he entitled to use up something which he does not renew, and to what extent is he entitled to obstruct its renewal? For that is what he is doing.

The universities within which these intellectual activities became concentrated, developed—whatever the legal arrangements—systems of internal government in academic matters which were de facto autonomous. The power of appointment was the most crucial of these academic matters. In the United States, as power passed from presidents and boards of trustees to teaching staff, the transfer encompassed the power of appointment. The transfer was not simply an outcome of a struggle for power; it was a result of the recognition that those members of the university who did the teaching and research were the best qualified to apply those standards which were inherent in the nature of the university and the ideals which were central to it. The transfer occurred as the quality of intellectual performances improved; each supported the other. Presidents, trustees, and deans recognized that only those who had achieved intellectual mastery of a subject could assess the attainments of others in this regard.

Every academic appointment is an action which affects the intellectual quality of the university. It determines the quality of teaching and research because it determines who does them. Furthermore it affects subsequent appointments in two ways. For one thing, it determines the composition of the bodies which recommend academic appointment. Mediocrities will choose mediocrities because they do not have sufficient sense of quality and because they fear comparison which would be invidious to themselves. Furthermore once a department is negligent in the application of strict standards, it tends to continue in that way. The appointment of friends, deferential former students, those with particular political convictions, just anybody "to do a useful job of teaching," all help to establish slackness as the prevailing rule and to place burdens on the future from which it is difficult to escape.

Of course mistakes are made and they remain a handicap, but as long as the standard is respected, care is taken not to repeat it—although it must be said that the presence of the "mistake" is itself a handicap to the resumption of the highest possible standard. There are many difficulties in the self-maintenance of academic staffs at a high level. Honest mistakes are made because it is not always possible to tell in advance with certainty that a person who is outstanding when young will remain so when older. There is moreover an ever-present danger of degeneration of departments, and the problem of what is to be done about weak departments which go on maintaining themselves in a state of weakness is still unresolved under conditions of departmental autonomy in the making of appointments. Until it is dealt with, universities are in danger of prolongation and reproduction of their mediocrity at a level lower than the state of the field and the supply of talented persons require. It certainly cannot be overcome under American conditions by governmental action in matters of appointment.

Caesar is now interfering with this process of appointment. He wishes to displace intellectual criteria and to diminish their importance in order to elevate ethnic and sexual criteria. He has placed himself in a position to do this by threatening to withhold financial support for research for which the government enters into "contract" with the universities. A university which does not meet the standard of appointment on ethnic or sexual grounds in one department is threatened with the refusal of funds for research in fields very remote from that errant department.

The federal government proceeds on the principle that one rotten apple spoils the barrel or that one department which does not have or which does not follow an acceptable "affirmative action plan" or which does not have a "target," as it calls its schedule for appointment by ethnic and sexual criteria, or a "quota" or a *numerus clausus* as it really is, can spoil the whole university. One need mention only the experience in this past year of the University of California at Berkeley where support for oceanographic research was withheld because the department of the history of art would not allow its records to be commandeered by officials of the federal government for the purpose of determining whether they contained evidence of actions contrary to the requirements of "affirmative action." Incidentally to its pursuit of the ideal of equality, the federal government claims the right to examine the confidential records of the universities in order to see whether they have behaved in the egalitarian way demanded by the government. The privacy of private bodies is disregarded in the case of the universities. Governmental agents, utterly unqualified, purport in order to enforce their targets or quotas to determine whether academic appointments have been made on intellectual criteria.

From this demand flow other intrusions into the interior affairs of universities. There are no records of the universities which are inviolable by federal investigators who wish to determine whether the universities are fit to supply a service which the government treats as a commodity being purchased from a seller. Once in the hands of the government, these confidential documents become available to whoever wishes to see them; this is provided for by the Freedom of Information Act. It is a little as if before purchasing a pound of butter or a dozen eggs from a shop, the purchaser demanded—and could enforce—the right to examine and take away copies of the personal correspondence of the owner or manager of the shop and his wife and then to divulge that correspondence to anyone who asked to see it. But at least in the latter case the purchaser is usually capable of passing a reliable judgment on whether the butter actually weighs a pound or whether the box has twelve eggs within it. The federal investigators are less competent than the purchaser.

VIII

The problem here is whether Caesar is entitled to regard universities primarily as instruments of his social, economic, and military policies, granting for the moment that universities are in fact capable of doing the things which are expected of them. The answer is that he is not entitled to do so. The universities are not the property of Caesar; they were not created by Caesar. They do things of overriding importance which Caesar cannot do and should not attempt to do. The discovery of truth, its promulgation and transmission, the understanding, as far as the mind can go, of the cosmos and its constituents, are not tasks which Caesar can perform. One need only compare the scientific achievements of governmentally operated laboratories with the achievements of universities: that alone should convince any reasonable person of Caesar's limited capacities. All that Caesar can do is to provide some of the conditions for the performance of this function. The performance of the function is the task of the universities. Caesar overreaches himself when he disregards, hampers, and undermines the performance of this function. He has no right to intrude into the internal processes which enable universities to perform their proper functions; he has no right, although he might legislate that right for himself until doomsday, to coerce the universities by policies which suppress or cripple that function. That fact that he has been so indulgent financially to universities does not give him the right to interfere with processes which if distorted, diminish the advantages conferred by the money, causing teaching to be less good, and research to be less good.

Now it must be said on behalf of Caesar that not all of his intrusions are on his own initiative nor have they reached their present scale against the will of the universities. The universities have a considerable amount of the responsibility for the distortion of the line which should separate them from Caesar. They have all too often nestled in his arms. They became dependent on him unthinkingly and often enthusiastically. Sometimes patriotism and pride in action for the public good have been the motives of their submission to his desires. Sometimes they have invited him to enter their sphere because grievances became too great to be borne, and sometimes these grievances arose from arbitrary action on the part of authorities within universities.

IX

Caesar does of course have his proper sphere and in that sphere he is entitled to make claims and to be affirmed and supported.

Caesar is entitled to expect that the universities will train enough young persons to practice well those occupations in which there is a substantial intellectual content acquirable only through systematic study in universities. There is no need for Caesar to become coercive about this or to exceed the limits which traditionally have left education and training for these occupations to the universities in matters of standards of admission, syllabuses and standards of examination and marking. Caesar is not entitled to blow hot and cold, to be willing to support profligate expansion and then to leave the universities to support the institutional apparatus—teachers and buildings—which had to be created in order to produce the expanded number of graduates.

Caesar is entitled to expect that universities which award degrees and certify competence should meet a minimum standard, but the definition of the level and substance of the standard must be left for the universities either alone or in consultation with each other.

Caesar is entitled to expect that the universities will undertake to admit and educate all those young persons, and those not so young, who meet the intellectual standards for admission. He is not entitled to insist that only a simulacrum of such education be provided. He is not entitled to require the universities to bear the cost of educating those persons for whom he wishes to obtain the desired certification.

Caesar is certainly entitled to invite the universities to conduct research conducive to what he regards as the proper purposes of government, but he must refrain from attaching to those "purchases" any conditions other than the supply of the "service" which is being paid for. He must avoid exploitation of the situation of his own creation whereby the universities have become dependent on the monopolist who has brought them into that state of dependence. He is not entitled to press universities to expand the numbers of teachers and research workers whom they appoint to produce the graduates and research results which he desires, and then to leave the universities to support those expanded staffs after his interest has lapsed.

In the United States opposition to Caesar has been the criterion for the establishment of one of the credentials of an intellectual; this was a common belief of many literary men, painters, sculptors, and literary critics. Academics, especially in certain parts of the social sciences, and in a few other branches of learning such as English literature and theoretical physics, have in recent decades taken up this attitude of opposition to the existing social and political order. Many of them are inert revolutionaries, i.e., they are revolutionaries in their belief and sentiments even though in practice they are law-abiding and even philistine.

No incumbent government has the right to demand that academics support it but it does have the right to expect—although it does not often have enough courage to demand it explicitly—that disagreement with its policies should be expressed in just and temperate language. An incumbent regime does have the right to demand that academics, not because they are academics but because they are citizens like any other citizens, respect the existing political and social order and do not take action to subvert it. Impressively enough, the tradition of infringement of the freedom of expression of academics, which was a blemish on the otherwise impressive respect of the states for universities in their proper functions, has not been taken over by the federal government in its recent career. Thirty years ago the situation was quite different. Caesar's self-restraint in this regard is a virtue which calls for appreciation but it does not call for us to overlook different vices which are fundamentally more damaging than those of thirty years ago.

II
THE CONFLICT OF GOD AND CAESAR: THE LEGITIMATE CLAIMS OF THE UNIVERSITIES

I

Jesus said, "Render therefore unto Caesar the things which are Caesar's, and unto God the things that are God's." The question of what the universities have to render to Caesar and what they have to render to their god is more complicated than that faced by Jesus when He answered the Pharisees and the Herodians who wished to entrap Him. The ordinary Palestinian Jew to whom Jesus addressed Himself did not live in a welfare state in which he was surrounded by the evidence of governmental power and benefit. Caesar was much remoter from the Jews of the beginning of the present era than he is from us. Our Caesar touches on our lives at many more points and we have more responsibility for the doings of our Caesar in this earthly realm. As Professor Arnaldo Momigliano has shown, the Jews had succeeded in holding themselves aloof from Hellenistic culture and when the Romans came to rule in Palestine, they did not saturate the society as modern governments have. Jesus was willing to recognize an earthly realm in which he had no intrinsic interest because he thought of the realm of God, His Father. We attribute more importance to the earthly realm and our sense of the spiritual realm is not as urgent as Jesus'. We too must establish a criterion of separation of the two realms.

American academics are in a more difficult situation from that of the Palestinian Jews to whom Jesus appealed and among whom He made his first converts. American academics are citizens of a democratic republic; the government is their government. Caesar is a Caesar partly of their choosing. In principle, they cannot regard Caesar's realm as a matter of indifference. They are co-responsibles with Caesar; they have an inescapable sense of affinity with the society with which their government is in very active reciprocity.

The state and society in its wider dimensions are very much more present to them than they were to a cultivator or craftsman or small trader in antiquity. There were no social scientists heightening the awareness of society by their investigations, no journalists reporting daily about their society. There were no scientists interested in a steady flow of money to support their research and looking to Caesar to provide what is needed.

There is another important difference. Jesus did not think that the right order of society was a theocracy. He did not expect God's realm to set the pattern for Caesar's realm. Some academics—not many—are secular theocrats. They think that scientists and social scientists should lay down the main lines of Caesar's actions. Most do not go anywhere nearly so far, but they do think that their knowledge should enter into Caesar's action, even if they do not insist that they should dominate it. They want to have some influence on it. They think that they owe something to Caesar—if not to the incumbent Caesar, then to a better one. They think that Caesar has legitimate claims on them, not just for the payment of tribute and abstention from rebellion but for positive contributions to the realization of Caesar's policies.

There is a further, paradoxical complication. Among the highly educated in the United States there has been a long tradition of thinking poorly of the earthly powers, of thinking poorly of the professional politicians as vulgar and susceptible to corruption. Sometimes they have seen them as part and parcel of a society fundamentally uncongenial to the muses or to the gods they worship; sometimes they have thought of themselves as living in a society consecrated to a fundamentally sound democratic idea, but which had gone sour because of the misrepresentation which it suffered at the hands of its elected representatives. These beliefs troubled the universities only around their edges.

The last decade of the nineteenth century was the time of change in this regard. The rise of the social sciences in the universities coincided with a period of increasingly disapproving judgment of contemporary American society by journalists, artists, and writers. They were joined by a number of social scientists who were a small sector of the academic profession, but they received a disproportionate amount of attention—given the smallness of their numbers and the few universities and colleges in which they held forth. Populistic radicals were few in American universities before the Great Depression of 1929. Marxist radicals were practically nonexistent. Yet there was a broad and unclear stream with many contradictory currents of discontent. The depression years widened and deepened the stream and it simplified its course and unified to some extent its divergent currents. But it did not eliminate the conflicting tendencies.

After the Second World War, the dominant current of opinion among academic social scientists and also among some philosophers and physicists came to be one which demanded a society in which government became the active principle, ubiquitous and omniprovident. At the same time the proponents of this kind of society and this kind of government were severely critical of politicians whose flaws were integral to the unsatisfactoriness of the prevailing society of private business enterprise, individualism, personal ambition, and private voluntary action in welfare and education. They were reformers in the two senses that they thought government could be reformed and that a reformed government could reform society. Since the reform of society could not be left to await the full reform of government, it was inevitable that an imperfect government, itself suffering serious ills, should be pressed into the task of curing society of its numerous ills. To summarize the contradiction: there was growing up a belief in the rightfulness of governmental ubiquity and omniprovidence, alongside the older half-heartedness about the legitimacy of the political realm. There was also a belief that scientists and social scientists should contribute to the improvement of the practical life of mankind, improving health, improving productivity in agriculture and industry, improving education and social institutions through their discoveries and their teaching, and latterly through their advice.

Thus, unlike the ancient Jews facing an utterly alien Caesar from whom they expected nothing, from whom they received nothing, to whom they owed only tribute and submission, and whose representatives were scarce and not usually visible among them, the American academic lives in a society permeated by Caesar. The Jews had a society with a center of its own, the Temple, and they trusted it. The center of the gentiles was not theirs; neither Rome nor Athens were their centers; their center was the Temple in Jerusalem. The American academic lives in a society with a powerful center from which he cannot and would not detach himself. But he is distrustful of it.

Overlapping and interpenetrating though we have seen the realm of Caesar and the ideal realm of the work of the mind to be, it is most important to try to define the boundary line between them, the line which delimits Caesar's claims on the universities and his duties to them on the one side, and the claims universities have on Caesar and the obligations which they owe to him and to their universities on the other. It is above all urgent for academics to make clear to themselves and their society the division between their obligations to Caesar and their obligations to their secular temple on the other.

II

American academics are in their actions profoundly attached to the ideal of truth and the ideal of the progressive achievement of more differentiated and more general truths; they adhere to rigorous standards in the discriminating assessment of what is discovered or excogitated. They would not have so many distinguished achievements to their credit in so many fields of learning if they did not act up to this ideal.

However, when it is a matter of explaining why they are doing what they do, when they are called upon to justify their strenuous and often productive exertions, they usually give an answer which does not quite correspond to their own actions. They will say that they are doing what they are doing because they hope that its results will be useful to society, that they will improve governmental practice, that they will be beneficial to the economy, that businessmen or farmers will learn from them and improve their processes and products, that public opinion will be instructed and aroused by the results of their research, and will attempt to influence on the basis of them the decisions of government. The more daring ones will say that they just want to satisfy their curiosity; a fair proportion will say that they wish to test a particular hypothesis. They find it difficult and sometimes even a bit embarrassing to give a justification for what they have done without adducing the practical consequences which they hope their discoveries will help to bring about. It seems to them to be selfish to say that they do it for the pleasure it gives them; nonetheless in private conversation, not in writing very often or in public, they will admit that the quest and the discovery gives them great pleasure. Sometimes a mathematician, or an astrophysicist, or a theoretical physicist says that an act of discovery gives him the same sensation as he experiences when watching a ballet or listening to a sonata. Very seldom does anyone in the academic world say that he regards pursuit of the attainment of truth as an ideal of ultimate value, that he is seeking to ascend through his mind and through the minds of his ancestral and present colleagues to a higher realm of being, the realm of symbolic construction of the ultimate order of things.

Even great scientists, who look back with yearning at the happy time in the 1920s and 1930s when scientific research was not connected with practical affairs in the way in which it is now, bridle at the suggestion that the justification for scientific and scholarly activity and hence of the existence of universities is the attainment of some fundamental truth about the universe or some part of it. They do not like the word "truth" used in this way. It has religious intimations which their secularist outlook does not welcome. Even those who devote the best hours of their days to this impassioned and dispassionate search, without a thought for the consequences outside the attainment of the intellectual goal, are nettled when they hear someone speak of the attainment of truth as an ideal. They do not mind quite so much when one speaks to them about a truth of physics, or a truth of biology, but the more general category and the notion of an ideal which transcends particular objectives in science and scholarship is disturbing to them. The notion of creating ideal entities, truths, propositions which exist in a realm outside the realm of practical activities or psychological experiences, does not go down well.

They know of course how interdependent they are with their colleagues in other universities and with those who just preceded them, but the notion of a vast, unplanned collaborative undertaking, moving forward on many fronts at more or less the same time, trying to understand the world in its infinite variety, is less appealing to them. The common element in these various movements is not acknowledged. Nor do they find easily palatable the idea that the university is the institutional incorporation of these movements possessing a common ethos and ideal.

III

These various *weltanschauliche* strands of the American academic traditions—collectivistic liberalism, individualistic utilitarianism, and the secularist aversion against the realm of the spirit which has an existence of its own, distinct from the existence of the individual organism or brain, and from the existence of society—all create difficulties for the American academic who has to decide what should be rendered unto God, or at least unto the realm of the secular surrogate of the spirit, as distinct from what should be rendered to Caesar. It is made more difficult by the fact that the secularistic collectivistic liberalism in the universities cannot see anything between their own department and discipline on the one side and their government on the other. Committed as so many American academics in the pure or theoretical parts of the natural sciences, the humanistic disciplines, and the social sciences are to collectivistic liberalism—the situation is somewhat different in the professional and technical schools—they also fail to appreciate that their respective universities are corporate entities animated by a common spirit which transcends the boundaries of disciplines and specialties and divisions. They almost always prefer, other things such as salaries being equal, to be at a university rather than in an industrial or governmental research laboratory, but they will not acknowledge that the university is what it is because it is a spiritual and intellectual corporation.

In other words, beyond and underlying the pursuit of particular truths—propositions or hypotheses or whatever they may be called—is the common orientation towards the realm of the symbolic constructions which depict the ultimate nature of things. The fact that this ultimate order is never attained does not belie the meaning of this great unplanned collaboration. Universities have been, in the nineteenth and twentieth centuries, and they are at present, the institutions where the various knots of this network are situated. The university is the institution in modern society to which this ideal has been entrusted, not by particular decisions of some representative organs of society but in consequence of those historical conditions, social, economic, and intellectual, which make it the site of this important responsibility of modern society.

The university sustains the pursuit of truth as a general value through adherence to its traditions. The pursuit of particular truths would not last if those who carried it on did not in fact sometimes unwittingly conceive of themselves as parts of a wider engagement on a front as wide as all the objects which engage the human mind in its efforts for fundamental understanding. The university is not just an administrative apparatus which schedules classes and finds rooms for them, which pays out salaries and administers research funds, keeps records or organizes graduation ceremonies. It is not just through the provision of intellectual companionship so that its members will not be isolated, by providing the presence of other intellectually alive and seeking human beings, that the university is the proper matrix for learning. The narrowest specialist—as many academics are nowadays—would be overpowered by the smallness of his undertaking if he were not carried forward by awareness that he is working alongside others who are, no less than himself, given over to the discovery of the truth about some part of the universe.

Each specialist hears the click as he brings events, previously perplexing and exasperating by their randomness, into a pattern. He might be satisfied with a small pattern but he knows and draws strength from the simultaneous activities of others also seeking patterns which are consistent with his own, which are consistent within a large pattern. He is as dependent on the presence of these other pursuits in his marginal awareness as he is on the accomplishments of those who precede him. He is carried forward not just by his own motives as he perceives them but by the motives of others in the past and present. It is not always easy to perceive this participation of the individual in the larger tradition as it is inherited from the past and as it is cultivated in the present.

The failure to see it makes for a blindness to the significance of the university as a corporate, spiritual, or intellectual whole. The failure to see the university as a corporate, spiritual, or intellectual whole is the crux of the matter because it makes it more difficult to discern the line which should separate the legitimate concerns and demands of Caesar from the proper obligations of academics to the realm of the products of the mind.

IV

This view is not commonly put in an articulate form. If it were it would be easier for me to discuss it; it would not even be necessary. Much more common is a view that the university is justified by its service of "social needs." According to this view, the university must constantly be adapting itself to changing conditions, not in order to keep that existence as intact as it can under conditions which impinge upon it, but rather because new "needs" require new satisfactions. This conception of the university is by no means wholly wrong but it is partly wrong. What is wrong in it is its implication that the university has nothing autogenetic about it, that it has no life of its own and no tasks of its own, that it is entirely a function of events outside itself and should be so. This is a view of the universities which has been taken by the university reformers of the past quarter of a century.

When in the early years of this century it was alleged that the universities were no more than what later came to be called "service stations" for the tasks put to them by economic interests, critics inside and on the edge of the universities, like Irving Babbitt and Abraham Flexner, wrote scornfully of this naive and insensate utilitarianism. But in the period after the Second World War this attitude towards universities, once attributed to the reviled businessmen, came to be taken over by the alleged friends of the universities.

It would not be surprising—although it would be wrong—if the politicians who have to answer more or less for the money which they vote to appropriate to the universities, were the ones to demand measurable results proportionate to what has been expended on them. Unfortunately there are those within the universities who take this view too. I leave aside, at least for the moment, the ignorant "educationists" and publicists who preach day in day out about "the need for innovation in the university," about the need to meet "society's needs," of which they define themselves to be the chief interpreters and spokesmen. These are the claimants of the "new university" as the adjunct of government and as the solvent of social problems, as the promoter of economic growth and of the individual's maximization of his lifetime earnings, as a device for changing society through criticism and as the redeemer of the past deficiencies of society.

It is the tradition of the collectivistic liberalism of so much of the academic profession which has been in formation and development in the United States since the 1890s and which has been the point of departure for this redefinition of the function of the university. Many years ago Richard T. Ely, who was certainly not a great economist but who was one of the most influential figures in the formation of the political views of American social scientists, said that he regarded the state as the religiously ordained instrument of the improvement of society. Subsequent academic social scientists did not go so far in the assignment of a divinely ordained role to government but the secular substance of Ely's idea was generally accepted. Ely was not alone in his generation and in the generation to follow. His conception of the academic social scientist as the critic of the existing social and political order and as the promoter of its improvement through political action and governmental intervention and regulation took firm hold.

If government is the vastly preponderant institution of society and the capacity for conferring good and ill fortune on its members is assigned to government, it stands to reason that the universities should be at the disposal of government in its efforts to accomplish those great ends.

That civil servants and politicians should believe these things seems to be in the nature of modern things—although they are relatively new beliefs. Nor does it seem out of the ordinary for political philosophers and journalists to believe them; the former have seldom been realistic and the latter have not enough time or experience to understand what is at stake. The striking thing is that so many academics believe this. They are very much in favor of academic freedom, by which they mean the freedom of individual academics to espouse whatever political views appeal to them without any sanctions being taken against them—the chief sanctions are the withholding of promotion or dismissal. They think less about the freedom of the university to be an academic institution and to devote itself to its proper calling, which is the cultivation of science and learning, which, whether it be useless or useful, is important for understanding the world and man.

In the United States today we have come to a situation in which one of the most essential components of this genuine academic freedom—the right of an academic body to select its staff according to criteria appropriate to academic appointment, namely, intellectual achievement and promise in teaching and research, and a minimum of academic citizenship—is being restricted by the federal government. Many members of the academic profession take this restriction "lying down." They are far less indignant about it than they were about the not wholly dissimilar harassment conducted by the late Senator McCarthy and other like-minded legislators. This intrusive restriction into the internal affairs of the universities is more injurious than Senator McCarthy and his friends and rivals were because it is more comprehensive and more systematic;

it is directed at institutions as wholes, not at individuals. It has moreover the force of the federal civil service and the weight of the whole executive branch behind it. It also has financial powers which Senator McCarthy, dastard though he was, did not dream of possessing.

The indignities visited on the universities at that time were deeply resented, even if not often publicly denounced. The present indignities represented in the spreading penetration of the Department of Health, Education and Welfare and of the Department of Labor into the appointive practices of universities seem to me to be less resented. One of the reasons is that the present efforts to penetrate into the universities are made in the name of egalitarian ideals and of social justice. Sometimes too the academics are muddle-headed and disingenuous. Thus, when the medical school of the University of California at Davis decided to diminish the weight of academic standards in determining the admissibility of applicants, it insisted that it did so on the grounds of social justice but it also insisted that the Supreme Court of California, in denying its right to do so, was infringing on the autonomy of a university to suspend academic standards. It claimed academic autonomy in order to act against the principles which justify academic autonomy. It is understandable that the desire of the University of California at Davis was supported by many nonacademic groups which stood to benefit from the suspension of academic standards. But when it was supported in a brief submitted as *amici curiae* by official representatives of Harvard, Columbia, Pennsylvania, and Stanford Universities, this was clearly evidence—on the best interpretation—of a deficient appreciation of the central task of a university, which is to maintain and advance in the best possible ways the search for truth and its diffusion.

In National Socialist Germany, many professors welcomed the new regime in 1933, which aside from its other monstrosities, did enduring damage to the then still great German universities. The Office of Civil Rights and related bodies are not to be compared in wickedness with the National Socialists, but the movement of the professors who went out of their way to welcome them was similar in its implications for universities to that of our professors, some of them—like the much worse German professors—very eminent.

The ends which the Office of Civil Rights or the Department of Labor seeks to realize are ends which are not to be disparaged. To spread opportunities to those capable of benefiting from them and to diminish the degradation of human beings are worthy ideals and the very opposite of the ends of National Socialist policy. Nonetheless, these ends, sought in the way in which they are being sought and applied by the federal government of the United States, are seriously in conflict with the no less important ideal of the pursuit and acquisition of truth and with the maintenance of the institutions to which consensus and tradition have assigned this responsibility.

I do not wish to dwell on the contradiction between the immediate end sought or the methods used by the federal government and the ideals which these measures purport to serve. I will repeat only the obvious points that these policies are contradictory to the ideal of equality of opportunity which permits rewards to be allocated on the basis of meritorious achievement and the prospect of such achievement in the future, and that every appointment which is forced primarily by the consideration of the ethnic or sexual characteristics of the candidate results in a defection from the ideal of equality of opportunity and the appreciation of meritorious achievement. It results in injustice to the better qualified persons who would otherwise be appointed and this in itself is a moral deficiency of the present measures.

But more important than the injury to individuals is the injury to the institutions which are to serve the cultivation of truth. And here I regret to say that much of the academic profession has been unfaithful to the ideals to which it is committed. The infidelity appears in various forms. There are the presidents, deans, and heads of departments who fear that to refuse to obey the damaging commands of the federal government will cut off their necessary income. Many professors acquiesce in it because they think that the burden of unsatisfactory appointments will be borne by some other part of the university and that their own research is so obviously important that the officials of the federal government will not allow that research to be endangered by insistence on the employment of insufficiently qualified persons. Still others think that the federal policies are right and that "justice" is more important than a few academically unjustifiable appointments in large departments. Some, and a few of them are themselves scholars of some distinction, are not only content to yield but are active proponents of the policy.

But the universities can properly reject this injurious policy only if they live up to the ideals which are inherent in the academic undertaking to search for and to transmit the truth up to the highest standards possible and by the best methods. If they are to resist the imposition of extraneous criteria of appointment, then they must themselves adhere to the intellectually most stringent standards in their appointive action. Their record is generally good but not as good as it must be. How many appointments are made because the candidate is a favorite pupil of one or more members of the appointive body? How many are made because "someone has to be appointed and he (or she) will do?" How many appointments and promotions are made on grounds of seniority of service, or because of friendship? And more recently, how many are made on political grounds?

The fact remains that misappointments, whether out of sloth, friendship, political partisanship, political ideals, or intimidation, do harm to universities. They do harm which lasts for a long time, longer than the villainous harassment of Joseph McCarthy, his predecessors and accomplices. They make departure from stringent standards the normal situation. They cause students to be less well taught than they need be, they accustom teachers to a lower standard. They bring a poorer quality of research workers into the university. I disregard all the tensions between colleagues which are produced by appointments of which the beneficiaries feel themselves to be unworthy and which hurt the morale of a department.

University teachers in American universities had already in the 1960s acquired considerable experience in defaulting on their obligations to their universities as intellectual institutions. They bear much of the responsibility for the disorders in the universities. These disorders are often referred to as "student disturbances" by "student activists" or by some such designation, which makes it appear that students were the sole actors on the troubled scenes of those years. But this was not so. Most careful observers of those years know to what an extent the students who were most active were encouraged by some of their teachers and of how, once the agitation became very audible and the disruption became tangible, university staffs were distracted by acrimonious conflicts. Closed ranks, honorable academic citizenship, loyalty to their universities and their tasks would have abated the student agitation and might have allowed it to pass without some of its disgraceful and persisting consequences, such as the deformation of the examination and marking systems which has become more common in American higher education than it should be.

No less injurious to the well-being of the universities is the cleavage which still exists between "the administration" and the academic staff in many universities. This cleavage continues a tradition which no longer has a counterpart in reality. It is the product of a set of images which is inherited from the time when the president of the American university was like the headmaster of a boys' school; he was "the college"; all the other members of the academic staff were his assistants whom he could appoint or dismiss either entirely by himself or in consultation only with the trustees of the college. This is no longer the case in any respectable institution of higher learning—although it turns out to have, here and there, some surprising persistence. The old images have however been sustained partly by unthinking prejudice and partly as a result of the expansion of the administrative section of the university. This bureaucracy was in part a result of a general movement in society to think that many things should be done which had not been done before and which have led to the disproportionate expansion of the administrative rather than the academic side of the university. The actual increase in the amount of administration was engendered by increased academic staffs, increased student bodies, increased amenities for students, increased funds, increased governmental regulations and demands for information, increased numbers of buildings and pieces of equipment to be looked after. The munificence and intrusion of the federal government in recent years has also increased the administrative staffs. All this has made administrators more visible as the powers of presidents and deans have diminished; as a result the traditional image of "we and they" received new vitality. The situation seems now to be much less acute than it was in the time of the disorder in the universities a decade and a decade and a half ago; at that time all the old wounds suffered by ancestors were laid open. Now they are closed again but the lines of the scars are still there, aggravated now by the constriction of funds and the consequent obstacles to new appointments to academic departments. The pettiness of the pretexts for starting a furor against the administration, even in well-ordered universities, is evidence of the persistence of this useless tradition.

The growth of membership in trade unions among university teachers is further and more visible evidence of how deeply rooted the tradition of "we and they" is, even at a time when the powers of the academic staff have increased greatly at the cost of the power of "administration." All of these things show how short the university teachers have fallen in their appreciation of the ideal realm to which they owe overriding obligations. Excessive devotion to the realm of Caesar, to the realm of incumbent Caesars and of oppositional Caesars, parochial departmental and generational interests, and philistine narrowness of sympathy and imagination, have all made university teachers less attentive than they ought to be to their obligation to the realm to which they are committed through their membership in the academic profession.

V

Of course, academics must render unto Caesar what is rightfully his. As citizens they have the responsibility both to aid Caesar, to guide him and to restrain him; citizens are now part of Caesar and not just his objects. Caesar's legitimate claims on the university on behalf of his own practical sphere are numerous. The first one is that of assuring the best possible intellectual training to all those young—and older persons too—who are capable by their intellectual and self-disciplinary powers to receive it. It goes without saying that this should be done regardless of color of skin, sex, or status of parents. A no less legitimate claim is that the university should train young persons for important practical professions, the practice of which have genuine intellectual component; these include medicine, law, engineering, business and civil administration, and some others. Caesar has also a legitimate claim that part of the research for which he pays will be directed to practical problems which he himself presents. He also has a legitimate claim for the dispassionate and unprejudiced counsel which scientists and scholars would be able to provide. He also has a legitimate claim that when he is criticized by academics, the criticism should be rational, and well founded and expressed in civil terms. He has a legitimate claim that academics should not abuse the freedom of expression which academics have as citizens by indulging in demagogy and giving patronage to subversion. Not least, he has a right to demand that academics should offer to their society some of the knowledge and standards of judgment which they have acquired, and that they should exemplify to their society the devotion to the ideal of truthfulness and rationality of which they should be, above all else, the custodians.

It would be a wrong and unjustly low view of man's nature not to see the capacity for the love of truth and for the appreciation of its intrinsic value. The love of truth and the obligation to cultivate it is fortunately not confined to universities; the audience of the universities is not confined to the student body; the intellectual functions the university performs are not just on behalf of itself or on behalf of practical things. In a good society at least some part of it cares for the ideal of truth about nature and the universe, about man and his works and its individual members. But the division of labor among the institutions of society has placed the special care of the ideal in the charge of the universities. The universities have other things to do as well, but all of them have or should have an inner affinity with the pursuit and possession of the truth about particular things and the truth as a general ideal and criterion. The professional training given by the universities, the technological research done by the universities, the advice and counsel which members of the universities give in publicistic and civil activities, all of these must be affected with the truth and with care for the ideal of truth as the first concern of the universities.

If this were not so, the universities would be like any business firm or any pressure group looking after the monetary advantages of its shareholders, managers, and workers or seeking to promote by political manipulation the ends sought by its leading members, sometimes to their advantage with respect to material things for themselves, sometimes on behalf of ideals referring to situations beyond their own material conditions. The universities are not institutions like business firms and pressure groups. That they are not is perceived—dimly perceived—by the general public. Even those who take a predominantly utilitarian view of universities or who assert that universities are an investment in economic growth or that they should be the instigators of "social change"—meaning the promotion of egalitarianism and the constriction of the ownership of private property—have an inkling that their utilitarian and political view is not quite adequate. They see that the universities enjoy prestige because of their disinterested cultivation of learning and they wish to exploit it for some ill-conceived practical end. Some teachers and students think that the universities should exploit their moral prestige—and the material resources which they have acquired because of their prestige—in order to advance some transient political cause in which these students and teachers interest themselves for a moment. In their foolish arguments they admit what they would not state explicitly.

Many teachers sense but do not wish or cannot find the idiom to acknowledge openly that the prestige which accrues to universities does so primarily and in the first instance on the grounds of their attachment to the ideal of devotion to the truth. When universities became "secularized" through their control by earthly powers, through the training of young persons for secular professions such as medicine, law and civil service, and then later through their increasingly specialized scientific activities, this fundamental spiritual property of the universities was partially lost from view. It still survived in the various conceptions of the university as a place for the training of character, especially in the English and in the Humboldtian tradition, but these are now ideals which most observers say are impossible of fulfillment. This conception of the university as a spiritual corporation is not much considered anymore, when the university has become defined as an institution for the performance of the functions of research, teaching, training, and service, to say nothing of the additional functions latterly laid upon it, such as criticism—meaning negative criticism—of government and society and the equalization of status through social ascent for all.

It has been common to say that professors have no sense of identification with their university, that they are identified with their specialized scientific or scholarly subprofession. This was one of the sociological slogans of the period after the Second World War. It was, fortunately, not entirely true; the assertion was a piece of academic cant, a self-vaunting act of disloyalty to the intellectual ideal on behalf of a misunderstood notion of what constitutes being a scientist. Nonetheless, the proposition was intended to legitimate disloyalty to the university as an institution, to one's own particular university and to the university as a general category or ideal. Then there were those who said that the university had ceased to be a university; it had become, they said, a "multiversity." There was some truth in this as well as a complacent affirmation that that was what universities should be. The very acceptance of the condition was a betrayal of the ideal. It was an effort to replace the university by a perversity.

If these statements that universities are "service stations," suppliers of "high-level manpower," satisfiers of the "need for social change" and the like are true, then there is no alternative to Caesar and his claims except individual self-indulgence, the following of idiosyncratic hobbies and enthusiasms at public expense or the expense of taxpayers and private patrons. Intellectual activity is reduced to a consumer good. (The economists have begged the question by declaring that intellectual activities can be only "producers' goods" or "consumers' goods." Everything must justify itself by its measured covering of its costs.) According to this view, there is nothing but the self-indulgent investigator gratifying his arbitrary curiosity or the demands of society represented by the state. There is no alternative to Caesar, if this view is taken, except the individual's arbitrary will.

This view is wrong, and not just when stated with the starkness with which I have put it. The individual who undertakes to explore systematically and methodically the cosmos in any of its parts, physical or social or physiological or cultural, and who undertakes to acquire and to transmit any of the results gained from that curiosity, does so under the auspices of a tradition of the results of prior exploration and with methods which have been formed in the course of prior exploration. He accepts these results as his point of departure and also as his accompaniments for much of his journey. In accepting, he affirms them and commits himself to the fundamental postulates of these undertakings, despite whatever he says to contradict this. When he enters a university, however "tough-minded" or—as those who would improve on William James say, "hard-nosed"—he is, he places himself into a setting which makes possible whatever he accomplishes, not just by its administrative services but by the provision of colleagues and artifacts which bear a tradition. This tradition comprises a general one which in turn comprises many specific ones. The general tradition pervades the specific ones. Even a narrow-minded experimental physicist or a very specialized entomologist regards himself as a "scientist" who shares with other "scientists" a set of general rules about the worthwhileness of knowledge, about the objective of a coherent view of anything which he investigates and its coherence with adjacent and superordinated things. He is committed to the postulate of a coherent order in all things and to a set of rules and scruples. Seeking that order without this postulate does not make sense. With this postulate, the academic is committed to respect for the larger collaborative quest by many persons investigating and teaching about many different things, all of whom are being driven forward by this quest of a collaboratively decipherable order in the universe.

The university is the institution which carries on that undertaking. It does other things as well, things which often look as if they have little connection with that undertaking, and indeed some of them do have a very attenuated relationship with that undertaking. The more of these there are, and the more that those who do them dissociate themselves from that fundamental undertaking, the weaker the institution as a whole becomes, the less it is able to impose itself on its members, the more it renounces the respect of the wider public and the less able it is to withstand any illegitimate claims by Caesar.

Our universities are no longer Christian universities in any literal sense of the word. Many of those who are in them as teachers and students stem from religious traditions other than the Christian one. Many of those who are Christian in their origin deny the validity of traditional Christian beliefs or they are indifferent to them. I accept this. Nevertheless, Jesus' command that rendering unto Caesar that which belongs to him must be accompanied by rendering unto God that which belongs to Him—rendering unto the ideal of scientific and scholarly truth what belongs to it is still a rule which cannot be denied without a further disordering of our lives. Caesar's failure to understand this makes it all the more necessary that the universities take it to heart and affirm it in principle and in action.

III
A NEW DECLARATION OF RIGHTS AND DUTIES

I

Jesus replied to the Pharisees that one should "Render therefore unto Caesar the things which are Caesar's; and unto God the things that are

God's." I accept this as the guiding principle of the constitution of government and universities, each according to its own principles in their reciprocal relations.

I proceed from the postulate of the rightness of a pluralistic society. I accept that there are many legitimate interests in society, the bearers of which seek to realize them. I accept that these interests contribute not only to the benefit of those who seek to advance them but to the benefit of other parts of their society and thus to the common good. I accept that these interests are not inevitably in harmony with each other and I do not think that some degree of conflict is a bad thing. Our whole system of representative government postulates the existence of conflicts; it is one method of compromising these conflicts. The task of compromise is rendered feasible by an acknowledgment of the legitimacy of the institutions through which the conflicts are compromised. It is also fostered by a willingness of each party or parties to the conflict to see their rivals as members of the same society, with legitimate interests and ideals of their own; it is fostered by the willingness to restrain one's own desires.

The task of compromising the interests of government and of the nongovernmental interests on behalf of which government often acts on the one side, with these interests which are not identical with the interests of government and its protégés on the other, is a major task of citizens and politicians and of those who have at heart the well-being and quality of their society. It is also a matter of finding the right principle of the division of labor among social institutions.

My aim in these lectures has been to contribute to that reconciliation and compromise. Matthew 22 gives us guidance in the search for a solution. It tells us that not everything belongs to Caesar, that there are things which belong to God. I am however not speaking here of the Church in the face of government; I am speaking of universities, and my invocation of Jesus' words is not intended to claim the protection of divinity for universities or to claim that the universities have found the way to God. My reason for doing so is that the universities in their essential activities seek and approach things which share something with religious things. The universities seek to discover—although they can never reach finality—the laws of regularities which govern man's existence, the earth's existence, the existence of the cosmos itself. They seek the truth and that is their primary justification for existence. They seek the truth not because of the idiosyncratic proclivities of their members but because it is something which mankind needs, because it is something their society needs. They need it not just because some of these truths can be incorporated into practical action and thereby increase wealth, improve health, and do many things which contribute to the physical well-being of human beings. They need it because it is in their higher nature to need it. It is not by accident that religion has played and continues to play such an important part in human life. The work of the university is in a sense parallel to that of the churches. It too operates in the realm of the ideal, that realm which has existence apart from physical objects, physiological organisms, and social groups. It operates with different methods and it does not claim or expect finality. The universities are great collaborative efforts in this search, a collaboration which has run over a long period of time, beginning long before universities began and before universities assumed approximately their present mode in the nineteenth century. It is collaborative effort which is the work of individual investigators, scholars, and thinkers working individually or in teams, within disciplines and beyond the boundaries of disciplines. It is an effort which is the matrix of the work of specialized scientists and scholars.

The accomplishments of this effort are numerous and particular and many of them have entered into the practical affairs of mankind. The young persons who have been educated in the universities have entered the learned professions and the civil service; the results of the inquiries of the universities have been drawn into many practical activities. University teachers have entered into practical activities as politicians, consultants, occasional administrators, and publicists. From its side, governments, wealthy individuals, businessmen, and landowners have supported universities, which have almost never been economically self-supporting. In wartime, governments have drawn upon university teachers and university plant for their purposes. Since the Second World War, the government of the United States has assigned much of the research which it has desired for a wide variety of purposes to universities and it has, through a variety of institutional arrangements, supported financially the scientific research done in universities.

As a result, although universities have their center of gravity in one sphere of existence, and government its center of gravity in another sphere, the relations between them are extremely complicated and very intimate. The universities are always in a weaker position. They have neither the physical force nor the legal powers nor the economic resources to resist a strong-willed government, and in a tug of war between them the universities could not resist the government. Yet, the government too is limited in its powers; it does not have the means of searching for the truth, it cannot educate the oncoming generations. It from its side depends on the universities. It can, up to a point, force universities to do what is against their will and it can deform the universities so that they cannot do what they alone can do. But this will never come to that pass if government and the university each recognizes its own obligations and the other's rights, and if the government returns to a more modest conception of its rights and powers in place of the inordinately inflated one which it has developed since the Second World War.

II

Caesar has the right to certain things from the universities and the universities have certain obligations to him. The universities have rights to certain things from Caesar and he has obligations to them. We know that the universities have obligations to the realm of the spirit, the realm of scientific and scholarly truth, the realm of the powers of reason; they have the obligation to transmit these truths and to train young persons for the practical professions in which these truths are applied. That obligation of the universities to the third realm is the first source of the rights of the university in the face of Caesar and society and of the obligation of Caesar and society to the university. Caesar and society and the universities all have obligations to this third realm but for universities those obligations must come before all others. If the university does not place its obligations to its intellectual calling above all others, it would render itself unworthy of the appreciation of Caesar and society, and it could not properly perform the functions to which Caesar and society are entitled. The university would be only a useful vocational training school if the attainment and cultivation of truth about the most serious things and the education of young persons in the spirit of this kind of investigation and analysis were not its primary concern and its achievement.

It has long been recognized by Caesar and his academic admirers and collaborators that universities are useful to society and to Caesar's own purposes. It was partly out of this recognition that faculties of law, divinity, and medicine were supported from the Middle Ages onwards. The faculty of philosophy—what we would call the arts and sciences—was also regarded as worthy of support. It trained teachers and it provided the rudiments of an important intellectual culture before its pupils turned their best attention to study in the other, more practical faculties. It was understood that the universities would do their very generally defined duties to state and society by accepting as a major obligation the training of clergymen, teachers, physicians, and lawyers, after the two latter came to require academic studies. They were not compelled by law to do these things. They did them in consequence of a deep consensus about their mutual dependence and independence, which most of the rest of society accepted without reflection and with only very vague expectations.

There was also a desire in the circles of commercial and industrial enterprisers in the United States that universities would not render their students utterly incapable of practical action in the future, and even that they would help by educating young men who would become leaders in the world of business. There were demands that the universities should teach practical subjects; in the American universities this led to the establishment of business schools and the growth of schools of engineering. These were adaptations of the German and French traditions of the eighteenth century which had not found a home in German or French universities. In Germany, from the eighteenth century *Akademien* of mining, agriculture, and other subjects, and in France from the military schools, there grew the *technische Hochschulen* and the *Handelshochshulen,* and the École polytechnique and the École centrale des arts et métiers. Their subjects were not admitted into the universities until much later, except in the United States.

By an unwritten agreement, the universities performed the services of training for the professions necessary for state and society, in return for support for those activities which had no practical value and which were respected because they were of the realm of the spirit, however attenuated the connection sometimes seemed to be.

There seemed to be an unwritten and unspoken pact between the universities, society, and state governments in the nineteenth century, which the federal government scarcely entered. There was a division of spheres and an acceptance, in fact, of reciprocal obligations. It worked quite well. Throughout the nineteenth and early twentieth centuries, the universities prospered intellectually and materially; society drew many benefits from the universities. It gained practitioners of the learned professions, it gained the material benefits, which came from research, in increased agricultural productivity, better health and many improvements in transportation, building, the preservation of foods, the coloring of textiles, etc., some of which were directly the outcome of scientific research done in universities and others of which were results of the application of scientific methods, which were not confined to universities but for which the universities maintained the standard. The universities also pursued learning and educated young persons in scientific and humanistic subjects; this was their primary obligation and it was recognized as such and appreciated widely in society.

It is often said that the universities have been supported in the United

States because of the anticipation of the practical benefits which they conferred on government and society, and there is undoubtedly much truth in this. But it is very far from the whole truth. There was an inarticulate reverence for learning in those states where the great state universities first developed through the nineteenth century and until the Second World War. This reverence for learning drew from the reservoir of Christian piety and respect for tradition. Academic learning, attempting to find the way to the ultimate stratum of being, the laws of cosmic existence and of human life, drew on the same stratum of piety as religious belief and respect for tradition.

It is reasonable to think that the universities would not have been treated so generously had they been only centers of learning and contributed nothing to the practical life. The fact remains, however, that their patrons often dispensed their funds with clear awareness that they would also be used for the pursuit of knowledge which was not practical in its intention. Their patrons, private and public, did not regard the universities solely as instruments of practical purposes; they believed that their societies had to have disinterested, pure learning; a society had simply to have that in order to be worthy of respect according to some deeper criterion.

Much obscurity lay over the boundary line between the sphere of intellectual activity which was maintained both because it was a part of the highest sphere to which human beings had reverently to submit, and because of it offered the prospect of practical advantage, and that sphere of practical action, governmental and private, which took the responsibility for increasing the wealth of society, pursuing and restraining the advancement of private interests and maintaining some degree of order in the everyday life in society. Nonetheless, the boundary was in the main respected. Occasionally, especially in the United States, governments and private persons became impatient because some university teachers criticized institutional arrangements and beliefs which they regarded as sacred; on these occasions they pressed for dismissal and they were from time to time successful. The teachers against whom they railed were few in number. Whatever their beliefs and sentiments, an only insignificant number of teachers associated themselves with *soidisant* revolutionary movements and not many more expressed beliefs which made excessively sensitive and not well informed laymen think that they were close to such movements.

State legislators and private donors from time to time expressed the wish that particular fields of study or research leading to practical benefits should be undertaken, but their interests usually coincided with those of some university teachers who were already intellectually interested in such topics. Teachers did not have to teach or do research against their will and intellectual interest on topics which were imposed upon them by external authorities; they did not have to espouse beliefs and, above all, they did not have to depart from standards of truthfulness and intellectual integrity. The application of intellectual standards remained inviolate, however practical the intention of the research. They were generally left to do as they wished; they often had more to fear from imperious heads of departments, deans, and presidents than they had to fear from legislators and private donors.

The peaceful relations between the universities and their public and private patrons were sustained by forebearance and mutual confidence on both sides. The earthly powers got much of what they wanted and they were willing to leave to the universities what was theirs. There were times when the powers were uncomfortable with universities but the friction always subsided although unpleasant memories were left. The academics generally appreciated the opportunity to infuse the light of the intellect into the practical affairs of mankind and they embraced the opportunity to devote themselves to intellectual things, despite the distraction of academic conflicts, low salaries, and careers not as successful as they had hoped.

III

If Caesar, as the agent of society, together with private patrons, should contribute to support the university financially, it should be because the universities are the places where truths are discovered, interpreted, improved, and transmitted. The universities perform services for society by educating at an advanced level its intellectually most talented young persons, enabling them thereby to provide the numerous professional services needed and to lead intellectually better lives, regardless of the professions they later follow. They perform services by conducting research, the results of which in varying and unpredictable degrees are applied to practical things desired in society. Above all, they serve society by exercising high intellectual functions, enriching the society in no practical way but by showing that it is capable of attaining the heights of human achievement and linking their society with ultimately serious things.

These are all good reasons why Caesar should contribute to the support of universities. The provision of these services imposes a corresponding obligation on Caesar. Just how large a sum of money should be provided for that support cannot be decided by any very exact criteria;

the mode by which the funds are granted to the universities is likewise not capable of any ideal solution but it is an important matter and needs to be discussed.

There are practically no Western societies where all the support for universities comes from government, whether central or provincial or in combination. France, Belgium, and the Netherlands are probably the countries in which practically all the support comes from the central government, through various research councils and from direct block grants. In the Federal German Republic the funds come in block grants from the state governments, special grants for building and research from the central government, and other funds from research councils and private foundations. In none of these countries do tuition, registration, and examination fees paid by students form more than a negligible proportion of the total revenue of the university; there is very little income from endowments. It is in Great Britain that the arrangements for supporting universities have been the most admired. An institution called the University Grants Committee estimates the financial requirements of all the universities for a five-year period. This sum is then negotiated with the Department of Education and Science—formerly the Treasury did this—and it is then allocated to the universities by the University Grants Committee in accordance with criteria which are not made public. Most research projects are supported by more or less autonomous research councils, the funds of which come from the central government; latterly, as a result of the report of Lord Rothschild, a large amount is paid by the various operational departments for investigation which, as the prospective users, they specify. Students' tuition and maintenance fees are supplied by local government educational authorities from funds which in turn are supplied by the central government. A relatively small proportion comes from private business firms and private philanthropic foundations. The colleges of Oxford and Cambridge receive no money at all from direct grants by government and they live almost entirely from the income from their endowments which have nothing to do with government, and from students' fees which come mainly from the central government through the local educational authorities.

All the European arrangements contrast markedly with those prevailing in the United States. There are many more universities and colleges in the United States than in any other country; they vary more in range of achievement; they differ more among themselves in their sources of income and their sources of income are more various than in any European country.

Could and should the American system of supporting universities be made more like the European? It is perfectly clear to me that the Continental system is unacceptable in the United States. In neither France nor Western Germany nor Italy has the central government been a wise Caesar. In Great Britain the still excellent University Grants Committee, with all the criticisms made of it for yielding too much to the government's desires and for "pushing the universities around," could not be applied in the United States. There is, for one thing, no need for the central government to provide for all the expenses of universities; the munificence of the state governments and of private donors renders it unnecessary, even if it were feasible. It simply could not be done. How could any government department deal with nearly three thousand higher educational institutions of the most various kinds, tasks, qualities, and excellences? However wise the members of a federal university grants committee, it could not deal with such a huge array of institutions except by mechanical arithmetical formulae which, despite their appearance of impartiality, would satisfy no one. Both the best and the worst would think themselves discriminated against. Discrimination in favor of the better institutions would arouse resentment on the part of those thinking themselves unfairly treated. It would moreover be impossible to overcome political considerations; representatives in the federal legislature would not wish to see the institutions of their respective states treated in what they would regard as an unfair manner.

IV

There is no widely divergent, desirable alternative, in my view, to the present system of federal financial support—if system it is—which has grown up haphazardly since the Second World War, whereby the federal government makes grants and enters into contracts for specific projects and purposes. It needs modifications and corrections, not replacement. In the support of research this existing system has on the whole worked quite well. The great progress of American science in the past 30 years is a testimonial to the excellence of this system in supporting research workers who could produce outstanding scientific results. It has permitted progress in both pure and applied science. Mistakes have undoubtedly been made, and of course, no one can know what perfect efficiency would be in the support of science. Nonetheless, it has succeeded in supporting projects and persons with often very striking results. One of the reasons for its excellence is that it has been competitive among individual scientists, the competition has been a competition of scientific skill and the judges of the winners have been the only persons capable of assessing the merits of competitors, namely, the scientists. Here and there, there has been some deliberate departure from the pattern of granting funds to the best qualified scientists where geographical criteria of distribution have been applied, but this has been marginal. Even when the government has laid down the subject matter or field of research, as is inevitable, and just as long as the practice coexists with larger areas of free choice of problems and fields by scientists of outstanding merit, the principle of allocating funds to the scientists, who by their previous accomplishments and capacities as judged by highly qualified practicing scientists were best qualified, has been faithfully observed and with results which have on the whole been very good.

The one deficiency of this system of "paying for research" which contributes to the financial support of the universities is that, despite its idiom which makes it appear that it is a commercial relationship between two contracting parties, the government does not pay for what it "receives." Leaving aside the recurrent efforts by the federal government to diminish payments for "overhead," the government does not conceive that, in this relationship, it is dealing with a university except in a narrow and superficial legal sense.

A university is not just a legally defined corporation. It is not just an administrative organization which provides space and administrative services for individual scientists. It is a culture which is maintained by the traditions of many men and women of learning, living and working in each other's presence, sustaining each other, keeping intellectual wits and sensibilities alert and sharpened. The culture is the product of past achievements and it is sustained by the copresence of many individuals of different generations who keep this tradition alive and active. If the tradition is not alive and active, the performance of each individual suffers, some more than others. The government's mode of granting funds for the performance of specific pieces of research does not provide for the maintenance of the institutions without which these traditions could not flourish. The government receives the benefits of these institutions and the traditions which keep them alive but it does not take into account their maintenance. The maintenance entails not only provision for libraries and pieces of equipment, the repair and cleaning of buildings, and provision for the salaries of scientists, scholars, technicians; it entails the careful appointment of new and old colleagues over a wide range of subjects, many of them remote from the field in which the research which is being supported is done.

This is a thing difficult to speak about with precision and probably impossible to measure. Nonetheless it is a tangible phenomenon to anyone who has lived and worked in a university. Such a person knows how much he owes to colleagues as well as to students in a university which has a tradition of strenuous devotion to high standards, how much it puts him on his mettle. It is a phenomenon which cannot be created by administrative order; it is something which can fade if the university deteriorates. It is maintained by the unceasing recruitment of new, young persons who are capable of responding to it, assimilating it, and expressing it in their intellectual demeanor. This is one of the things which the government obtains when it supports a particular piece of research. Yet under present circumstances nothing is paid for it by the government.

The central part of the university is the teaching staff. It is the teaching staff which does most of the research; not all of the teachers do equal amounts of research and the funds obtained for research do not pay their salaries for teaching. The government pays for their "released time" from teaching; it pays neither for what has been "invested" in them, nor for the teaching they do while doing the research which is ostensibly "paid for." The least the federal government should do is to pay for more than "released time"; in this way, the government would pay for the maintenance and replacement of the intellectual "capital" on which it draws when it makes a "contract" with the universities.

Nor do funds made available by the federal government for payment of the tuition fees of students cover the costs of teaching them, to say nothing of the costs of maintaining the university as an intellectual institution. It is left to the states, to gifts from private patrons, and to the returns on endowment and income from fees to cover the rest of the budget of the university; this comes to about two-thirds of the total budget and in some cases more. The inadequacy of these funds for the purpose of maintaining the quality of teaching and research of the university is evident in the number of leading private universities which have been in deficit in recent years and which are having to consume their endowment, which, in any case, is being dissipated by inflation.

I propose therefore that it is an obligation laid upon Caesar to contribute to the maintenance of the capital which he is using. I suggest that in addition to the payment of the narrowly defined overhead, each university receive an additional payment proportional to its total receipts from government for the support of research. This would assure that those universities whose intellectual capital is most drawn upon would receive proportionate compensation for its use. As long as the prevailing system of judgment by juries of qualified scientists allocated the research grants, there would be no danger of political bias or arbitrariness in the allocation of intellectual capital grants. This leaves out what are called "developing institutions," "black colleges" and other special concerns of the federal government. The contributions to the support of these institutions entail a different criterion of support and I do not deal with this matter here.

The maintenance of the intellectual capital of the university is clearly one of the most essential conditions for the universities to continue to perform their obligations to Caesar's practical demands on behalf of society and to the ideal of rational scientific and scholarly understanding. It is imperative that this intellectual capital be maintained; it is no less imperative that nothing be done to cause it to deteriorate.

At present the government draws upon but does not want to maintain the intellectual capital of the university. It is at present engaged in actions which are deteriorating the stock of intellectual capital, and which threaten to damage it further in the future. It is doing this by its insistence on the diminution of emphasis on intellectual criteria in academic appointments. In its support of scientific research, the government, through its use of juries of qualified scientists to recommend which proposals and applicants should receive support, is applying a principle which it is hindering in the appointment of teachers from whom the applicants for research grants are sooner or later to be drawn. Instead of enabling criteria of prospective scientific fruitfulness as assessed by qualified scientists to be applied, it insists on an adulteration of such intellectual criteria when it comes to the appointment of teachers.

Any appointment of a mediocre and incompetent young person who later gains permanence of tenure is a weakening for years to come to the university in which the appointment is made. It reduces the pressure for intellectual alertness and scrupulousness within the university as a whole. It is a dilapidation of the sustaining intellectual capital of the university; it cheats the students. The weakening affects in the first instance the department as a whole in which the poorer appointment is made, but this weakening is not confined to that department. It spreads the consequent slackness throughout the university. This is what the federal government is attempting to impose on the universities although it does so on behalf of a worthy ideal.

I refer here to the "affirmative action" policies of the federal government, which in effect demand that ethnic and sexual criteria must be given precedence over intellectual criteria, so that the academic staffs of universities will become in composition much like the composition of the population as a whole. The universities are being harshly pressed by the federal government to move actively towards the meeting of certain quotas or proportions for blacks, women, and other "minorities." It seeks to enforce this system of quotas by threatening to deny all applications for the support of research coming from universities which do not have any affirmative action plan which satisfies officials of the Departments of Labor and of Health, Education and Welfare.

The scrupulous avoidance of the application of ethnic and sexual criteria in academic appointment is necessary not only because justice to the able, of whatever color of skin or ethnic ancestry or sexual characteristics, requires it, but because the maintenance of the very highest intellectual standards of a university requires it. Criteria of justice and intellectual standards coincide where academic appointments are scrupulously made. These two criteria cease to coincide if justice is interpreted as requiring that ethnic and sexual criteria should be accorded precedence. The present policies of the federal government point menacingly in the latter direction.

In doing so, this policy contradicts the policy which the government has hitherto followed in supporting scientific research, both applied or fundamental. Yet the poorer the intellectual qualifications of the teachers who in their other capacity are the research workers, the poorer the results of research will be. It should be observed that the government, when it allocates funds for research, does not insist that the staff which is to do the research must meet the "targets" which it demands in the appointment of teachers. Instead it insists that all other parts of the university be composed according to its targets. Perhaps it does not wish to reduce the likelihood of scientifically and practically valuable results from the particular piece of research it is supporting. But it is also possible that it has not thought out consistently the right policy to follow. In any case what it is doing is an unprecedented and damaging intrusion into the very center of the university.

The government, in the pursuit of its objective, has repeatedly claimed the right to copy and take possession of documents which were written by referees with the clear expectation that they would be treated as confidential by the person to whom they were addressed. It does so on the assumption that its civil servants are capable of assessing the merits of the various candidates who are considered in fields of science and scholarship in which they have not even the slightest competence.

The weighing of assessment by referees and the assessment of published and unpublished works as evidence of scientific achievement and as promise of future achievement is obviously something which can be done only by qualified scientists. The federal government has acknowledged this hitherto in its arrangements for the allocation of support for particular pieces of research. The assessment and recommendation of appointment of teachers in universities and colleges are also actions which can be competently done only by persons who know the problems of the fields in which the appointments are to be made, who know the state of knowledge, the literature, and the workers in the field. What does a civil servant know about the history of art, or classical studies or linguistics or anthropology or biochemistry or mathematics to enable him or her to pass judgment on whether one candidate is better qualified for appointment than another in one of these departments? How can he or she assess the published writings of candidates or the written testimonials of referees? The only criteria which civil servants are capable of applying in passing judgment on academic appointment are utterly irrelevant to the intellectual academic qualifications of candidates. They can tell whether the person appointed is black or white, male or female, but there their competence ends. Nonetheless they cannot avoid going further and passing judgment on whether whites and males merit appointment on academic intellectual criteria. The very insistence of governmental officials on assessing the process of assessment in cases of appointments inevitably entails their application of criteria which are irrelevant, at best, to the tasks of education and research and, at worst, in most cases, injurious to the effective performance of these tasks. This is why academic appointment must be autonomously made within the university and not prescribed by persons who do not have the necessary knowledge. The appointments must be made on the basis of dispassionate intellectual assessments of the merits of candidates by persons who are competent to assess their worth and who can assess them honestly. At present the federal government is attempting to subvert this method of appointment. It does so in disregard of the judgments made by those qualified to judge and by rendering it more difficult to obtain honest judgments from those who are so qualified.

The federal government of the United States is a very leaky container of information. On behalf of the ideal of "open decisions, openly arrived at," to adapt the maxim of Woodrow Wilson, the Freedom of Information Act permits interested persons to obtain unpublished documents in the possession of the executive branch of the federal government. Letters by referees about candidates for university appointment come under the category of unpublished documents which are obtainable by an interested person, such as a rejected candidate for appointment in any university to which the federal government has turned its attention. This is a deterrent to the writing of frank and unambiguous assessments by referees and such assessments are indispensable to the appointment of the intellectually best qualified. Thus when a civil servant takes a copy of documents bearing on academic appointments, he does so as a step in the exercise of his coercive powers over the university. But at the same time, he is also causing an adulteration of the evidence on which academically acceptable appointments are made. Stringent criteria cannot be stringently applied unless there are stringent assessments regarding the candidates. A pincers-movement is underway. On the one side the federal government wishes to cause the proper criteria of academic appointment to be suspended; on the other side it is obstructing the establishment of truthful evidence by which academic appointments can be made according to the appropriate criteria.

I recognize that it is doing these things on behalf of worthy ideals but in doing so it also damaging institutions which are responsible for ideals which are certainly not less important and which also perform invaluable services to society—the very services which Caesar prides himself on helping to bring into existence.

V

The entire apparatus which the federal government has built up to prevent discrimination on grounds of sex and ethnic origin in academic appointments cannot be anything but damaging to the quality of education and research. It should be discontinued and the universities and the colleges of the country should be allowed to do for themselves the job which only they can do. The federal government has certainly contributed to the movement to diminish certain gross forms of exclusion of blacks from opportunities which must be open to them to compete for in their capacity as citizens. Nonetheless, it is not the sole agent, probably not even the major agent in the tremendous improvement in American society which has occurred in this regard in recent decades. The government has been able to do what it has done because it has ridden on the crest of a powerful wave of opinion. The improvement in the attitudes of whites towards blacks is part of a process which has been going on since well before the Office of Civil Rights began its activities in their recent form. Much of the credit for this change in opinion in the white parts of American society goes to the movement of the black population for its civil rights, to the courageous activities of young black students and of the leaders of the movement who helped to make white Americans more aware of the wrongness of the arrangements which they tolerated and in which they participated. But the change of opinion had already been going on before the massive movement for civil rights began. The practical disappearance of anti-Semitism which was common in the United States up to the end of the 1930s has not been in the slightest a result of governmental measures. No more has the improvement in the conduct of whites towards blacks been a result of governmental measures. The federal government must recognize that it did not begin the movement for the more civil treatment of blacks and women; this was a result of a moral transformation in the American people. The federal government could not have undertaken its civil rights program if it had not been borne forward on this wave of moral transformation. The academic profession in the United States showed after the Second World War that it could extend the application of strictly intellectual criteria in academic appointments to Jews. Why should it be thought that it could not and would not apply them to blacks and other so-called colored candidates and to women unless it is menaced by the often inept agents of the federal government?

The federal government should therefore cease its threats to withhold research contracts and grants unless "acceptable affirmative action plans" are submitted and "compliance agreements" are signed. It should cease its demands for inspection and possession of the confidential documents of universities regarding appointments, on which it is not competent to pass judgment.

I do not make this simple and radical proposal merely to spare the universities the wearisome harassment by mediocre civil servants and the large expenses which are entailed and which they can ill-afford in this time of straitened circumstances. I make it because it is necessary to avoid wanton damage to our universities which, with all their shortcomings, have served both Caesar and their secularized conception of the highest ideal so well.

VI

It is very difficult for the government of the United States to comprehend what a university as an institution of advanced teaching and discovery is, when for so many years it has proceeded on assumptions which are not conducive to that comprehension. But even on the assumption that the universities are "contractors" who supply the services of research and training—this is the assumption on which the federal government has proceeded during the several decades of its active relationship with the universities—it will not serve its own purposes or the good of American society if it persists in these policies which will further run down the "contractors" capital on which it draws without a serious concern for its maintenance and improvement.

The federal government should recognize that universities depend for their existence on the maintenance of their intellectual capital, i.e., the institutional embodiment of beliefs and sensibilities which the members of a university help to keep in force in each other. This is the achievement of centuries of exertion and devotion in the whole world of universities and in particular those universities which, by living in the matrix of these traditions and arrangements, can thereby perform intellectual activities and produce intellectual works of high quality and thus justify their existence.

Not everything which everyone in a university wants to do can be done because the resources are not adequate for that, whether they come from private or governmental sources. Not all the persons who are candidates for appointments can be appointed because resources are not adequate for that—nor would it be desirable in most situations, even if it could be paid for. If funds are limited, they must be used to support the most important research by the best scientists and scholars and to support the teachers best able to arouse the intelligence of their students and to bring before them the best of human intellectual and cultural achievements. To interfere with these processes of decision, to obstruct them and to adulterate them, would be ungrateful and frustrating to the state governments and private patrons and to the taxpayers—businessmen and workers—who have produced the surplus which has supported the enrichment of human understanding over numerous generations.

VII

The generosity and self-restraint which Caesar has shown in the past and which I am urging that he extend calls for corresponding action on the part of the universities. The confidence and support of government must be marked by a corresponding devotion and self-consecration of the universities to the tasks arising from their transient ideal. They must also accept Caesar's legitimate claims.

Political parties and groups of citizens joined together for the pursuit of private ends to seek to influence the policies of government through contention in elections and through the representation of their own parochial or transcendent interests. They are legitimate bodies pursuing legitimate ends, but the ends of universities are not their ends, however much individual members of universities agree with one or another of these parties and civic groups. Except in totalitarian countries, political parties do not seek to have a formal voice in the management of university affairs.

Business enterprises are entitled to own property, buy, produce and sell what they need to make a profit for their shareholders. They have their proper sphere of activity in which they are entitled to be free of external regulation. They are also limited in their rights outside this sphere. One of the common criticisms of business firms often made among social scientists in universities is that they have attempted to influence the process and outcome of political contention. For the purposes of this argument at least those who make this charge imply that there is a sphere of business enterprise—"the private sector"—and a sphere of government. They admit when making this criticism of business firms that in a pluralistic society each sector and type of institution has its own legitimate objectives and responsibilities; that the objectives of one sphere are not always in harmony with those of another sphere; that one should not arrogate to itself the tasks of others or attempt to dominate them; and that in seeking its own distinctive ends, each group also contributes in some measure to the common good.

When we come to spiritual activities—those carried on in churches and universities—we find that those pluralistic principles are sometimes suspended. Some churchmen have attempted to make the churches into arbiters of the whole range of social life. Yet the entire principle of the separation of church and state by law or in custom was intended to work in both directions. Political life was intended to be preserved from theocracy, the churches were to be preserved from exploitation for political purposes by the reigning powers. The relationship has been interpreted differently in recent years: some collectivistic liberals think that the churches should be free of the government but that the government should be under the dominion of the churches, not by a theocratic organization of authority but rather by its morally authoritative prescriptions for conduct. But this is not universally shared by collectivistic liberals and it is sharply rejected by more traditional liberals and conservatives.

Many universities were once religious institutions affiliated to and governed by one or another church or sect. It is now generally and rightly regarded as improper for a church to govern a university in a way which requires that the members of the universities should adhere to or at least submit to the articles of faith of the parent or founding body. It would be contrary to the responsibilities which are incumbent on a university if it were, as a corporate body, to adopt a theological position. It is indeed one of the achievements of universities to have succeeded in gaining release from such a necessity and to concentrate their powers on the service of the ideal of truth, rationally and methodically pursued, and in transmitting the truths so gained by themselves, their colleagues, and ancestors to those who seek them. The university is not a church, whatever the religious beliefs of its individual members. Churches have their very legitimate tasks but their tasks are not the tasks of universities.

These observations are very pertinent to the obligations of universities as corporate bodies. Their obligations and responsibilities are for research and teaching; these touch on political matters in many ways but the fundamental point is that universities are not political institutions. Their standards and objectives are not political. That is why they are justified in not being subjected to political or other nonintellectual criteria in appointments in method of teaching, in the mode of conduct of research, in the publication of results, or in determination of the policies necessary for the realization of their primary obligations. They are not entitled and should not be required to take political positions on any matters which do not directly affect the performance of their primary intellectual obligations of inquiry, teaching, and training.

So much for the corporate obligations of the university with regard to matters in public contention. The situation is different when it comes to the political activities of individual members of the university. University teachers are citizens and they have the rights and obligations of citizens to espouse whatever ends they believe right and to contend for them within the limits of the law. But they also have a special obligation outside the university and that is to conduct their political activities in a civil manner. This is an obligation of all citizens but it is especially incumbent on academics who, for good or poor reasons, claim, or at least accept, special prominence on the grounds that their views are founded on dispassionate study and careful reflection. To do otherwise is to exploit the respect which is accorded to universities, while being unfaithful to the ideal for which they are respected.

Within the universities their obligations are to teach and to do research, in varying proportions, and not to promote their political beliefs. I know that this is not an easy matter to apply, especially in the social sciences, but the principle is clear and, in particular situations, it is also clear when the boundary is exceeded. Even in the social sciences it is not too difficult to respect this distinction.

Individual academics have as their primary obligation within the university fidelity to the standard of truthfulness, of strenuous exertion and intellectual scrupulousness. This applies in teaching, as I have just said. It applies in research; this goes without saying. It applies in the assessment of the intellectual merits of candidates for appointment and promotion. If academics wish to be free of intrusions from outside the university in the making of appointments, they have to show themselves worthy of the trust which this claim implies. The claims of ethnic or social origin, of sex, of political sympathy, of friendship and of mere seniority or presence and of patronage must be studiously expelled from all consideration when appointments and promotions are discussed and decided. This follows automatically from the commitment of universities to the ideal realm of the understanding of the world, of man and his works. Anything less is treason.

VIII

The federal government of the United States launched itself about a third of a century ago, unthinkingly and with the best of intentions, on a course which should be modified. It found the universities of the country ready to hand and it thought that they were ideal instruments for many of its newly found purposes. As it added new purposes to its program, it sought to use the universities for those purposes as well. The universities had not come into existence for those purposes; the universities existed before the government began to pursue those purposes. The government only thought of those purposes and regarded the universities as no more than an instrument.

In its first delight, the government was very pleased with its adaptable and productive instrument. It made more demands of it but all the while the instrument was not completely absorbed into the tasks laid upon it by the government. There were zones of activity within the universities into which the government did not penetrate, to which it contributed little, from which it demanded little, at least explicitly, and from which it nonetheless benefited greatly. It did not acknowledge these benefits. In the course of time, as it took on new purposes, the government became aware of the possibilities for its new purposes of these hitherto disregarded zones. It paid no attention to what was done in these zones, it cared nothing for them except insofar as they could be used for its own purposes.

The government became frozen in its posture of demandingness. It began to think—contrary to tradition and constitutional custom—that its own purposes should override all other purposes in society. This is a very dangerous course and it is injuring the pattern of consensus and collaboration of autonomous institutions so necessary for the common good. It is a course which breeds distrust among institutions.

Universities were not placed on earth for the service of government. They have served the purposes of governments well but they have always, whenever they were vital and productive, had their own purposes, which were the practice of science and scholarship and the transmission of learning to the most talented and ambitious of the young generation of their society. When government comes to think that the purposes it espouses are the only purposes worth fulfillment, it is undoing its own good work and affronts the common good. It arouses more distrust than is beneficial to society.

American society today is beset by mistrust. The ordinary citizen distrusts his government—while demanding more and more from it. There is distrust of the police, distrust of businessmen, distrust of the "industrial-military complex," distrust of lawyers and physicians. Intellectuals distrust professional politicians. The government for its part distrusts the family, municipal governments, the medical profession, businessmen and the universities. This is a situation which cannot go on without adding to the burdens of life in our society, making it more difficult for every section of society and for every institution to do what it is best qualified to do.

The division of labor among institutions and occupations and the exchanges of services among them, all so necessary for our society, presuppose and require mutual confidence. The relationship between Caesar and the universities requires not only that the universities should provide for Caesar—and society—the service which their consecration to intellectual things qualifies them to provide. It also requires a fundamental confidence in and respect for Caesar. But these will not be forthcoming unless Caesar recognizes the nature of the universities, enables them to maintain the institutional foundations of the traditions which produce the services of research and teaching he desires from them, and shows in them the confidence they merit and must have.

But to bring Caesar to appreciation is a slow process. An indispensable element in the process is the universities' consecration to their own imminent ideal. Self-respect, self-discipline, and self-restraint in the universities will bring with them confidence, respect, and self-restraint on the part of Caesar. These are the things they owe to themselves and to their traditions and to their ideal. By attending to what they owe to their ideal, they will also give Caesar not all that he demands but what he is entitled to have and can justly demand.

The Idea of the University: Obstacles and Opportunities in Contemporary Societies

I

There are odd goings on in American universities. Quasi-professional football, pre-professional basketball, the teaching of acting, creative writing, and remedial reading for students, training in ethnic sensitivity for teachers, and the like. All these oddities and many others notwithstanding, the idea of the university which still prevails is that propounded by Wilhelm von Humboldt about 180 years ago.

Humboldt conceived of the university as an institution of research and teaching. He very explicitly declared the unity of teaching and research. He also required the freedom of teaching. While he was a liberal, he was also a Prussian official who thought that the university was an institution of the state. Nonetheless, he thought that teachers must be free to teach in accordance with their studiously and rationally arrived at convictions. The principles of the unity of research and teaching and of the freedom of teaching were both clearly enunciated by Humboldt in his memoir "Über die innere und äussere Organisation der höheren wissenschaftlichen Anstalten zu Berlin."[1] They became guiding maxims of the German universities. The principle of university self-administration (*akademische Selbstverwaltung*) was not put forward by Humboldt, although he wanted the state to forbear from intrusion into academic matters as had been commonly done in Germany in the eigh-

Reprinted with permission of Kluwer Academic Publishers from *Minerva* XXX/2 (Summer 1992): 301–13.

1. Published in English translation as "On the Spirit and Organisational Framework of Intellectual Institutions in Berlin," in "University Reform in Germany," Reports and Documents, *Minerva* VIII (April 1970): 242–50.

teenth century. Despite his reserve or silence on this matter, I think that academic self-administration was the only practicable alternative to governmental control.

Humboldt did not imagine his principles out of nothing. He was drawing on the achievements of the great European universities from the twelfth century onwards—from the University of Bologna to the Universities of Leiden and Utrecht in the Netherlands and the Universities of Göttingen and Halle in Germany. He was also writing against a strong current of opinion in Germany which favored the abolition of universities and their replacement for teaching and training purposes by specialized professional schools—as Napoleon had done in France—and by concentrating research in academies or learned societies.

Humboldt did not think that a university was either a machine for producing professional persons—lawyers, civil servants, engineers, and physicians—for which there was an effective (mainly governmental) demand, or for turning out scientific knowledge. He thought that fundamental to both of these was the cultivation of the ideal of the pursuit of truth and the ordering of life around that pursuit.

Only Wilhelm von Humboldt ever formulated so clearly those properties of a university which could be conducive to the effective discovery, transmission, and reception of truth—of particular truths which shared in the dignity of the ideal of truth in general. No one else except Humboldt ever left such a deep mark on a particular university and then on the universities which followed thereafter. The University of Berlin, which was formed as the realization of Humboldt's proposal, was different even from its greatest predecessors—but it was also like them in its insistence on the crucial importance of methodical investigation, and systematic teaching of serious matters on the basis of the result of that methodical investigation. The founding of the University of Berlin in 1810 was a turning point in the history of universities. Nearly all universities that were founded subsequently were profoundly marked by the type of university of which the University of Berlin was the first example. Nearly all universities which already existed underwent changes in the direction of that example.

Humboldt's postulated and implied properties of a university remain the fundamental postulates of universities wherever they are. Sometimes the postulates are more proclaimed than they are adhered to in practice; they are overlaid with many other ideas of what universities should be. The fact is that whatever deformations the Humboldtian postulates have undergone in the one and three-quarter centuries since they were first promulgated, they still constitute our idea of what a university should be.

But even the departures in practice are connected with their persistence. Indeed, when departures from the Humboldtian pattern take place, they are justified by making it appear as if they are not departures but only applications.

Some of the difficulties which afflict our universities at present may be traced in part to this persistent adherence to the Humboldtian pattern. For example, the surfeit of uninteresting research in certain fields is attributable to the steadfastness with which the Humboldtian principle of the unity of teaching and research persists in our present academic practices.

The widespread acceptance of the requirement of possession of a doctorate, awarded on the basis of achievement in research as a condition of appointment to a teaching position, is in the Humboldtian tradition. Reappointment and promotion require evidence of achievement in research assessed by the number of the candidates' publications. It has become clear that in certain fields, like English literature, there is more research than ought to be done, there is more research that can be done with intellectually valuable results, which enrich the minds of the investigator and of the reader of those results in published form. It persists nonetheless, with harmful effects, and I do not see how it can be stopped. Alternatives have been suggested which would change the requirements for the award of the doctorate, but they have been without effect. Grave disorders in the humanistic subjects are repercussions of this requirement. The malformations of universities testify to this clinging to the Humboldtian postulate of the unity of teaching and research.

Freedom of teaching, the freedom to teach in accordance with one's intellectual convictions, has persisted. No one would disavow it. It has become a dogma of the academic profession. In liberal-democratic societies, governments lean over backwards to avoid any charge that they do not respect the freedom of their teachers to teach and investigate as they see fit. The governing bodies and administrators of universities do the same.

Similarly, the idea of university self-government persists as an ideal, in the face of the temptations and necessities of large sums of money for research, which would locate authority outside the universities. There are infringements on this ideal, and it is possible that they will become more numerous as universities seek income from the discoveries and inventions of their scientists and enter into joint ventures with business firms. I refer here to the creation of research institutes which are parts of universities, but which are under the joint control of a university and a body external to the university; in such institutes, academic appointments do not lie entirely within the powers of the university. The criticism of such ventures is evidence that the ideal of university self-government has not lost its vitality. It must be recognized that Humboldt and those who accepted his implicit principle of university self-government also accepted the governmental approval of academic appointments. The idea of academic self-government has, in fact, moved so far that the power of administrators, presidents, provosts, and deans and heads of departments in the making of decisions in academic matters has been greatly reduced. The ideal of university self-government originally meant freedom from governmental control in academic matters; it now has come to mean control by the teaching staffs of departments.

II

The Humboldtian university has been a very great success. The extraordinary efflorescence of science and scholarship in the German universities, and their movement into a central position in German society in the century between the realization of Humboldt's idea of the university in the University of Berlin and the First World War are certainly to a considerable extent a consequence of the firm implantation of his ideas about what a university should be. The improvement of the British and French universities of the last quarter of the nineteenth century was a response to the achievement of the Humboldtian universities in Germany. In some cases, that improvement has been a consequence of the adoption of some aspects of the German pattern. In other cases, it has been a response to the challenge presented by the achievements of the German universities and the impetus which that challenge gave to national pride and imagination and the fear of being left behind. The transformation of American higher education, beginning with the formation of Johns Hopkins University in 1875, is too well known to need reiteration here. It was clearly an effort to implant, in the United States, the idea of a university like that was embodied in the German Humboldtian university.

The status of universities in society has also changed markedly and that has occurred partly in consequence of the triumphs of the Humboldtian idea of the university in the creation of new knowledge and in the education of young persons. From having been wards of a particular church, the universities have to a large extent supplanted the churches. The prestige of universities has grown throughout modern societies. From having been small institutions, with places only for a tiny percentage of the young persons from the upper and middle classes of every

European country and North America, they have reached the point where attendance at a university—or in the United States, a college—has become a norm by which societies are assessed. There have been forceful and, on the whole, successful demands for education at a university—or an approximation to a university—to be available to all young persons who aspire to it and who have the necessary formal qualifications for it.

The expansion of the European and later the North American pattern of the university to Asia, Africa, and South America has been the expansion of the Humboldtian idea of the university. Where the model was originally the British model exemplified in Oxford and Cambridge, or the Spanish model exemplified in the University of Salamanca, it has had, superimposed on it, the Humboldtian model. So it was in the United States and in the British colonies and dominions. Where the model was the French university, it was one which included the changes wrought in French universities in response to the challenge of the German universities in the second half of the nineteenth century.

Scientific research has become indissolubly wedded to universities. This remains so, even though the total amount of research done outside universities in independent research institutes and governmental and industrial research laboratories has increased so markedly. The scientific knowledge produced in universities has become a prominent object of public opinion. This was not an intention of Humboldt, but it is a consequence of his fateful memorandum.

The Humboldtian idea of the university, by providing a model and a standard for emulation, has indeed in this and many other ways helped to change the world, for better or worse.

III

Yet, despite its triumphs, the Humboldtian university is in danger of submergence.

It is often said, particularly in Germany, that there is no longer any prospect for the survival of the "Humboldt university." It is pointed out that the mass university is the antithesis of the "Humboldt university," which it was taken for granted was a small university. Some of the most eminent German universities had only five hundred students in the last decade of the nineteenth century; the University of Berlin—the Humboldtian university par excellence—was called a *Riesenuniversität,* when before the First World War it had about eight thousand students. A university of twenty thousand or thirty thousand or forty thousand students seems to be entirely incompatible with the principle of the Humboldtian university, which aimed at the formation of character through the experience of research.

Against the existence of the "mass university," with all its obstacles to the fulfillment of the Humboldtian idea of the university, the principle of the unity of teaching and research is still defended. Several recent surveys of academic opinion in Germany disclose that most teachers wish to adhere to it, despite the difficulties. It has been, until recently, unchallenged in Great Britain, while in France, governmental science policy persists in its tradition of placing much research outside the universities. It is, as I have remarked earlier, still espoused in the United States, although the practice departs from the ideal.

It is well known that many university teachers in the United States are reluctant to teach undergraduates; they are, generally, very ready to supervise the dissertations of doctoral candidates because that does not interfere with what they regard as their first, perhaps even sole, obligation—namely, research. At the other end of the academic hierarchy, the ideal is affronted by the existence of great numbers of teaching assistants, students for the doctorate who are supposed to be working on their doctoral dissertations but whose time and energy are demanded by teaching. Then there are those multitudes of teachers who, once they are appointed, do little or no research and very seldom if ever publish a scientific or learned paper. The last group like the first testify to the less than universal observance of the Humboldtian principle of the unity of teaching and research. The group which does little research, while representing a departure from the principle of the unity of teaching and research, at the same time offers evidence of the continuing persistence of the principle. The persistence of the principle is manifested in the fact that many of those who do no research feel inferior to those who do; they thereby proclaim their belief in the rightfulness of the Humboldtian principle that those who do research in universities should also teach and those who teach should do research. These however are only sentiments and beliefs. In practice, there are many departures from the Humboldtian ideal of the unity of teaching and research.

There are also other developments which are strains on the Humboldtian idea of the university. These strains have not obliterated the ideal, but they have constrained its practice.

IV

The world is now more complicated than it was in Humboldt's time, although it was not all that simple even then. The stock of knowledge has increased beyond what Humboldt conceived; the numbers of universities, students, teachers, and investigators have all increased to an extent unforeseen and unforeseeable in 1810. The universities have become much more differentiated internally and more bureaucratized, as Max Weber observed about seventy-five years ago. Not less significant is the multiplication, complication, and intensification of the relations between universities, governments, business firms, and civil organizations. When Humboldt wrote his memorandum, the scientific knowledge discovered in universities scarcely moved at all into application to practical affairs; that process began only several decades later.

Technology has increasingly acquired a scientific content. As a result, academic science—fundamental science carried on in universities—has become more interesting to managers and technologists engaged in industrial and commercial activities. This has brought the universities and industrial and other business enterprises closer to each other. Businessmen, technologists, and administrators of health services, farmers and agricultural administrators are now more eager to know and use and to support and cultivate the knowledge produced in academic laboratories.

Something recognizably similar has occurred in the activities of government—legislative, administrative, military, educational, medical, etc.—in relation to the social science research done in universities. The capacities for relatively exact descriptive social research on contemporary social conditions have advanced unmistakably in the last half-century. The various branches of government have become very eager to have the kinds of concrete descriptive information and the relatively concrete interpretations of causal connections which are produced by social research. The data produced by census bureaus and by departments of agriculture, industry, and commerce from the reports which enterprises submit regularly are not looked upon as sufficient for the ambitious activities of governments. They want more knowledge than these official reports provide. That is why they commission research to be done by university teachers of the social sciences. Much of this research could probably be carried out by governments themselves, but the availability of university teachers and their graduates has led governments to support university teachers to perform such research while they continue their work as teachers, research workers, and supervisors of doctoral dissertations within universities.

How much and in what way this knowledge produced by academic social research is "used" by governments is unknown. The important thing here is that the governments want to have it and are willing to pay for it, either through direct commissions, by contracts, or by grants through the various grant-awarding agencies of government for research proposed by academics, individually or as groups. Here too, one of the results is a more intimate intertwinement of governments and universities.

Governments are even more eager—much more eager—to have the results of research in the natural sciences. They are prepared to allocate unprecedentedly large sums to pay for research and to train young scientists.

Universities have become correspondingly more dependent on payments for research by governments. The academic physical sciences, biological and medical sciences and the social sciences, live to a large extent on the financial support of government for their research. This is as true of public universities as of private universities. It is as true of continental European universities which have traditionally been state universities as it is of British and American universities. In the American universities, the public universities have been supported by the separate states, while the private universities have been supported from their endowments, the gifts of private philanthropists, either as individuals or as foundations, and from the fees paid by students. In both the state and private universities, which were before the Second World War untouched except marginally by the policies of the federal government, the latter has now come to be a major source of funds. But even the financial support of central governments has been insufficient to pay for all the research which university teachers wish to do.

In Great Britain, the decision of the government to limit its support has heightened the necessity for universities to embrace whatever opportunities can be discovered to engage in close relations with private industry in order to gain additional revenue. The same is true in the United States where part of the payments made by government for research is taken by the universities as "overhead costs"; funds acquired in this way are used by the universities for their other activities. Such charges for "overhead costs" are necessary for the universities. This does not obtain in the European universities, either British or Continental.

In the humanistic subjects, in which in the past research was done by individuals on projects on a small scale, and which was supported with small philanthropic gifts and from the teachers' own salary, the increased frequency of large projects—learned editions, dictionaries, etc.—has also increased the demand for governmental support. In France and Germany, such funds have been provided by the Centre national de la recherche scientifique and the Deutsche Forschungsgemeinschaft; in Germany, these funds are supplemented by grants from private philanthropic foundations. In the United States, the establishment of the National Endowment of the Humanities has linked academic research more closely with government, but since such research in humanistic subjects does not ordinarily offer any prospect of practical applications, the pattern of relationships between government and the humanistic parts of universities is less intense, although far more elaborate and intimate than it used to be.

In all these instances, one common result is an increase in the amount of administrative activities within universities. The size of university administrations has grown disproportionally. Whereas in the past, university administration was largely performed by university teachers and by quondam university teachers, not by full-time administrators, this situation has changed since the Second World War. Careers are now made in university administration.

Other developments in universities have also contributed to their internal bureaucratization. Although the rule of *in loco parentis* has practically disappeared from British and American universities—it has generally been absent from continental European universities—the scale of services for students such as medical, dental, psychiatric, recreational, vocational counselling and employment services, etc., have multiplied and, with them, the number of administrative employees. Universities in the United States, and latterly in Great Britain, also have considerable staffs for soliciting funds from graduates and from philanthropic sources. (In the United States, these are called "development offices.") Closely connected with this is a concern for the "public image" of universities, which has meant officers and staffs to maintain good relations with the press and to foster publicity for the achievements of universities.

Some of the internal bureaucratization of the universities is a consequence of the more far-flung and more penetrating impingement of government on universities. Universities are scrutinized, ranked, cajoled and threatened by governments.

In the Netherlands, the government has intruded rather penetratingly into the internal affairs of the universities, even to the point of attempting to regulate the number of hours which teachers must and may spend in the buildings of the university. On the Continent the universities are governed, to a greater extent than was the case until several decades ago, in accordance with prescriptions laid down by the central government. I cite as an example the *Rahmengesetz* of the German Federal Republic.

The American federal government, in a way which is unique, has also intruded into the affairs of universities in matters of appointment. A presidential executive order, No. 11246 of 1965, has required that there be no discrimination with respect to race or sex in any institution having contractual relations with the federal government. When applied to universities, which receive grants and other financial support from the federal government, this had led to marked intrusions by the federal government. It has been called "affirmative action"; sometimes it is called "reverse discrimination"—an ugly usage, but a more accurate description. Universities have been required to show that they have not discriminated in the appointment of blacks, Puerto Ricans, women, etc. Although defenders of the policy have repeatedly asserted that this has not required the setting of numerical quotas, that has in fact been the standard by which the achievement of a university in the avoidance of discrimination has been assessed. At first, there were some open conflicts between the universities and the government, which withheld or threatened to withhold payments for research, whether as grants or on contracts; the agents of the federal Department of Labor exercised close and not always reasonable scrutiny of the records of universities. These conflicts have since ebbed. Some universities, often under the prodding of the "affirmative action" officers whom they have appointed to give evidence of their *bona fides,* have indeed established quotas. (Duke University is one of these; so is the University of Wisconsin.)

Conflicts within universities have been endemic but they usually smoldered or were pushed aside by other conflicts. They were seldom the subject of appeal to the courts. The courts usually refused to claim jurisdiction in university affairs. In more recent years, however, the judiciary has intruded into the affairs of universities to a greater extent than previously; this has been particularly the case in the United States. In the German Federal Republic, the federal high court confirmed the *Gruppenuniversität.*

None of these developments was foreseen by Humboldt. His idea of the university made no provision for them. Although he expected government to provide the financial support needed by universities, and agreed that the training of civil servants had to be done in universities, he certainly did not anticipate the complexity, intimacy, and intrusiveness which has since developed in all liberal-democratic societies. His principles—both those which he made explicit and those which remained implicit—still obtain, but under constricted conditions.

V

Thus, the universities, driven by financial necessities, governmental compulsion, the natural development of their intellectual interests, and the growing differentiation and specialization of their intellectual interests, and by the changed relationship between fundamental scientific discovery and technology—to say nothing of the changes in public opinion—have found themselves in a situation very different from the *Freiheit und Einsamkeit,* i.e., the freedom from political interference and from distraction which Humboldt thought of as the condition needed for fruitful learning and discovery and which he thought should prevail in universities.

The universities have been so successful in following the course which Humboldt prescribed for them that they have come into a situation very different from that faced by the University of Berlin when it was formed in the light of his memorandum. Many of the features of this new situation have been created by the success of the universities in carrying out just those tasks which they were set on the path of doing. The new situation, which is thus partly of their own making, has been made possible by the essential spirit of the Humboldtian university which is the love of truth, sought by exigent methods. The universities and their societies and governments are more dependent on each other than ever before. Neither the universities nor governments can get along without each other; neither the universities nor their societies can get along without each other.

In the course of their development in the present century, universities have changed nearly out of recognition. They have not gone the whole way yet. If they do, they will cease to be universities, except in name. They will cease to nurture and inculcate the moral and intellectual standards and aptitudes indispensable to research; they will cease to deal with fundamental problems for their intrinsic interest. If they complete their departure from the Humboldtian ideal, they will become more broken up into specialized institutes, departments, and research projects, often connected only in name with each other through their common legal membership in the university.

VI

This is the way the world is. The external situation of universities is not likely to change its directions. Student numbers might not continue to increase at the same rate as they have done since the Second World War, but they certainly will not decline. The activities of government, even if they cease to expand as they have done for nearly a century, are certainly not going to be reduced to the level of the period between the two world wars. The clamor for welfare services will not grow fainter; the cognitive inquisitiveness of governments is unlikely to diminish. The sophistication of the costs of research is an uncertain factor, but is unlikely to grow more slowly; the technology of research becomes more and more expensive. Nuclear research and radioastronomy, which take such a considerable percentage of the "science budget" of most of the major scientific powers, will probably not become less expensive.

The universities, if they are to protect themselves by keeping their best scientists, their best professors of law, medicine, engineering, and economics within the academic profession, will have to pay them salaries not far below, if not equal to, what they could receive in private practice or private employment. In their competition for students in the United States, and particularly for students from the "minorities," more money will be needed for amenities, services, and scholarships.

None of these things is likely to change as long as the universities are thought by their societies and their governments to be so important. Large sums of money will be forthcoming, although not in quantities large enough to satisfy the desires of university administrators and teachers. With those large sums, universities will continue to do many of the things which are asked of them. The question which should be asked is: what will happen to the universities when they are so engaged in meeting the demands of their societies? My answer is that the universities must be alert to save their own souls. By this, I mean that they must remain universities. They must be careful to avoid disaggregation. They must avoid being drawn by the powerful centrifugal forces which they themselves have generated and encouraged, further and further from what is central, namely, the pursuit and transmission of fundamental knowledge in all the fields of science and learning. These are the defining functions of the university.

Thanks to Humboldt's imaginative coupling of research and teaching, the universities have become powerful devices for the creation of new knowledge and for the multiplication of its future creators. If the universities reduce their performance of the latter function, they will run down their own capacity and that of other types of scientific institutions to perform the former function as well.

There might come a time when the fraction of research done in universities by active university teachers will be only a very small part of all the research done in any advanced society. There is already a movement in that direction, but if the movement culminates in the nearly complete removal of research to places outside universities, the continued growth of knowledge will be obstructed and broken because there will be very few scientists to carry forward from points already reached. There will be no *Nachwuchs,* because there will be practically no scientific training. On this point Humboldt's program is as valid as it ever was. Scientific teaching can only be done by experience in research, the experience of the teacher and the experience of the pupil. Every subject must be taught in the context of research. Otherwise, it becomes a litany of settled and accepted propositions which raise no problems for further investigation.

Of course, it may be said—there are some persons who already say—that more research can be done if scientists are relieved of the distractions of teaching. As for the training of future scientists, they say that can be done in independent governmental and industrial research laboratories. This is only partly true. (I cite the experience of the Bell Telephone Laboratory when its very distinguished staff members tried to develop the quantum theory of solids by seminars within the laboratory; they had in the end to go to Columbia University and study the most advanced basic science needed for their purpose.)

The university is a place especially endowed for the training of scientists because it offers knowledge of many different fields. It offers that knowledge over a wide range and therefore, despite all the excesses, both necessary and avoidable, of specialization, the various subjects are adjacent to each other, not only intellectually but spatially. To learn any particular subject in the context of other subjects has had an effect of broadening the imagination which is needed to open up new fields of inquiry. Molecular biology could be created only on the basis of the study of physics, chemistry, and genetics. Separate institutes dealing concentratedly with each of these subjects could not have performed the functions of a university.

Study in a university, in the presence of persons teaching, studying and investigating a large variety of subjects, helps to precipitate and maintain the academic and scientific ethos. One of the main functions of the university is to instill the academic and the scientific ethos. This was one of the things that Humboldt had in mind when he spoke of the formation of character by research in the setting of a university. Where teaching and supervision are neglected, and where all that an aspirant young scientist does is to run the "rat race," there is no scientific ethical inhibition placed against his ambition.

Fraud in research is in large measure a result of this failure of the scientific ethic, and it is a consequence of the failure of the excessively busy older generation of scientists to inculcate it into the young. I certainly do not mean to say that this failure of inculcation is a result only of specialization and busywork which separate the teacher from the pupil. I do not mean to say that the maintenance of the traditional combination of teaching and research will always avoid it. I do not mean to say that separation of research from teaching will result in boundless dishonesty in research, while the maintenance of the traditional Humboldtian principle will avoid all traces of dishonesty in research. After all, the cases which have recently been brought to public attention have occurred in a period when the separation has by no means been thoroughgoing. Nevertheless, the cases should be seen against the background of large laboratories in which the superiors were so preoccupied with many different projects that they could devote little time to any one of them or to any one of their investigators. It should be pointed out that the malpractices were committed by persons trained in the period after the Second World War when research and teaching began to draw apart, in consequence of the increase in the number and size of research projects.

It is not, however, only the scientific and academic ethics which are being endangered. The danger threatens the concentration of the minds of academic scientists on phenomena and problems freely chosen for their intrinsic intellectual interest and investigated to discover their nature and interconnections, and without regard to their practical utility or profitability.

The enmeshing of the research done in universities with the interests of practical institutions can have a distracting influence. It can offer larger financial rewards to the individual, more resources for research, and the gratitude and appreciation of administrative superiors for "bringing in money," etc. The desire for publicity and, hence, fame—at least for a short time—can be another distraction to the minds of academics in the present circumstances of universities.

VII

The topic on which I have been asked to speak refers to "opportunities" and "obstacles." In certain respects, the opportunities are themselves obstacles to the idea of the university and its fulfillment.

The opportunities for universities to serve society in a great variety of ways are numerous and are unlikely to diminish. These opportunities entail increased activity in research, large student bodies, large teaching staffs and more participation by academics in the activities of external institutions. These opportunities are seized upon by universities; they increase their revenues and they offer occasions for public service and interesting and financially rewarding services to society and government. Except, however, for the increased numbers of students and teachers, they are not central to the existence of universities. They are diversions from the primary tasks of universities. It is a task for the universities to decide how many of these opportunities are conducive to the realization of the ideal of the university, i.e., to what is essential to their existence as universities.

The obstacles I have referred to are mainly external obstacles; the opportunities likewise. But what of the interior of the university? For it is upon the interior of the university that depends whatever can be preserved and restored of the Humboldtian principles, of the unity of teaching and research, of academic freedom and academic self-government, of freedom from distraction, and of the ends of discovery and the ethos of discovery. The situation is not entirely favorable.

University teaching staffs have embraced with open arms the opportunities which have been generated by the success of the Humboldtian university. They have benefited to a great extent from the conditions generated by the Humboldtian university, especially the freedom of inquiry and the appreciation of research. They have also benefited from academic self-government and interpreted it to mean departmental and individual self-government. They have allowed the university as such to look after itself. They do not see that their achievements were made possible by the fact that they were made in the setting of a university, which is more than an administrative facility. They have left the university as such in the hands of presidents and administrators whom they do not usually esteem.

Presidents were once powerful and imperious figures, usually supported by their boards of trustees and rendered self-confident by that support. Provosts and deans were small-scale presidents, chosen and appointed by presidents, and they enjoyed self-confidence because of their confidence in the president's support. I think that Robert Maynard Hutchins was the last such president, and he came early to grief in his attempt to do what great presidents had previously done without any difficulty, namely, appoint a professor to a department on his own initiative.

The new generation of presidents are of a different breed. They are usually far from imperious; and, in view of the incessant and urgent demand for money, they have to spend much of their time in seeking it. They have become the victims of academic self-government in its latest form of departmental self-government. In strong and able departments, this is beneficial to discovery, although not always equally so to teaching. In weak departments and departments in weak disciplines or disciplines in crisis, such as the study of modern literatures, the results of departmental self-government are not at all beneficial to scholarship or teaching or to the university as a whole.

Under better conditions, the president of a university could act as a balance wheel, or as a governor to slow down the process of disaggregation of the university as a whole and of the reign of proud frivolity in fields in which no intellectually valuable work is being done. Contemporary presidents, in so far as they are not wholly diverted to the financial side of the university, do nothing—perhaps they cannot do anything—to halt the active efforts of certain parts of their faculties to saw off the branch on which they themselves are sitting, perhaps even to saw down the tree of knowledge on which the entire university sits.

One seldom hears of a university president who would call a halt to this effort to discredit scientific and scholarly knowledge. Rather one comes across efforts by presidents to boast of the immense salaries which they are able to pay to attract such characters to their universities.

Now university presidents usually acquire some common sense in the course of their duties. They usually know better—with half their minds—than to believe the nonsensical things which the expensive prima donnas of their English or other departments so confidently assert. But they would never allow their better judgment to be expressed. It would be too disagreeable for them to be denounced as reactionaries or tyrants, as agents of a corrupt and power-seeking ruling class. Instead they act like Benito Cereno.

The Modern University and Liberal Democracy

At a time when the governments of liberal-democratic societies attribute so much importance to universities, and when many publicists and university administrators and teachers respond symmetrically, it is desirable to give some thought to the relations between liberal-democratic societies and universities.

The first thing to be said is that the university as a particular type of institution is not a creation of liberal-democratic society. If we take the long stretch of seven centuries when universities became integral parts of European countries, and when despite numerous ups and downs in their achievements, they had many achievements in science and learning to their credit, it is obvious that the period of their establishment was not a period of liberal democracy. Some of the distinctive features of universities—of the universities of the past century and a half as well as those of earlier centuries—were settled in these early centuries. Instruction at an advanced level, the pursuit and transmission of fundamental truths, institutional autonomy and financial support by external powers, are now in practice and at least in declaration, characteristic of universities everywhere. These features were certainly fixed long before the emergence of the liberal-democratic order which took root over the past two centuries. They were the creations of the medieval and early modern churches, absolutist monarchies and empires, princely states and oligarchical municipalities, and commercial republics.

The Impact of Liberal Ideas on Universities

The American universities and the American colleges which later became universities—for example, Harvard, Yale and Princeton—unlike the great European universities, were all founded in a time when what we now call liberal ideas were being much discussed by philosophers

Reprinted with permission of Kluwer Academic Publishers from *Minerva* XXVII/4 (Winter 1989): 426–60.

and publicists. Nevertheless, the ideas which presided over the founding of American universities and colleges in the earliest years of the eighteenth century were not the ideas of liberal democracy. The private colleges established before the Revolutionary War and the formation of the United States were not intended to serve a liberal democracy. They were intended to instruct young men who would enter the clergy or who might play a part of significance in oligarchical colonial societies. Neither in their course of study, nor in their policy of recruitment, nor in the careers towards which they sought to guide the youths who were under their care, did they think of a democratic society. There was no expectation that colleges and universities would educate a large part of the generation between the ages of fifteen and twenty-two, nor was there any intention that the institutions of higher education in the colonial period would take their places as exemplars or propagators of liberal ideals. There certainly was no notion that they would enable their graduates to contribute to the wealth of their society. Fragmentary approximations began to appear in the eighteenth century. The universities and colleges of the newly independent United States offered curricula which were much influenced by the undergraduate courses of study at the ancient British universities, teaching mainly mathematics and classics. They did not regard the classics as subjects contributing to the training of citizens of a liberal society, although the study of Cicero, Aristotle, and Locke did help to form the minds of the founders of the republic.

The American colleges and universities began to introduce subjects drawn from the Scottish universities—moral philosophy, political economy and the history of civilization. In this way they were affected by the Scottish Enlightenment. The first opening of American higher education to liberal ideas came with the establishment of the University of Virginia by Thomas Jefferson. (Jefferson had recruited and appointed teachers from Scotland. Some of these later returned to University College London, thus bringing to that college, which was already under Benthamite influence, Scottish ideas about higher education admixed with Jeffersonian liberal rationalism.) The writings of Adam Smith began to appear in the syllabuses of the American colleges and universities. With them came a breath of European liberalism in its beginnings.

Liberal Scepticism about Universities

Liberal thinkers did not have an especially high opinion of universities, nor did they think that they had any great part to play in liberal society.

In France, neither Tocqueville nor Constant thought seriously about universities, and they had no great expectations that they would contribute much to the effective operation of free institutions. In Scotland, Adam Smith had a rather low opinion of universities and university teachers, although he was a university teacher for a great part of his life. He certainly did not regard universities as the intellectual engines of liberal society. John Stuart Mill did not expect any great help for liberalism or democracy from universities. (Von Humboldt's ideas about the *Grenzen der Wirksamkeit des Staates* were taken up in part by John Stuart Mill in his *Essay on Liberty,* but not his ideas about universities.)

The vocation of the university was differently seen in Germany. Belief in the formation of the character of cultivated autonomous individuals was much more the product of idealistic German philosophical thought. Fichte's idea of "the calling of the scholar" could be said to be a liberal idea, but it did not envisage the individual as a citizen in a liberal society as much as it did the individual as an end in himself. Freedom was necessary for the development of character, of a harmonious whole within the individual, rather than as a condition which would enable the individual to pursue his own freely chosen ends by the use of his own reasoning powers and his own cognitive assessment of the situation of his action.

The first influence of liberalism in European universities occurred with Wilhelm von Humboldt's memorandum on "the state of our learned institutions" from which emerged the University of Berlin. The liberalism expressed in the memorandum was the idealistic liberalism which looked to the universities for the formation of the character of the autonomous cultivated individual. The ideals of the unity of research and teaching *(Einheit der Forschung und Lehre),* the freedom of teaching and learning *(Freiheit der Lehre und des Lernens)* and of academic self-government *(akademische Selbstverwaltung),* were liberal ideals but they were not products of the individualistic liberalism of British provenience. Von Humboldt did not think of the practical utility of what is discovered and taught in universities, although he took for granted that they would produce higher civil servants educated in law. Nor did he think of universities as providing training for civility in the leadership of society. The highest good to which universities would contribute was the formation of individuality or character and the means to this was the disciplined, methodical search for truth, i.e., free and unhampered research. The ideal of academic freedom became an integral feature of universities of many countries in the nineteenth century, not least of those with quite a different tradition of liberalism.

Academic Freedom: Humboldtian and Benthamite Liberalism

The academic freedom which became a major part of the program and constitution of the German university was a different sort of thing from what academic freedom became much later in the United States. As propounded in Germany, it was intended to culminate in the realization of the autonomous character. For that, freedoms of the kind mentioned were necessary. It also required the civil or political freedom of academics, but that was not an end—only a means. The justification for the political freedom of the academic later became a most important element in the argument for academic freedom, when that ideal began to be discussed in American universities in the last two decades of the nineteenth century and throughout the twentieth century. This was a significant change in part of the substance of a tradition consequent on the shift from idealistic to rational-individualistic liberalism.

Another point of contact between liberalism—individualistic and utilitarian—and the foundation of universities is to be seen in the history of University College London. This institution was founded by the liberal utilitarians led by Lord Brougham and George Grote, the historian of Greek liberty—under the inspiration of Jeremy Bentham. One of the main intentions of the founding Benthamites was to offer higher education for the offspring of the professional and business classes at a lower cost than at Oxford and Cambridge. In so far as it was the intention of liberals to promote the middle classes, then the foundation of University College London could be said to have been a step in the direction of a liberal and to some extent democratic society. But the intention was not clear and unambiguous. University College London became the first institution of higher education in England to cultivate the full range of modern academic subjects, and its development was parallel to and in frequent contact with the German universities as they were developing in the nineteenth century under the influence of von Humboldt's liberal ideas and of the University of Berlin which embodied those ideas. University College London was a liberal institution also in the sense that it deliberately refused to have any requirements of subscription to any church or religious belief as a condition of admission as a student or appointment as a teacher.

State and Private Universities

In the United States, when the new republic launched itself on its career, state universities were formed mainly in the states (recently colonies) in which there were no dominant private established colleges. For example, Massachusetts, Connecticut, New Jersey, and New York had no state universities until very recently, since they already had Harvard College, Yale College, Princeton University and Columbia College (called King's College during the colonial period). The first state universities, formed in the southern seaboard states, were little different from privately founded and supported colleges. Private colleges and universities continued to be created in the United States throughout the nineteenth century, even in states which had state universities. In Great Britain, the major modern universities—London, Manchester, Birmingham, Leeds, and Liverpool—were founded by private initiative and they were also supported almost entirely by private patronage. Private patronage is still very important to American colleges and universities, even to some of the leading state universities.

Liberal-democratic societies are pluralistic societies; voluntary associations and free corporate bodies, privately founded and conducted, are parts of their constitutions. Yet the independent private creation of a university has, with the exceptions of the United States and Great Britain and territories which were once parts of the British Empire, been very rare. The Université libre de Bruxelles founded in 1834, the Vrije Universiteit of Amsterdam founded in 1880, the Libera università di Economia e Commercio "Luigi Bocconi" of Milan founded in 1902, probably had none to follow in their footsteps until the University College (University since 1983) of Buckingham in Great Britain founded in 1973, and several institutions in Western Germany.

It is sometimes thought that private universities and colleges in liberal-democratic societies enjoy a greater measure of autonomy and academic freedom than do universities which are supported by government and which are legally under the jurisdiction of the state. This would seem to be the case in principle. In fact, however, there are numerous exceptions. Although the modern British universities were private universities, in the sense that the term is understood in the United States, and their teachers have accordingly had exceptionally wide academic and civil freedoms, this was almost as true of the German universities—all of them state universities—from the foundation of the German Empire in 1871 until the accession of Hitler. In contrast with these, in the United States, there were some infringements of academic freedom and relatively numerous infringements of the civil freedom of college and university teachers, both in state and in private universities. The United States Constitution provided for the separation of church and state; many colleges and some universities were founded and governed by churches. In the institutions which were under ecclesiastical authority, there were many infringements on the freedom of their teachers in their teaching, their civil activities, and in their private affairs.

The investigative commissions established by legislative bodies have not hesitated to take private universities into their purview; of course, the private universities have been less susceptible to the sanctions of legislation—only a few of them have had the courage to resist the demand for restrictions on academic freedom.

Liberalism and the Development of Universities on the European Continent

Germany

The German academic profession in the first half of the nineteenth century was not only permeated by the liberal ideals of the freedom of research and teaching; it was also liberal in its public political activities. The liberalism of the "Göttingen seven," who were dismissed for their criticism of the unconstitutional activities of the King of Hanover in 1837, lived on in the German revolution of 1848 when, in the liberal parliament meeting in Frankfurt, about one third of the deputies were university professors.

After the unification of Germany in 1871, political liberalism faded from the German academic profession but the liberal ideals of the unity of research and teaching, of the freedom of teaching and study, and of academic self-government did not fade. They persisted undiminished. Even in the period of the Weimar Republic, when many German professors were hostile to the liberal-democratic republic, these particular ideals remained largely unimpaired.

So strong was the conviction of the dignity of scientific and scholarly knowledge that any derogation from its traditions was resisted. There were limits on the consistency with which this conviction was observed in practice. Before the First World War, socialists were not looked upon as fit to teach in a German university. Jews too were frowned upon when it came to university appointments. There were genuinely liberal professors who tried to undo this limitation on the primacy of strictly intellectual standards, but they were not successful. The situation in these respects changed under the Weimar Republic, but at the end of that period the German universities lost nearly all the virtues which they had acquired from universities of the age of absolutism and humanism and princely states, and from the idealistic liberalism of the neoclassical period. During this time, which ran for more than a century, the German universities maintained certain features which although not liberal in origin, became part of the tradition of universities in liberal-democratic societies.

It should be pointed out that the German universities at the height of their devotion to academic freedom never questioned that they were "institutions of the state," and that the government retained the final and definitive decision regarding appointments and the establishment of new subjects and new chairs. It was accepted by academics that the statutes and by-laws of the university lay within the province of government, and were not merely to be approved and enacted, but also to be promulgated by the government. In comparison with the situation of American and British universities, the autonomy of the German university was relatively restricted, and these restrictions were accepted. But the restrictions very seldom intruded into the freedom of teaching and research of a teacher once appointed. The cases of infringement of academic freedom in Germany were invariably infringements on the civil freedom of academics. One case is that of Theodor Lessing. Two cases of infringement on the civil freedom of academics involved *Privatdozenten* whose appointments were legally not under governmental jurisdiction at all; these were the cases of Leo Arons in the 1890s and of Ernst J. Gumbel in the 1920s.

France

The French universities did not enjoy the prerogatives conferred by liberalism, either before or after the Great Revolution. They progressed towards the freedom of research and teaching only very slowly. For much of the nineteenth century, the central ministerial authorities—French educational administration was very centralized—sought to deny the freedom of teaching to teachers in the provinces. They also denied the civil freedom of academics; university teachers who expressed political opinions distasteful to the government were dismissed.

Perhaps in response to these indignities, French academics in the second half of the nineteenth century became more and more demanding of academic freedom. Thus, whatever might have been the case among French academics previously, liberal attitudes became more common among them by the latter part of the century. When, in 1893, almost 104 intellectuals signed the letter drafted by Émile Zola—"*J'accuse*"—in support of the assertion of Captain Dreyfus's innocence, for publication in *l'Aurore*, about one third were academics, mainly in humanistic disciplines (including the social sciences). There were very few academics among the public supporters of the government in its condemnation of Dreyfus and its refusal to reopen the case.

The position of the academic, as well as the literary signatories of "*J'accuse*," was clearly a liberal one. It was a matter of equality before the law, religious toleration, equality of opportunity ("careers open to talent"), free scrutiny of governmental actions, the appreciation of the power of public opinion, etc. All of these are among the primary and derivative articles of liberal belief. There were undoubtedly conservatives and reactionaries in the Sorbonne and in the École normale supérieure and in the École pratique des hautes études, but the running was made by the liberals and democrats who were also often socialists. They were secularists, if not anticlerical. They were in short the embodiment of the academic ethos of the Third Republic. Albert Thibaudet was right to call the Third Republic the *république des professeurs*. This was a period of academic freedom inside and outside the universities, i.e., in the content of teaching and research and in the expression of political attitudes. French scientific activity was marked by outstanding individual achievements, but neither the government nor the public did much to promote and increase the scale of that activity by greatly increased support. Although de facto autonomy increased in the universities—they became corporate bodies instead of an informal cluster of separate faculties only in 1893—the ministry of education kept a firm and highly centralized control over syllabuses, requirements for degrees, the creation of new chairs and other aspects of university autonomy. Indeed, the universities, especially the provincial ones, were financially neglected by the government and by the wealthy classes.

The *grandes écoles* were favored institutions which operated at a high intellectual level. They were intended to prepare intellectually outstanding men for the civil service, for the technological departments of government, and for teaching in secondary schools. In brief, these great intellectual institutions within which intellectual freedom flourished de facto, with correspondingly high achievements, were to some extent continuations of the traditions of the absolutist regime.

France was, like Germany, notable for the fact that its universities were state universities. One exception was the École libre des sciences politiques founded in 1872 in response to the defeat by Prussia in the war of 1870–1871, by private initiative (Emile Boutmy) and by private financial support (the Duchess de Galliera); the other was the Institut catholique founded in 1875.

Liberalism and Academic Freedom in the United States

In the United States, liberalism, verging towards collectivistic liberalism, gained ground among university teachers, although the majority, especially in natural scientific and technological subjects, had relatively little interest in politics, did not share in and, above all, were not sympathetic with the collectivistic liberal view. As university teachers became more liberal in their political views, so the university became a more liberal institution in a more liberal society. The establishment of the elective system and the greater diversity of courses of study in the education of undergraduates increasingly displaced the fixed and narrow curriculum of the earlier period. Specific religious qualifications for academic appointment—within the universities and colleges of Protestant foundation—were less frequently invoked. Jews and Roman Catholics continued, however, until the end of the period between the two world wars, to be considered very charily. Until the 1930s, Negroes were never appointed outside predominantly or exclusively Negro universities and colleges; when the situation changed in that decade, it changed only very slightly. It is not that there were many aspirants among the Roman Catholics and Negroes. Jews on the other hand were available in large numbers but, until the 1930s, they too were seldom appointed in the universities.

Academic freedom, in the sense of the civil freedom of academics, was occasionally sharply reproved in the United States until after the Second World War. There were many cases of the infringement of the civil freedom of academics in the early part of the century, and this in turn heightened the demand by academics for their protection from such infringements. This led to the formation of the American Association of University Professors in 1915; its main concern was with the protection of university and college teachers from infringements on their academic freedom, and particularly from infringements on their civil freedom.

Between the two world wars and after the Second World War, there were a number of investigations by legislative bodies, federal and state, into allegedly subversive organizations and activities, and university and college teachers not infrequently came within their purview, resulting in embarrassment in many cases and in dismissal in a small number. We may say that to the extent that in American society there were such departures from strictly intellectual criteria of academic appointment on grounds of religious belief or ancestry or racial features, and that such infringements on the civil freedom of academics as occurred in the United States, to that extent the United States departed from the model of a liberal-democratic society.

The Intended Function of Universities in the Liberal-Democratic Age: The Infusion of Ordered Knowledge into Society

One motive for the establishment and expansion of universities in the United States was an aspiration to realize one of the ideals of liberalism, namely, to introduce rationality and soundly based knowledge into the management of the affairs of society. Another motive for the establishment of universities and colleges in the United States, both private and public, was respect for the spiritual sphere and an acknowledgment that a society must make provision for the cultivation of the spiritual sphere; these attitudes long antedate the origins of liberal society. (In the Middle Ages, the church was the predominant object of such respect and acknowledgment; universities in time began to share that position. This motive also included the desire for an educated clergy. The desire of rulers for officials who would free them from dependence on aristocratic families, and who would be loyal and relatively rational administrators of the royal will, was another motive.)

The belief in the value of reason and sound empirical knowledge for society had been given a vivid presentation by Francis Bacon in *The New Atlantis,* at the threshold of modern times. English liberalism, in the form of the Benthamite maxim of "Investigate, agitate, legislate," did not reach the universities of its home country for a long time; but in Scotland, Adam Smith's and Adam Ferguson's teaching and writing represented a step in that direction. It was, oddly enough, in Germany, where the Baconian and Benthamite beliefs in rational statecraft—in the case of Benthamism, working through intellectual influence on public opinion, and of public opinion, in turn, on government—were philosophically repugnant, that the idea of the guidance of government through social inquiry found a firm footing in the work of the Verein für Sozialpolitik in 1872. This institution, with its steady flow of meticulously documented monographs on the economic and social problems of German society, acquired a firm footing in the universities. Germany was at that time a less liberal and less democratic society than Great Britain, yet it was in Germany that the specifically liberal idea of empirical social inquiry as a means of illuminating public opinion and thereby guiding government settled in the universities. The British Social Science Association, which had rather similar aspirations, had no impact on the British universities. The next society to take the social sciences into its universities was the United States.

Universities in the United States took to the entire range of the social sciences with much enthusiasm. The movement which began in the last quarter of the nineteenth century, first at Johns Hopkins University and then at the University of Chicago on a much larger scale and in a much wider variety, gradually spread to other universities, at first mostly the state universities in the Middle West, and somewhat later to the older Eastern universities.

The inspiration for this kind of social investigation—now established as an indispensable part of a liberal-democratic society—was first experienced by American academics during their period of study in German universities from the 1870s onwards. American academics saw in the Verein für Sozialpolitik a model for the enlightening influence of social investigation of public and political opinion. This was at the bottom of the teaching of economics at Johns Hopkins University; it was there that American academic collectivistic liberalism first became rooted and from there that its seed spread to other American universities. The more traditional individualistic liberalism of British, especially Scottish, political economy also took root in the American universities. The latter kind of liberalism in the universities—mainly in departments of economics—was as interested in influencing governmental policies as was the academic collectivistic liberalism, but it wished to influence them in the opposite direction, namely, in the direction of fortifying the workings of the competitive market and individual enterprise.

The foundation of the National Academy of Sciences in 1863 was another step towards realization of the ideal of liberal enlightenment, by proffering scientific advice to government on the basis of knowledge gained through scientific research. This took place before American universities were producing much knowledge of that kind. Nevertheless, two of the moving spirits in the foundation of the academy were Asa Gray and Louis Agassiz, both of them professors at Harvard University.

The American universities never attained the predominance in training for the highest levels of the civil service that was achieved by the German universities and the University of Oxford. One reason why the universities did not come to the forefront as sources of recruits to the higher civil service was because the "spoils system" remained for a long time the chief method of recruitment for the civil service; the higher positions in the service just below the cabinet were filled by the incoming party with persons who had become eminent as politicians and as lawyers. Nevertheless, the reform of the civil service at all levels—which aimed at the recruitment of officials by competitive examinations, to which only persons with a specified amount of education were admitted—was the work of university graduates who had studied in Germany and who had in mind both the German and the British civil services (the latter after the reform of 1853).

The highest positions in the German civil service had been reserved for graduates of the law faculties of German universities. The policy of looking upon the universities as the institutions which train young persons in rational judgment and technical knowledge for public service is far older than any liberal-democratic society; to aid this policy was one of the tasks of European universities in the age of the formation of the absolute monarchies of prerevolutionary Europe. The British reforms both at home and in India were the product of Whig and radical liberalism, which intended to replace primordial criteria of recruitment, by recruitment on the basis of performance in competitive examination to which admission was restricted to young men with high academic qualifications. The recruitment of highly educated experts for the service of the rulers was originally a policy of absolute monarchies; joined with the liberal principle of "careers open to talent," it later became an article of faith of more or less liberal-democratic regimes. The universities played a vital role under both kinds of regimes.

The Universities and Specific Features of Liberal-Democratic Societies

Dispersion of Authority

One of the chief features of the liberal order is the autonomy of corporate bodies. The autonomy of universities is consistent with the principles of liberalism and with the pattern of a liberal-democratic society. (It is less well situated under conditions of collectivistic liberalism or populistic democracy.)

The tradition of the autonomy of universities is one of the oldest of all the traditions of universities. It is nearly as old as universities themselves. It is much older than liberal-democratic societies. While the substance and most of the methods of teaching, and the subjects and techniques of research, have changed almost beyond recognition, the tradition of autonomy has persisted. It is perhaps all that is left from the medieval tradition of corporate liberty.

Nevertheless, it has never been complete. Universities have been dependent for practically all of their history on external financial support, and this has affected the degree of their autonomy. They have had to concern themselves with the external demand for the services of their graduates, and for the requirements of the professions for which their students have had to be trained. They have also intermittently been forced to submit to the powers of the rulers of their societies, and they have had to adapt themselves to the demands of external opinion. Despite these constraints, the universities have managed through most of their history to enjoy a very considerable measure of autonomy.

This autonomy became well entrenched in the course of the nineteenth century—earlier in the Netherlands and the Germanic countries—but it was never complete. In the liberal-democratic countries, it reached a high point in the first half of the twentieth century, within the limits permitted by the constitutional and political traditions of their respective societies. In the first two-thirds of this century, central governments of liberal-democratic societies by and large abstained from intruding upon the sphere of autonomy of universities. Intrusions have begun to become more substantial since the middle of the 1960s.

This has happened in nearly every liberal-democratic society. In Germany, the central government which had hitherto always abstained from dealing with universities, except in the interwar period to provide funds for research through the Notgemeinschaft der deutschen Wissenschaft, enacted the *Rahmengesetz* which has imposed a certain degree of uniformity on the university laws of all state governments; there is also now a central admissions office for all German universities. Similar actions have occurred in other countries as universities and their research have become more costly. In the United States, an executive order of the federal government has intruded very influentially into decisions regarding academic appointments. Most universities have been compliant with the ambiguous demands of the central government, and some have recently gone beyond what has been governmentally required in the suspension of the application of intellectual criteria in academic appointment.

It is not that central governments have taken action against the resistance of universities to these trends of central control at the cost of autonomy. On the whole, academics and academic administrators have been rather supine in the face of these intrusions into what had previously been regarded as the legitimate autonomy of universities.

Indeed it is not unreasonable to go further and to say that a great deal of the impetus to the movement towards greater centralization of authority in the government has come from academics of liberal-democratic societies, and particularly from economists, political scientists, and sociologists. Many of them have been the prophets of collectivistic liberalism and have denigrated traditional constitutional liberalism. This does not mean that academics have not been jealous about their academic freedom, and especially about their civil academic freedom. On the contrary! Nevertheless, much of that civil academic freedom has been exercised on behalf of policies of centralization.

Separation of Church and State: Consequences for University Autonomy and Academic Freedom

The liberal ideal contained at its very center the idea of religious toleration. Toleration entailed, if not necessarily the legal or constitutional separation of church and state, at least the right of diverse religious communities to believe and worship in accordance with their own reasons and visions—as long as they respected the widened limits of public order. The realization of the liberal ideal of the separation de facto of church and state has made a very great difference to universities. In general, it has strengthened the corporate autonomy of universities and the freedom of individual college and university teachers. It has done so by decreasing—not eliminating—the capacity of any major religious community to intrude into the affairs of any university not established, governed, or supported financially by itself.

The autonomy of universities originally was, to a great extent, indebted to ecclesiastical powers which wished to protect the universities from their rival earthly princes and from municipal authorities. That autonomy was not, however, an autonomy vis-à-vis the church. Nevertheless, the idea of a more far-reaching autonomy came into existence. In the oligarchical states of Germany, a *modus vivendi* between the states and the universities was found; this, except for a small qualification regarding chairs of theology, excluded the churches from any direct or constitutional influence on universities. In France, the progress of autonomy was unsteady, but the more the regimes moved towards the separation of church and state, the greater the autonomy vis-à-vis the church became. In England, after 1870, the church ceased to play any direct part in the affairs of universities although, in ancient universities, the Church of England was always a visible presence without any formally assured powers.

In the United States, which, alone of the major liberal-democratic countries, has had from the very beginning a constitutional separation of church and state, ecclesiastical bodies continued to exercise influence in colleges of their own foundation until well into the twentieth century.

Yet with all the differences in constitutional provisions and in the role of churches on the highest governing bodies of universities, the modern university has come to enjoy an almost complete autonomy with respect to religious bodies. This is true even in universities which are still legally governed by churches; even in these, the churches without the reinforcement of constitutional establishment have in many instances renounced much of their former power to dominate their universities.

The invaluable gift of the autonomous university with which the societies of modern times, and then the liberal-democratic societies of the nineteenth and twentieth centuries, were endowed by the Middle Ages has needed revision. It has needed this revision in order to improve it and to bring it to a higher degree of realization of the idea of freedom of investigation and teaching. It is not that teachers in medieval universities were uniformly servile agents of an ecclesiastically or officially prescribed syllabus and pattern of thought; teachers frequently strayed from the path of orthodoxy. That is why many universities were forbidden to teach theology and why that subject was confined to particular universities which, it was thought, were easier to control. Nevertheless, the preoccupation of powerful intelligences with ordered knowledge could not but lead to new interpretations of traditional ideas and therewith to discoveries. What was needed by these powerful intelligences was the assurance that their lives and careers would not be damaged by infringements. The idea of academic freedom gradually became installed as the mark of a proper university. It has continued to be so up to the present. Some of this may be attributed to retraction of the churches of their older claims to authority in intellectual matters.

Market Economy and Private Property

Traditional or constitutional liberalism, which restricted the powers of government, supported the freedom of contract, and hence the market economy. This too has had many consequences, most of them beneficial for universities. Universities have prospered from the market economy. The market economy has made the wealth of which universities, whether governmentally or privately supported, have been the beneficiaries. The universities could never have done the many things they have accomplished in research and teaching, and in the participation of academics in public life, if the economies of their respective societies had not been so productive. Nor could universities have accomplished so much if private businessmen had not given large monetary gifts to universities and created philanthropic foundations which have also made large gifts. They have benefited too from the capacity of persons made wealthy by the market economy to pay taxes assessed at high rates from which universities have been supported by governments.

There are, however, other sides to the relationship. One side to the relationship between universities and the market economy is rather different. Academic economists have not been as generous to the market economy as the market economy has been towards the universities. Economics—theory and research—was more sympathetic to the market economy before it became an academic subject. It did not cease to be so once it was given a place in the teaching program of universities. Nevertheless, academic economists—teachers and students of economics—also became more critical of the imperfections of the market and more insistent on the desirability of some governmental intervention to hold in check the injurious effects of the market on those who had failed in it. The humanitarian opinions and activities of academics have helped to darken the reputation of the market economy and have encouraged efforts to supplant it entirely or to restrict its freedom.

Some academics in the United States and Germany have denounced the market as an immoral institution. At the same time, other academics have not yielded to such arguments. The economists of a few major academic institutions contended strongly for the market, even when its reputation in academic circles and in government was at its lowest ebb. Over the past forty years they have been vindicated.

This touches on another side of the relationship. Businessmen have at times been sensitive to the criticisms made by "socialists of the chair" and other academics of the market economy and the regime of private business. In the United States in particular, where they have usually made up a large part of the membership of boards of regents, they have allowed their displeasure to become known. This has sometimes resulted in infringements on the civil freedom of academics.

The Rule of Law

The training of lawyers was from the very beginning of universities one of their major tasks, and the teaching of law to future lawyers has remained an unceasing activity of universities. (Great Britain, and to a smaller extent the United States, were for long exceptions to this generalization, but have become much less so in the course of the present century.) In Germany the practical rule of law, and especially the doctrine of the rule of law, was to a large extent the brainchild of university professors of law. Yet it must be recognized that the "free school of law"—*die freie Rechtsschule*—in Germany, and "sociological jurisprudence" in the United States, were also to a large extent professional creations.

The universities have benefited from living under a regime of the rule of law which has restrained the power and ambitions of civil servants and, in the United States, of state legislators as well. They have benefited also from the self-restraint of the judiciary in dealing with universities. By and large, until quite recently, judges have abstained from exercising jurisdiction over universities out of respect for university autonomy. Academics and students have become more litigious in recent decades, the courts have accepted jurisdiction more frequently. Their recent record with respect to academic autonomy is mixed.

Governmental and Internal Representative Institutions

Representative institutions are essential to liberal democracy. Universities, even those with academic self-government ("*akademische Selbstverswaltung*"), lived for most of their history without internal representative institutions. When they were ruled by rectors or by presidents, there was seldom provision for representation of the teaching staff in the governing body of the university. The rector or the president ruled—in so far as church or king or emperor permitted him to do so—without the aid of a council, although he might seek the advice and support of deans of faculties, as later in American universities, where the heads of departments were his agents and not the representatives of the teaching staff. Academic self-government had a place for internal representative institutions but that place did not become open for a long time.

Oxford and Cambridge colleges had no need for representative institutions since the fellowships were small; all fellows were members of the governing body. Of course, the head of the college was sometimes a tyrant and was often indifferent to the governing body; sometimes he disregarded it. (Bentley as master at Trinity College, Cambridge was one of the most notable examples.)

The German faculty senate was not a representative institution inasmuch as all the teachers, except for *Privatdozenten* and assistants, were professors. The senates became more representative when extraordinary professors were allowed to elect representatives from among their number to sit in the senate alongside the ordinary professors, who were automatically members of the senate in their own right.

The modern British universities began to develop internal representative bodies when readers, senior lecturers, lecturers, and assistant lecturers elected colleagues of equal rank to represent them alongside the professors in the senate. American universities came late upon the scene of internal representative government. The powers of these bodies, when they did come into existence, were at best consultative. They had little or no legislative power, either positive or negative. Representative bodies of the teaching staff are now widespread in universities throughout liberal-democratic societies.

Governmental representative institutions provide for the civil freedom of academics, as well as of all other citizens. The participation of academics in governmental representative institutions goes very far back in Great Britain. There the ancient universities were represented by seats reserved for them in the House of Commons and filled through elections by an electorate consisting of masters of arts of the universities. The appearance of the modern universities was met by the provision of one seat in the House of Commons for London University and another seat for all the other universities combined. No such arrangements have existed in other countries; they no longer exist in Great Britain. As representative institutions grew with the spread of liberalism, university teachers began to stand for election to national and state legislatures. I think that this began earlier in Germany and in Italy than in other countries. Nevertheless, in the present century there have been many academics who, either on leave or having resigned their academic posts, have stood for election to national legislatures and have sometimes been elected. If they persisted in parliamentary careers, they usually always discontinued the intellectual side of their academic careers, although they sometimes nominally retained their appointments.

By and large, academics have approved of parliamentary government, although many of them, especially in Germany, looked on the growth of democracy with misgivings. At a time when many of them were liberals, representative institutions had a place in their articles of faith. Conservatives too accepted them. In the 1920s, with the triumph of the Bolsheviks in Russia and the rise of fascism in Italy, the criticism of popularly elected parliamentary bodies became more widespread; academics, however, were not usually among their more vehement critics. Even in the United States where academic intellectuals stood apart from "party"—and "machine"—politics, they were not severe critics of the national legislatures and they were not especially active in seeking to reform them. Woodrow Wilson was an outstanding exception. The interest of academics in the United States was much more drawn to the reform of the civil service.

Even when many academics were most hostile to liberal-democratic societies, from the 1930s to the 1950s, they did not especially single out parliamentary bodies as objects of hostility. Those who took a more or less Marxist view regarded such bodies as part of the "executive committee of the bourgeoisie." Nevertheless, during the administration of President Franklin Roosevelt, when many important reforms were enacted by the Congress, they followed them avidly and accepted their legitimacy.

However, in the United States not many academics have sought elected office, although their numbers have increased since the Second World War. The reason for this reluctance to seek electoral office in the United States has been that selection as a candidate has generally required an apprenticeship in local or state politics. This was not welcome to any but a few. The opportunity to exercise power seemed more attractive when it was offered in the form of an appointment to a high position in the executive branch. This was very true in the time of Franklin Roosevelt when American academics, for the first time in the history of the country, entered government in relatively large numbers. (There had been such an entry during the First World War but it was on a proportionately much smaller scale, and it diminished markedly in the postwar decade.)

Here and there, distinguished academics have risen to high office in liberal democracies, for example, Woodrow Wilson, Thomas Masaryk, Amintore Fanfani, Luigi Einaudi and Raymond Barre. But, on the whole, the electoral process does not attract them, in part because it is too arduous and too distracting from the academic mode of life. Academics are much more inclined towards serving as advisers, as members of specially appointed commissions, and in periods of national crisis, as temporary civil servants at a high level.

Intellectually, they have tended to disparage legislatives and legislators. The popularity among academic social scientists of the idea of the "bureaucratization" of "mass society," is an expression of a denial of the value of representative institutions. The fact that so many leading and less leading academics in France and Great Britain before the Second World War, and in most liberal-democratic societies after the Second World War, admired the Soviet Union so passionately is evidence that many of them did not really consider representative institutions to be all that valuable.

Freedom of Expression of Beliefs and Academic Freedom

Although academic freedom is not the same as civil or political liberty, it has greatly benefited from the expansion and consolidation of the latter in liberal-democratic societies. Much of the progress of genuine academic freedom and of the civil freedom of academics is owed to increased acknowledgment by the educated public of the dignity of learning, of learned institutions, and of the profession of learning.

Freedom of expression in teaching, research, and publication was needed if the universities were to achieve what they wished and what was expected of them. This is what the unevenly emergent liberalism provided. It did not have an easy birth. It was probably the universities of the Netherlands, the Universities of Leiden and Utrecht, which led the way. Most other countries lagged behind, some very far. The French universities of the ancien régime were among the most retrograde in Europe in this respect. The Revolution which appeared to break the ancien régime did not improve the situation. The age of Napoleon was scarcely an improvement and the successive regimes which followed were little better. The German universities exhibited a closer approximation to academic freedom in practice in the eighteenth century. Perhaps even more important for the establishment of academic freedom was the promulgation of the ideal by von Humboldt and some other German thinkers. By the end of the nineteenth century, the freedom of research and teaching and publication had become a standard for the assessment of universities through the Western world. This does not mean that it is always observed.

Methodically Gained and Ordered Knowledge

The liberal ideal accepted, indeed it stressed, the indispensability of rational reflection drawing upon the most reliable information or scientific knowledge for the making of private and public decisions. The market was regarded as the best mechanism to make available the knowledge needed for reaching private decisions about exchanges of goods and services. The market required a wide dispersion of that knowledge.

The liberal ideal also proposed or required a wide dispersion of the knowledge needed for public decisions. The original intention of academic social sciences was to make available the results of social science studies to the widest possible public. It was the expectation that on the basis of such knowledge, produced by academics and transmitted to the public, individuals could adapt themselves, i.e., they could control their own actions in ways which would enable each to realize his or her individual objective, and to enable participants in collective actions, especially those in which authority is exercised, to perform in ways which would be optimally beneficial to all concerned.

The growth of scientific knowledge has not, however, turned out to be compatible with the liberal ideal of the equal distribution of knowledge to the adult public. The liberal ideal of a rationally and mutually adjusting collective life is not so readily adaptable in the affairs of large societies with a high degree of concentration of authority, and a fairly high degree of specialization of institutions and of occupational specialization within institutions.

The idea of representative institutions is a concession to inequality in the distribution of knowledge. It was in that respect also a departure from the ideal of complete *Mündigkeit* of all individuals. The development of modern scientific and technological knowledge has placed a strain on the liberal ideal because it renders inevitable a varying, but always rather high, concentration and specialization of knowledge. The problems created for liberal democracy by the growth of knowledge and its distribution have not been resolved.

This anomaly is a ramified consequence of liberal democracy. It is liberal-democratic society which has given such a free scope of action to the universities, and it is the universities which have generated so much scientific and scientific technological knowledge. The universities, which have been to such a great extent the beneficiaries of liberal democracy, grew up and flourished at various times under other social and political regimes, but they have flourished especially under the regime of liberal democracy. By their very efflorescence and their fidelity to the task laid upon them by the multiplication of knowledge, they have created a situation which might become a troublesome embarrassment to liberal democracy, as well as to themselves.

The esteem in which universities have been held in liberal-democratic societies has been strengthened by the belief that the universities, as centers of scientific research, have contributed and will continue to contribute to the economic well-being of their societies. In the early nineteenth century, before universities had become sources of practically beneficial and economically profitable knowledge, they were esteemed as parts of the spiritual sphere in which the churches were beginning to renounce their claim to monopoly or at least preponderance. The universities owe much to their standing to this latter belief in the intrinsic value of methodically gained and ordered knowledge.

Rewards Commensurate with Achievement

The superiority of individual achievement as a claim to preferment and reward over the criteria of birth, religion, race, etc., is one of the major features of modern liberal-democratic societies. This has many sources. One of them is the metaphysical–moral belief in the value of the individual human being as an intrinsically valuable entity; it has gradually gained the upper hand over belief in the legitimacy of status derived from lineage and role within the family. The value of individual intellectual achievement is almost inherent in universities, although there have been times—for example in Oxford in the eighteenth century—when individual intellectual achievement was only one value among others, and not usually the main one.

In the nineteenth century, however, this changed. It was not merely the assimilation of the ethic of individual achievement from the surrounding individualistic liberal society. The change came about from within the universities when increasing emphasis was laid upon intellectual achievement through research. In the course of that century, when degrees and prizes were awarded, when honors were conferred and when appointments were made, they were made for the intellectual achievement of individuals.

Thus in consequence of the spread of the ethic of intellectual achievement, universities became purified. Idlers and spellbinding placeholders became relatively more rare as the capacity for an actualization of individual academic achievement became more widely regarded as the proper criterion for admission, graduation, appointment, and promotion. The application in matters of appointment of the criterion of past and prospective academic intellectual achievement has always been appreciated in universities, but it has not always been applied in practice. For a long time, religious affiliation and affirmation were either explicitly or implicitly treated as being among the criteria of academic appointment, admission to university, sitting for examinations, and proceeding to degrees. These have gradually been abandoned in universities in liberal-democratic countries. Intermittently, political criteria have been applied at the cost of academic intellectual criteria.

In the United States, where for a very long time Negroes were never considered for academic appointment, the governmental program of affirmative action and a perverse egalitarianism have reversed but not nullified the earlier situation. At the same time, the program of affirmative action imposed by the federal government, the politicization of universities by their own teaching staffs, and the agitation by small circles of students have weakened adherence to the criterion of academic intellectual achievement in the award of marks and the making of academic appointments.

Humanitarianism, Liberal Democracy and the Universities

Humanitarianism is not usually associated with traditional or constitutional liberalism. They are frequently thought to be antithetical to each other, and in some aspects they are. But they have much in common. Both extended the boundaries of society and incorporated previously peripheral sectors of society; both accorded much value to the individual; both espoused a puritanical ethic, regarding the working, self-supporting individual as the norm. Nevertheless, it is wrong to say that liberalism of the traditional or constitutional sort and humanitarianism are identical.

Nor would it be correct to say that humanitarianism and democracy are identical or always harmonious with each other. But like liberalism and humanitarianism they overlap with each other. Liberalism and democracy together have incorporated a good part of the humanitarian program of the nineteenth century. In this, the universities of liberal-democratic societies have played a great part. At the same time, the espousal of humanitarian attitudes has helped to change the universities within themselves and in their position in society.

Humanitarianism had nothing to do with universities in their early centuries. The improvement of the conditions of life of the society, and especially of the lower classes, was not thought to be anything of interest to universities. It might have been to some extent the coming of political economy under a variety of names into universities—first in the German and Italian universities in the seventeenth and eighteenth centuries, and then in the Scottish universities in the eighteenth century—which marked a turn of attention of some academics towards the wealth of societies and their populations, and to the physical conditions of the people. (Political arithmetic had a transient connection with Brasenose College, Oxford, through William Petty who was a fellow there while serving as professor of anatomy in the university, but there is no evidence that he taught political arithmetic while at Oxford.)

It was really in the nineteenth century that persons holding academic appointments began seriously to consider the wealth of nations, and incidentally the condition of the poor.

The Verein für Sozialpolitik in Germany with its numerous academic members had a deep impact on universities in the United States. The establishment of the Johns Hopkins University in 1875, the University of Chicago in 1892, and the London School of Economics in 1895, greatly widened the institutional provision for inquiries into the conditions of the poor. (Previously in those countries, such inquiries had been conducted by private individuals and private charitable societies.) This new field of academic work was often associated with the emergence of a divergent current of liberalism, namely, collectivistic liberalism, which in the course of time pushed aside the great liberal tradition which required the free control and disposition of property as an essential feature of the competitive market and the regime of liberty. This new collectivistic current of liberalism brought academics, especially in the social sciences, into public agitational activities.

In universities, both in the United States and in Germany—in France and in Great Britain the universities were much slower—the provision of teaching in the social sciences gave much attention to "social conditions." Social science departments of universities—some universities were very reluctant to create them—were from the beginning intimately related to activities outside the universities to improve the conditions of the poor, orphans, widowed and deserted women, prostitutes, alcoholics, immigrant labor, and the whole panoply of activities and conditions called "vice" and "poverty." The turn towards humanitarian concerns among academics fostered the study of economics and "social economics" in the universities and, early in the present century, the establishment of "schools" within the universities for the teaching of "social work" or "social administration." (This happened especially in some universities in Great Britain and the United States.) The surge of humanitarian beliefs in academic circles was accompanied by actions of academics on behalf of "social reforms." These actions were intended to arouse public opinion and to impel governments into measures to alleviate poverty and to control "vice."

From at least the last decade of the nineteenth century, university teachers appeared in reformatory and civil activities performed outside the universities. Academics served on commissions of inquiry appointed by governments and they carried out investigations of their own, sometimes with the aid of students. They also agitated for reforms. These agitational activities, directed towards the larger public, raised questions about the propriety of such activities and sometimes, particularly in the United States, precipitated small crises of civil academic freedom. It also brought with it an increased participation of academics in academic activities which inquired into or which purported to "solve" social problems.

From the early twentieth century, critics of the universities, especially critics of radical progressivistic inclinations, had censured the universities for their failure to find places in their student bodies for the offspring of the working classes and from the poorer sectors of their societies, more generally. Numerous statistical studies had demonstrated in the decades before the Second World War that the students of universities came mostly from the middle and upper middle classes and more specifically from the families of members of the learned professions—the clergy, medicine and law, business enterprises and higher civil servants, and in the United States from the families of more prosperous farmers. Neither university administrators nor university teachers worried much about these facts.

After the Second World War, governments and publicists, and particularly the expanded breed of higher educational publicists, began to take these matters to heart. Everywhere the numbers of university students increased, first through support for demobilized members of the armed forces, then through determined efforts by governments to further the admission into universities of candidates who, without financial support from outside their families, could not attend them. As a result, after the first surge of students who had been kept from university studies by their service in the armed forces, there was a further and almost uninterrupted surge. This was made up to a large extent of students who benefited from grants by governments and by the universities from their own resources.

In the United States, with its large Negro population, and demand for an increase in the percentage of students from "minorities," the insistence has been greater. It is not so pronounced in other liberal democracies, but it is likely to increase in those societies, given the increase in the major countries of the numbers of "foreign workers" who are mostly Asians and Africans.

The admission of such students represents more than a mere increase in the absolute size of student bodies which brings with it severe problems in the supply of qualified teachers, the provision of physical facilities, refectories, hostels, etc. The introduction of many students from cultures alien in their traditions of language, religious belief, and outlook in life, and often with a secondary education inferior to that of earlier generations of students, makes the situation more difficult.

A similar demand for the appointment of university teachers from the "minorities" has occurred. This has been associated with a readiness to suspend or qualify the application of strictly academic or intellectual criteria in academic appointments.

Those changes in the composition of the student bodies and the academic teaching staffs have brought with them demands for changes in courses of study and syllabuses. "Black studies" and "women's studies" are among the new subjects introduced. There has also been a demand to change the content of teaching away from emphasis on Western civilization and to give more attention to the "contributions" or work of Asian and African authors and female writers, who, it is argued—quite wrongly—have not been sufficiently appreciated in teaching.

Rationality, Rationalization, and the Universities

Liberalism, both constitutional and collectivistic, has laid emphasis on the superiority of reason over custom, knowledge over ignorance, in the conduct of institutions. Each current of liberalism has stressed its greater efficiency and rationality. Scientific knowledge and rational analysis as the basis of practical action have been fundamental in liberalism.

Between the two world wars, there was much worry about the adequacy of representative institutions and the other institutions of liberal democracies to deal effectively with the problems of contemporary liberal-democratic societies. The firm grip of the Bolsheviks on the empire which they extended, the abolition of liberal democracy in Italy by the fascists in Italy, and the tribulations of liberal democracy in Germany and its overthrow by the Nazis against the background of the apparently insuperable economic depression, shook confidence in the capacity of liberal-democratic institutions to act effectively. The powers of analysis and discussion, indeed of rationality itself, were thrown into doubt. Irrationality found spokesmen inside the universities as well as outside.

On the whole, however, within the universities persistence in the pursuit of scientific knowledge and the use of such knowledge in the polity and in economic life held the upper hand in the liberal countries. The prophets of irrationalism were scarcely represented in the universities of the liberal-democratic societies. The critics of capitalism and of representative institutions, the proponents of socialism and communism, stressed the superior rationality and the more scientific character of their preferred types of society.

The Second World War silenced the doubters about the capacities of scientific knowledge in the service of practical ends. After that war, the scientific side of universities—now greatly extended—brought a new eminence to universities. Governments began to spend much larger sums of money on scientific research and scientific education. The chief beneficiaries were the universities which appreciated greatly the benefits and thought little about the costs of these greatly increased expenditures.

When governmental expenditures on science and universities were relatively small, little public attention was directed towards them. The prestige of scientific knowledge and of the universities were generally very high in the first two decades after the Second World War, and the great expenditures were neither begrudged nor closely scrutinized. This seemed to be a very happy moment in the relations between universities and liberal-democratic societies. However, it was only a prelude to a continued but more captious largesse, and a greater demandingness. No largesse could ever be generous enough to meet the much expanded demands of scientists and universities for financial support on a scale which was sufficient to meet their ever expanding demands. The intensified scrutiny which accompanied the largesse was not wholly in accordance with the traditional freedom of academic scientists to choose their problems and to do their work without having to worry about very detailed accountability.

The reversal of the tradition of scientific freedom was never as far-reaching as it could have been. Academic scientists retained a great deal of their traditional freedom, but they lost some of it. In fact, the relationship between universities and the governments of liberal-democratic societies had become more differentiated, intimate, and intricate than ever before.

Concurrently, new scientific discoveries and their applications in scientific technology in private industry and commerce also became much more intimately connected with each other. Scientific discoveries in certain fields have turned out to be much more immediately and specifically applicable than had been the case up to the beginning of the Second World War. This has made industrial and commercial entrepreneurs more eager to profit by the application of scientific knowledge and to encourage such research by the provision of financial incentives. Thus, academic scientists have been drawn into connections with private business enterprises more closely than they had ever been. The academic scientists have been attracted by the prospect of additional support for their research which was becoming ever more costly; in some cases they have been attracted by the prospect of private enrichment.

These new relationships have been embarrassing experiences for other reasons as well. The demand for funds for research is insatiable; at the same time, universities have become more costly to administer as they have grown in size and in the scale of their teaching and research activities. University teachers and administrators are in search of funds in ways which they have never been before. Universities have never before been expected to pay their own way, except for institutions of marginal intellectual importance which have supported themselves mainly from the tuition and other fees paid by students. Nowadays, at least in Great Britain and the United States, they are being pressed by their own administrators to engage in money-earning activities to meet their increased costs—as well as to contribute to the economic growth of their societies. These situations have added to the difficulties of conducting autonomous universities with internal freedom along traditional lines.

Ambivalent and Hostile Attitudes towards Tradition

Neither the liberal, nor the collectivistic liberal, nor the democratic streams of thought which have entered into contemporary liberal-democratic societies have looked with affection on traditional beliefs and institutions. It is true that each of them has appealed to its own traditions, but they have been very critical towards the traditions of others and they have all tended to deny the value or supportability of tradition. Their ideal of society would be one in which traditions were set aside by scientific and rational analysis, popular will, and calculations of collective-individual advantage ("interest").

The scientific and technological parts of the academic world have had little patience with tradition; many of their practitioners deny that they have had traditions of their own. Social scientists likewise have lacked understanding of the traditional elements of their own societies. The specialization of humanistic scholarship, while studying traditions and practicing their transmission in their own research and teaching, placed the more fundamental understanding of the nature of tradition into a marginal position. All this notwithstanding, many academics in liberal-democratic societies have had a genuine appreciation of the traditions of their own universities, and a sense that there were traditions which ought to be continued. These attachments to the traditions of their universities, and hence their attachment to the universities, did not make them indifferent to the importance of traditions in society.

The developments of contemporary liberal-democratic societies have had a deleterious effect on these attachments to university traditions. The appearance of the mass university, the increase in size of administrative staffs, the large classes and seminars, as well as the high degree of specialization and the increased frequency of close collaboration with colleagues in other universities, have had a debilitating effect on the morale of university teachers and students. The creation of so many new universities has offered a poor soil for the growth of university traditions.

The student disturbances in so many liberal-democratic countries in the 1960s and 1970s, the idea that a university is a "constellation of interests"—the basic idea of the *Gruppenuniversität*—the numerous conflicts among teachers arising from the disturbances, and the increased intrusion of central governmental bureaucracy in the internal affairs of universities, have had disaggregative consequences.

On top of all this, the birth of the ideal of individual emancipation from the ties of institutions—itself a noxious outgrowth of liberal democracy—has accentuated these disaggregative tendencies within universities.

What Universities Have Given to Liberal-Democratic Societies

The universities have contributed to their liberal-democratic societies through training for the various professions which have helped those societies to function, and they have affirmed—although far from unqualifiedly—certain beliefs which are constitutive of liberal democracy.

On the most practical side, they have trained physicians, scientific research workers in medicine, biology, agriculture, and the physical sciences. They have trained all types of engineers, who, taking over the task from engineers trained by apprenticeship and periods of study in very specialized institutions, have continued, together with chemists, the elaboration of the technological apparatus of the modern economy and contributed to its productivity. They have trained medical research workers, have made it possible to control many diseases and, with the agricultural research workers who have increased agricultural productivity, they have lengthened the life span of human beings in many countries and not just in the liberal democracies. They have provided both systematic theoretical and relatively precise particular knowledge about the workings of economies and societies. They have trained a very large fraction of the persons who have administered modern governments and business enterprises, more or less efficiently and honestly. They have trained the lawyers needed to apply the law and to represent individuals and institutions in the conflicts which are inherent in a free pluralistic society, and to bring them to peaceful solution. They have increasingly educated the journalists who supply the factual information needed by citizens and rulers.

They have not only performed research and applied the results of research, they have also offered expert advice to governments and large organizations and perhaps helped them, by their advice, to function more efficiently, and thereby maintained the morale and confidence necessary for the effective functioning of liberal democracy.

Universities, by their research and teaching, have greatly increased the stock, breadth, and depth of knowledge of nature and of man; they have increased our knowledge of the history of human societies and civilizations and of the achievements of mankind in religion, art, literature, etc. They have, directly and indirectly, through the lower levels of the educational system, given to the citizens of liberal-democratic societies some knowledge of the history of their own societies and the ability to see themselves as participants in them. They have made human beings in modern liberal-democratic societies cognizant of the place of their civilization among the civilizations which appeared in world history. They have above all enriched their knowledge of their own civilization. They have disciplined many minds by making them aware of how truths are discovered and of the moral discipline which is required for attainment of those truths. They have given to many the exhilaration of discovery and contemplation of the intricacy and coherence of the world, or at least of sectors of it. They have enabled some human beings to grasp the dignity of rational, methodical thought and reflection. On a level intellectually less important but not less important for a liberal-democratic society, they have enabled many individuals to improve their lot in life by offering them the training and certification to enable them to enter the occupations to which they aspire.

What Universities Have Not Given to Liberal-Democratic Societies

What have the universities failed to do? They have failed to replace a lost religious faith in many human beings whose lives have become more troubled—intermittently—by their inability to hold confidently a view of the world which gives meaning and value to cosmic and human existence. That, however, is a task the universities never undertook. As long as the churches were able to do what it was in their province to do, the universities worked alongside them in a division of labor which left the final truths of cosmic and human existence to the churches, while the universities attempted to understand and explain according to the methods of valid and reliable empirical knowledge. When the churches declined in credibility, the universities, except for those "grown-up children"—as Max Weber called them—who thought that scientific methods could supply answers to all the questions which serious inquiring minds could ever ask, continued to perform with increasing success the tasks which were appropriate to them. The universities have in fact taught theology for most of their history, but have done so under ecclesiastical supervision. They still teach theology but the other departments of the university do not regard the maintenance of theological belief as their responsibility. Hence to charge the universities with the failure to replace religion would be to charge them with a failure which they share with the churches. The protection of the traditional religion was never the responsibility of the whole university; it was the responsibility of the churches and of the divinity faculties.

Wisdom

A society without wisdom is bound to go astray, and a liberal-democratic society is no less liable to do this than any other type of society—perhaps more so, as university graduates who have not received some of the intellectual preconditions for wisdom come to constitute an increasingly large fraction of the adult population. This is where the humanities are failing to serve the good of a liberal-democratic society.

The study of the great works which are the subject matter of the humanities may foster the growth of wisdom in those who study them. Wisdom cannot be taught and the students are too young and too inexperienced to give birth to it. It can be elicited only by those who have a mind for it, and that can be achieved only in the years of maturity. Still the study of the great works—the "canon" now disparaged by teachers of the humanities—can lay the foundations for it in youth, if teachers are attentive to the opportunities offered by teaching. But that is not the way in which teaching is done nowadays by many teachers of the humanities.

Humanistic studies moved from the task of finding and living in accordance with the right pattern of life through the study of the great intellectual works of antiquity, to the pedantic emendation of texts of important authors, and later to the pedantic study, in great detail, of unimportant authors and events. The transformation came about gradually and unwittingly. At first, the secondary task of humanistic scholarship was the discovery and collation of surviving manuscripts, with the aim of making the texts as pure as possible, that is, as close as possible to the state of the text when it left its author's hand. This was a work of tremendous importance. It was also a task which challenged great intelligences and called for impressive qualities of memory and imagination.

When, with the increasing sensitivity to contemporaneous truths, the study of modern languages and literatures came into the program of academic humanistic studies, the emendation and purification of texts aiming to establish what an author had really said declined in prominence. The invention of the printed book had rendered much of that important activity superfluous, as far as modern languages and literatures were concerned. There were not many modern authors as great as Plato and Aristotle or Horace and Virgil, and the study of the contemporary, recently living great authors offered little in the way of an exemplary pattern of life in accordance with which a scholar could hope to form and live his own life. Nor did modern authors offer the same legitimate opportunities for philological textual study and emendation.

In consequence, and with the attendant increase in the number of research students writing dissertations for the doctorate, from quite different causes, innumerable doctoral dissertations were produced and many of them were published. They had to be as detailed as the much richer documentation of recent events permitted. The small number of worthy subjects and the great number of persons to work on them, with the obligation of making an original contribution to knowledge, resulted in a widespread trivialization of subjects. Such "original" research led to the production of a flood of boring books and an inevitable weariness and uninterestedness of much postgraduate research, which had to continue long after the dissertation was completed. The requirement of long lists of publications as a criterion of academic appointment and promotion accentuated this drudgery. The academic calling became a profession in which the bare fact of publication was the sole mark of merit. Research became increasingly specialized and self-contained. It looked upon its objects without the benefit of any large perspective.

It is no wonder that, as humanistic scholars became experts without vision and with no end in life except promotion and more publication, teaching sank in importance alongside this all-consuming treadmill of exhaustive and exhausting research. The vision of a way of life faded away nearly completely. That is one of the causes of the crisis of the humanities which has been aggravated by the wantonness of a desperate profession. What is now called "theory" in the humanities is the misguided effort to find new tasks for the humanities.

The movement towards "theory" in the humanistic disciplines has received an influential embodiment in the technique of "deconstruction" which has recently gained the ascendency. Its derogation of the "canon" is an effort to deny the validity of the tradition which ranks literary works in accordance with intellectual and literary criteria other than individually variable likes and dislikes. It is against the traditional canon. What it is really trying to break is the tradition of Western liberal-democratic society. It is a form of antinomian political radicalism with scraps of Marxism and psychoanalysis, supported in the most far-reaching and subtle form in some of the work of the philosopher and historian Michel Foucault. It is hostile to intellectual traditions, even to knowledge itself which, because it has been received from the past, is regarded as "oppressive." Even language, according to this new movement, is "oppressive" because it provides established forms for expression.

This antinomian body of beliefs is prominent mainly in the humanistic disciplines and particularly in the study of modern literatures. It has, however, made inroads into the social sciences, and even into the classical and oriental parts of the humanistic disciplines. In the social sciences—not in economics—the work of "deconstruction," i.e., of devaluation, takes the form of "unmasking" and "demythologising."

The current efforts made in the humanistic disciplines to overcome their desiccation by launching themselves into "theory" cannot be accused of narrowness. They are very broad. Their leaders hold forth on all sorts of subjects which they have not studied, e.g., economic history, sociology, philosophy, comparative religion, etc., etc. There is no subject which they do not venture into to rediscover their own image of the world. Nor can it be said against them that they are not interested in a way of life. They are interested in a way of life—it is nothing other than complete emancipation from all traditional ways of life. Humanistic "theory" is very political but its politics are those of antinomianism—although probably in any particular situation their views are those of the radical or emancipationist variant of collectivistic liberalism. This is not very fertile ground for the growth of wisdom or for the growth of civility, either within the university or within society. In any case, they find liberal-democratic society utterly abhorrent. It embodies all that they would destroy.

Their political sympathies are generally populistic and anarchistic. In the United States, this hostility to the tradition of liberal-democratic societies has another facet: the accusation against the great literary and philosophical works of Western civilization as "sexist, racist, and imperialist." (The discussion about the required course for undergraduates at the Leland Stanford University, which has been amply documented in *Minerva,*[1] exhibits the aggression of the critics and the compliance of those who otherwise know better.)

This is of course not the entire picture. Traditional modes of scholarship are still strong in many of these fields, but the practitioners of those modes are timorous and on the defensive. Although these practitioners of the traditional modes of study do not wholeheartedly support the antinomian views, they are reluctant or afraid to oppose them. Only a small minority speak out against them and they are pilloried as dogmatic reactionaries.

Thus within the universities in which they hold remunerative appointments and in which they exercise their authority over students, they oppose the traditions without which universities could not exist. Needless to say, they are irreconcilably hostile to liberal-democratic society.

Civility in the University and in Society

Specialization is an inevitable and fruitful condition of scientific discovery. But it has dangers for the university and for liberal-democratic society. Hyperspecialization is often attended by an attrition of perspective, i.e., of breadth or comprehensiveness of curiosity and understanding. Specialization is like the leather tanner's view that "there is nothing like leather"; for the leather tanner there is nothing in the world as worth-

1. "The Discussion about the Proposals to Change the Western Culture Program at Stanford University," Reports and Documents, *Minerva* 26 (Summer–Autumn 1989), 223–410.

while as leather. Specialization is incivility in intellectual treatment of the realm of material substances, it is indifference to the larger scene. Pedantic specialization in the academic disciplines is part of the attrition of civility within a university; nothing in the university is of interest to the specialist—neither the work of other parts of the university, nor the university as a whole. Only his own department or his own research project interests the specialist. This is one of the sources of the damage from which universities are suffering at present. Indifference to what is happening in one's own university is a companion to indifference to what is happening in one's own society, an indifference qualified only by an unthinking partisanship, pervaded by cliches.

Scientists, pure and applied, and technologists have, through their specialized research, already made great contributions to liberal-democratic society. They have also presented it with problems which are beyond their capacities to solve. The problems generated by the advances in biomedical sciences and biomedical technology are unprecedented. They have raised questions about the prolongation of human life and the manipulation of species with which no societies have ever been faced before. Scientists, having contributed their mite to the abandonment of traditional religious beliefs and their associated ethical beliefs, now find themselves confronted by problems which they are ill-equipped to solve. It is not that the traditional religious beliefs and ethics offer any clear solutions. It is only that the new problems disclose the moral threadbareness of the scientific and technological professions. They also disclose the moral threadbareness of the population as a whole in facing problems of a sort which have never been faced before.

It is not that there have not been some great scientists and physicians who have also been humane and generous persons and who have taken seriously the future of their respective societies and of all mankind. There was such a wave of naive but genuine civility at the end of the Second World War among scientists who had been engaged in the work which was directed towards the invention and construction of nuclear weapons, but this did not last. It fell into the groove of collectivistic liberal partisanship and helped to make internal discussions about nuclear weapons more vehement and less civil. (I refer here to the Federation of American Scientists; the American Association of Scientific Workers had always been a "front" for the Communist Party, than which nothing was more uncivil.)

The once widespread notion that scientific training purged an individual of prejudice and partisanship and that scientists could therefore speak for the whole, since scientific knowledge itself offered such knowledge of the common good, has turned out to be a generous delusion. I do not intimate by this statement any slur on the character of scientists, many of whom are guided by a disciplined love of truth which is exemplary.

The vast majority of scientists are probably little interested in public affairs except in so far as they affect resources for scientific research and training; they are also little interested in what goes on in their universities. They are not antinomians in the way which many members of the departments of the humanistic disciplines have become. However, public spirit is not among their striking features, nor is academic citizenship.

Social scientists by their professional obligations know more about societies than their colleagues in the natural sciences and the humanities. They have also become very specialized as the social sciences have become more scientific. Their specialization within each discipline tends to be focused on "social problems," i.e. the poor, the outcasts, the broken reeds of society. That is the tradition of empirical sociological research; that is the tradition which they have inherited. This focus of attention is kept in place by the readiness of governments and philanthropic foundations to support such research.

This partiality of vision has laid them open to the ravages of the last few decades. Sociology, anthropology, and political science all have somewhat more intellectual discipline than does the present-day practice of the humanities, but they have not been resistant to the infectious spreading from the humanities and from the radical epidemic of two decades ago. Whereas among natural sciences a high degree of specialization may be accompanied by indifference to or ignorance of society, among social scientists it produces a superficial view of society. Superficiality is quite incompatible with civility. Those social scientists whose procedures were more rigorous or more "scientific" have been less susceptible to the infection of uncivil radicalism than those with purportedly "theoretical" interests. There, antinomianism found more acceptance.

The Universities as Bearers of Civility

This is a very rough but approximate account of the relationships between the universities and the main features of liberal democracy. It is clear that the universities owe a great deal to liberal democracy and that liberal democracy owes a considerable part of its successful functioning to universities.

Liberal democracy needs civility, i.e., a concern for the common good. What have the universities contributed to this? Before attempting to answer this difficult question, it is desirable and reasonable as well to suggest that civility—which involves detachment from conflicting interests, and an imagination capable of envisaging a solution which is more than a compromise between the conflicting interests and which takes into account consequences for third parties—is a rare quality and it is probably never found unalloyed. It is mixed with partisanship within the mind of the individuals who possess it.

Despite their often crude and unashamed espousal of partisanship, civility is probably most often found among politicians with long experience because it is they who see the entire society somewhat more frequently than other persons, except experienced lawyers who often have a comprehensive perspective over the entire society. What about academics? Can they achieve and exercise the civility needed by a liberal-democratic society for its maintenance?

Karl Mannheim thought that the "*freischwebende*" intellectuals—the detached intellectuals, free of obligations of devotion to political parties—might be capable of speaking for the common good. He thought that they could do so by amalgamating the partial perspectives of the contending parties into a single wider perspective. For this he was almost everywhere ridiculed. (In the recent revival, by radical sociologists, of interest in his ideas about the sociology of knowledge, this is one aspect of his work which has been allowed to rest in oblivion.)

Yet Mannheim's idea should not be rejected without further ado. It ought to be seriously examined. Scientists and academics achieved the high status which they long enjoyed because it was thought that being disciplined to observe and analyze, despite their own personal predilections and pride, they possessed the objectivity necessary for dispassionate judgments, as true as the evidence allowed.

Governments over the past half-century have frequently turned to academic scientists to do research on particular problems. They have also been invited to give advice to politicians and administrators at the higher levels of authority because there was confidence that scientists could rise above vanity and partisanship. They have been asked to tell what "science" knows on particular problems and to recommend alternative policies. They have even been encouraged to recommend the adoption of particular policies, because there was confidence that they would assess fairly arguments for and against any particular policy and that they would bear in mind the interests of the entire society.

Their association with universities was thought to be a further guarantee of disinterestedness. The university was believed to be an exigent institution; nothing less than truth was to be expected from it or from those who were members of it.

In serving governments in advisory capacities in this manner, academics conformed with the liberal-democratic ideal of infusing sound scientific knowledge into the conduct of practical affairs. They were able to do this because of the good reputation universities had acquired as institutions devoted, in an utterly disinterested manner, to the discovery and enunciation of truth.

The advice given by academic scientists has not always been good advice, in the sense that the results of policies based on their advice did not turn out as had been hoped. Often the advice given by academic scientists, including social scientists, has been disregarded because the persons advised received contradictory advice from other advisers, or because they themselves had opinions of their own which were inconsistent with the advice they received. Nevertheless, the advice of scientists was frequently sought because it was thought that scientists were politically disinterested, desired to serve the common good, and were capable of objectivity in judgment.

Politicians and administrators, i.e., laymen without the discipline and knowledge provided by scientific training and experience, cannot themselves assess the validity of the knowledge drawn upon by their scientific advisers. The validity of the results of research gained by scientific methods can really be judged only by other scientists who have mastered the field into which the investigation falls. Scientific studies are often so highly specialized that even an authority in one field of science often cannot pass judgment on the knowledge gained in another field. Certainly very few laymen can verify the scientific assertions made by a scientist. If a layman consults scientists who have divergent views about the same subject, he is scarcely in a position to adjudicate their differences and to decide correctly by himself which one is right.

It is important that the scientists be regarded by the laity as trustworthy. Being a scientist has been thought to be a guarantee of trustworthiness. Universities have been respected because they dealt with what were thought to be very important subjects and because it was also thought that those subjects were dealt with honestly and impersonally, that is, without concern for private pecuniary gain or for fame. That is why, in the course of the nineteenth century, liberal-democratic societies and those which were less liberal and less democratic fostered the development of universities. They believed that universities, like the church and judiciary, were necessary for society; they attributed a high moral value to them. It was thought that they served the ideal of the disinterested search for truthful knowledge. The functions of universities were not just practical; even when they performed such functions, they were esteemed for producing the truthful knowledge which was necessary for practical functions such as the care of health or the practice of law. But the main function—seldom if ever adequately articulated—was the custodianship, transmission, and enlargement of the various bodies of truthful knowledge.

Universities were maintained because the centers of their respective societies wanted them, not necessarily for their own practical or spiritual benefit, but because they thought that universities were needed for society in the way in which religious institutions, literature and art, justice and internal peace, majesty and ceremony, were needed. A society without these things would be an incomplete society.

Universities moved forward as the churches diminished in their centrality. The universities overlapped in their function with the function of the churches which was to link the society with a transcendental realm, i.e., a realm which transcended the material interests of individuals and of the various groups making up society and which held forth a higher ideal. The universities, like the churches before and alongside them, represented to their societies an objective value or values beyond the interests or desires of any given group within the society.

The universities and their academic staffs usually did not think in these terms which envisaged the university as an earthly church. But they did accept that the universities should stand above or beyond the practical interests of any class, and that they must make the scrupulous methodical pursuit of truth in research and in teaching their first obligation.

This was an important function to perform in a liberal-democratic society. The liberal component of the market, the aspiration towards individual achievement and the working of the mechanisms of the allocation of rewards commensurate with achievement, sometimes produced injurious consequences which had to be moderated by the idea of the moral order of the whole of society. Similarly the democratic element in liberal democracy had a tendency towards populism which placed the desires of the populace and of its proponents and their conception of its interests above all else. This too is not the only thing in democracy, but there is a tendency in that direction which has to be kept in check for the concern of the whole.

What Can the Universities Do for Liberal-Democratic Society?

Liberal democracy is the ideal form for societies which are highly differentiated, in which the various individuals and sectors of society, each of which has interests and ideals which are in conflict with the interests and ideals of the others, have an opportunity to strive to realize some part of their interests and ideals. This differentiation is an inevitable consequence of the size and tasks accepted by the society. It is also the ideal form of society for vigorous individuals with ambitions and ideals of their own. Liberal democracy is a regime which acknowledges this differentiation of ideals and interests. Other types of regimes, and particularly totalitarian societies, attempt to suppress them and attempt to bring under their own central authority those which cannot be suppressed, and to deny the existence of those types of differentiation which they cannot suppress and which they cannot dominate.

Because it is differentiated and calls for differentiation, liberal democracy requires some measure of consensus, i.e., a collective self-consciousness embracing most of society. Not everyone in the society needs to be completely civil to the rest of society or to a particular group at all times. Even if it were desirable, it is neither necessary nor possible. The centers of society must be more civil than the peripheries, although these peripheries too must possess some civility; there must be subcenters of higher degrees of civility scattered throughout the society. A liberal-democratic society is incompatible with complete consensus; complete consensus would render liberal democracy largely superfluous. In any case, complete consensus is an impossibility. It does require a measure of consensus or collective self-consciousness. This collective self-consciousness is sustained by a common language, the strength of a common authority making and applying law over a common, bounded territory. It needs traditions which keep before it an image of a long, common past. It needs emblems of effective centers and subcenters. It needs institutions and individuals who are emblems of the whole and who can speak and act in ways which bring forward the image of the whole so that it overshadows its parts.

The different sectors of liberal-democratic societies must be kept in a peaceful balance or equilibrium with each other. It is not possible for this balance or equilibrium to be achieved or maintained only by the rational bargaining of individuals and corporate bodies with each other and by explicit compromise. Some differences of interests can be bargained over and fixed by contract, but not all can be rendered compatible with each other by this technique.

The concern for the whole is a transcendental value. It is not only transcendent of the material interests, of the various sectors of society; it is also transcendent with respect to power and the desire for it, with respect to authority and the desire for it, and with respect to prestige and pride and the desire for them.

Can the universities perform this function nowadays when they are needed more than ever, now that the churches have renounced their aspiration to provide for mankind an objective transcendental ideal which stood for the whole in time and society?

I do not think that the universities, either the greater or the lesser, are representing this civility to their respective societies. They are not very civil inside themselves, having become disaggregated by earnest specialization and by a self-indulgent antinomianism. The tendencies which make them uncivil internally make them uncivil in their activities and beliefs regarding the public sphere.

Concluding Observations

My conclusion from all these observations is that the universities in the liberal democracies will continue to perform important functions in training for those professions which require, for admission and practice, knowledge of the matters which universities can and should properly provide. They will continue to do important research, although as the results of intellectually important, as well as practically useful, research can nowadays be more speedily converted into practically useful and profitable activities, more of such research will be done outside the universities.

They will continue to nurture and display a relatively small number of persons of exemplary devotion to truth in their respective fields. All of these are functions necessary to the well-being of liberal-democratic societies. They will continue to provide consultants and advisers.

As to the provision of an infusion of civility in liberal-democratic societies, I do not see the universities performing this function. They have become too uncivil—internally—and also too self-indulgent and lacking in firmness of character to withstand the pressure of external incivility. Administrators of universities are usually too weak in character; they are harassed by costs which exceed revenues and by the ceaseless desire to increase their activities and to stay on the right side of uncivil proponents of external and internal demands. If universities were less before the eye of the public, it would be better for them and for their liberal societies. But I do not think that this is likely to happen in the near future.

I think that, for the time being, liberal-democratic societies, which cannot do without many of the functions which universities perform for them, must make do with a very small contribution from them to the exhibition and diffusion of civility throughout their societies. They will have to do as well as they can with the civility produced by some politicians and lawyers and by the saving remnant of ordinary citizens scattered throughout liberal-democratic societies.

Index